Dresden Rüstkammer

The Firearms Gallery in the Long Corridor

Dresden Rüstkammer

The Firearms Gallery in the Long Corridor

Published by Staatliche Kunstsammlungen Dresden
Marius Winzeler

Stefano Rinaldi, Gernot Klatte

Deutscher Kunstverlag

Staatliche Kunstsammlungen Dresden

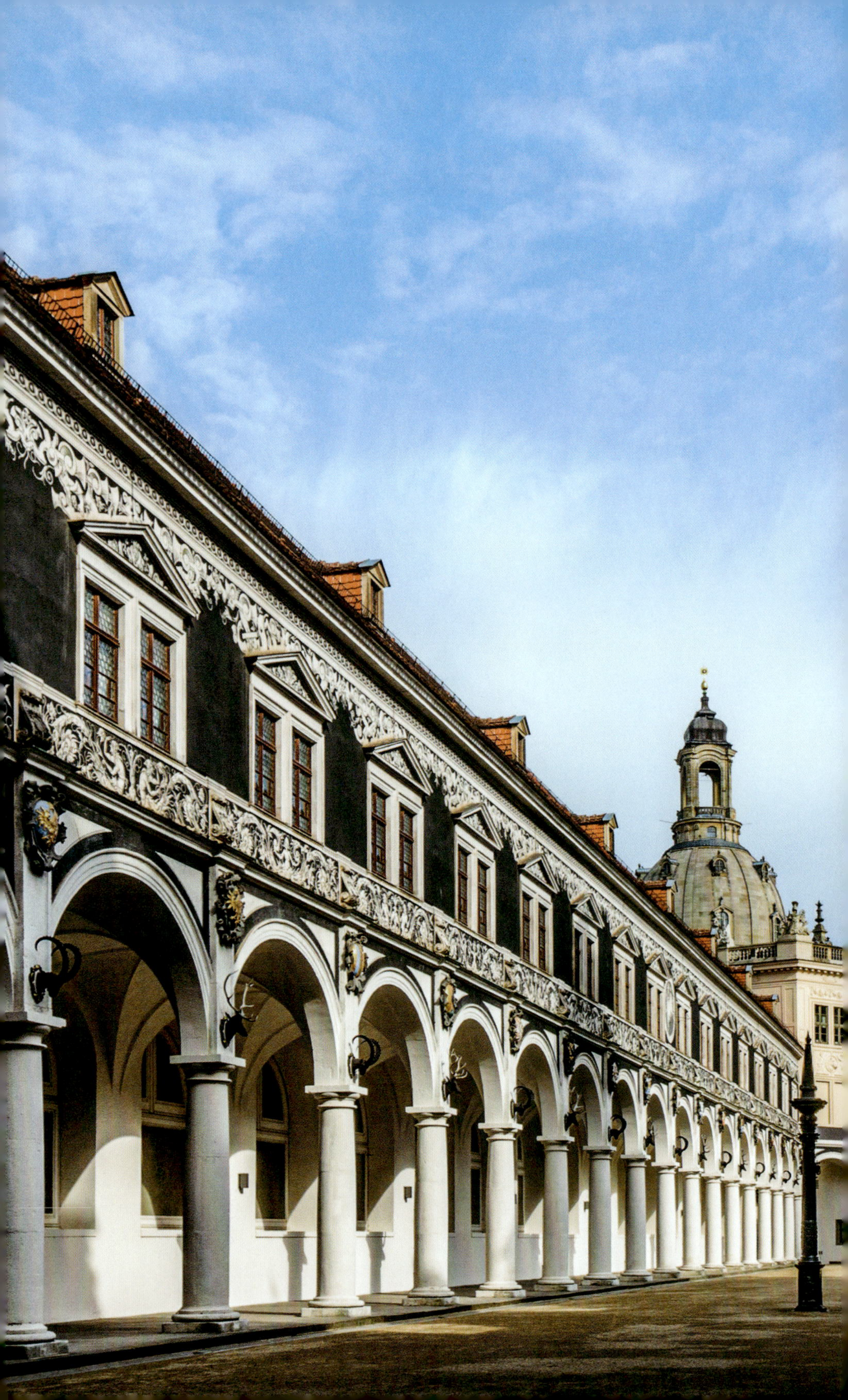

Content

The Firearms Gallery in Dresden's Residenzschloss

MARIUS WINZELER

The Firearms Gallery in the Long Corridor of Dresden's Residenzschloss presents a unique collection of more than 500 outstandingly crafted firearms dating from the sixteenth to the eighteenth century in an equally unique late Renaissance setting. Here, visitors can experience a contemporary take on an eighteenth-century museum concept in its authentic location.

Starting in 1709, the Elector of Saxony and King of Poland, August the Strong, began reorganising his collections. He founded the Kupferstich-Kabinett and the Grünes Gewölbe, had the Rüstkammer moved from the New Stable Building into the old War Chancellery, and designated the Zwinger as a *Palais Royal des Sciences*. From 1722 onwards, the ruler also decreed that the firearms, which had previously been stored in various locations, should be brought together. However, it was left to his son Friedrich August, later King August III of Poland, to set up a dedicated display of the personal arms of the Elector (the so-called *Leibgewehr*) in the Long Corridor in 1733, which he continued to expand over the course of his reign. The Firearms Gallery remained in place until the Second World War and was reestablished in 2021.

When it was first built, between 1588 and 1590, the Long Corridor had had a different function: it connected the Georgenbau wing of the Residenzschloss with the New Stable Building and served as an ancestral gallery. The young and ambitious Elector Christian I used it to demonstrate his sense of tradition and his political will to shape the future. The New Stable Building designed by Paul Buchner for the most precious of the Elector's personal horses and the holdings of the Rüstkammer, some of which dated back to the early sixteenth century, gave the palace complex a new façade looking towards the city. It was thus a prestigious extension of the palace premises. It also redefined the urban space. The medieval city wall facing the Elbe had lost its defensive significance owing to the Renaissance fortifications (today's Brühl Terrace) that had been built in front of it. The Elector purchased 24 adjacent plots of land and had a spacious tournament ground, the Stallhof (Stableyard), laid out between the palace and the stables. An elegant arcade was set in front of the old city wall, and the Long Corridor was built on top of it. This design was undoubtedly inspired by Giovanni Maria Nosseni, who had come to Dresden from Florence in 1575 as a sculptor, architect, and festival director.

View of the Firearms Gallery facing west, toward the entrance

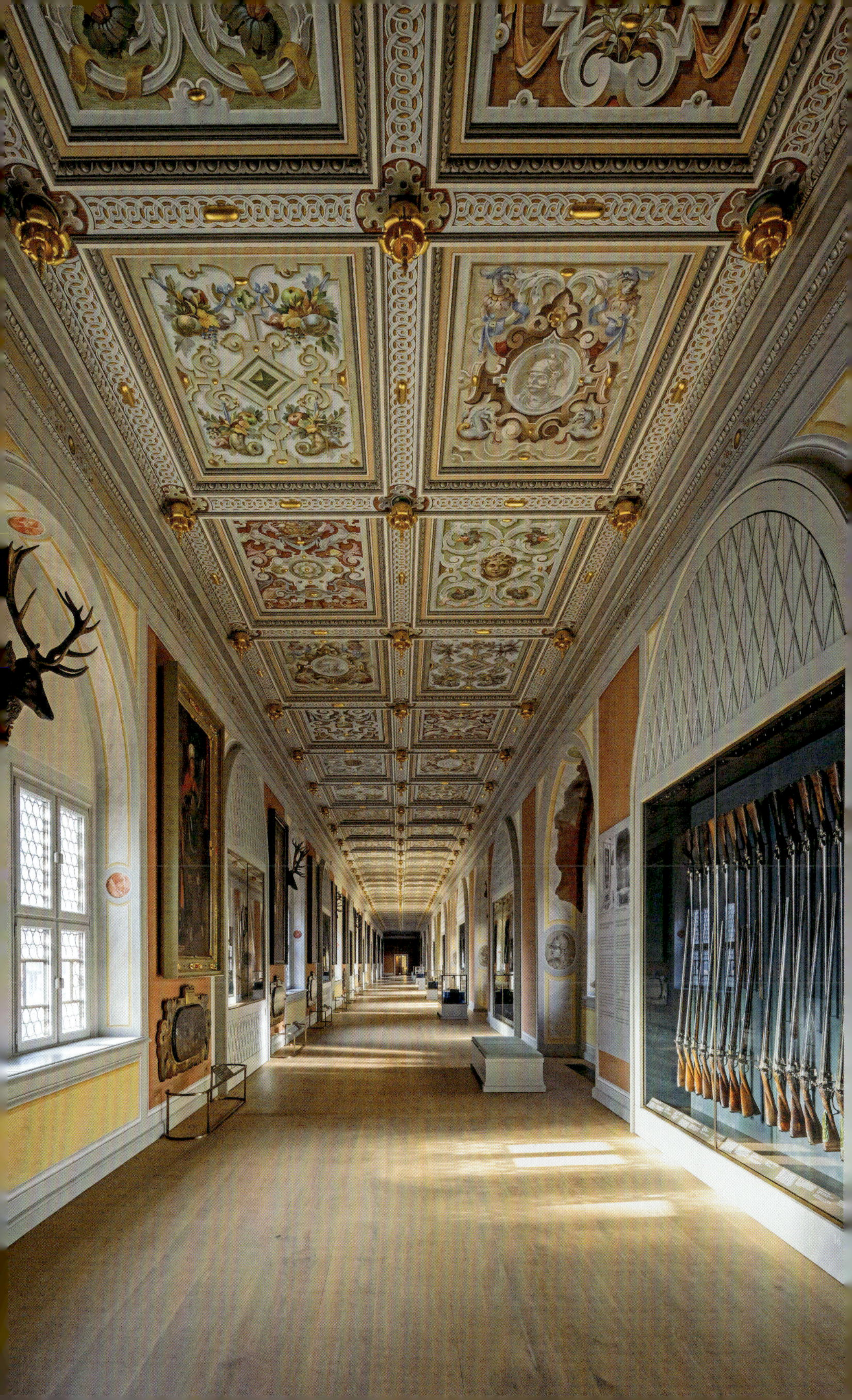

Christian I's innovative architectural concept was modelled on precedents from France and Italy: King François I of France had had the first comparable galleries built in the Palace of Fontainebleau. Their idea – of using long connecting rooms as presentation spaces for dynastic, allegorical, and topographical picture cycles – was immediately taken up in the Papal Palace in Rome, by the Medici in Florence, as well as in the Town Residence of the Bavarian dukes in Landshut, and in Cardinal Albrecht of Brandenburg's New Building in Halle an der Saale. At the same time as the Dresden Stallhof complex, the new wing of Prague Castle was constructed, commissioned by the Emperor. This comprised a magnificent two-storey stable building with a hall and a gallery above it. These were connected to the living quarters of Rudolf II by long corridors that were also used to house his collections.

While in Dresden the exterior façades of the Long Corridor and the Stable Building were painted with sgraffito-style depictions of ancient battles and triumphal processions, the Stable Courtyard featured scenes from the myth of Hercules, referencing the designation of Christian I as *Hercules Saxonicus*. To underscore his eminence, he had an equestrian statue made, which stood imposingly at the Pirna Gate, located directly along the axis extending from the Long Corridor. This exaltation of the ruler culminated in the ancestral gallery in the Long Corridor, created by Heinrich Göding the Elder and his workshop. With its in part fictional ancestry dating back to biblical times, it emphasised and vividly illustrated the claim to power and high status of the Albertine House of Wettin in Dresden. It was one of the most extensive portrait cycles of the late Renaissance in one of the longest galleries north of the Alps. Later, the Baroque founder of the Firearms Gallery was obviously aware of the significance of this concept, and so the interior decoration was left unchanged. The adaptation of the room to house the royal *Leibgewehr* was limited to blocking up every second window to accommodate the wall cabinets for the firearms.

Then as now, the Dresden Firearms Gallery was one of the largest and most important princely firearms collections in Europe. Comparable collections exist only in Paris, Stockholm, and Vienna, none of which are exhibited in such a magnificent setting as that of the Dresden Firearms Gallery. On the one hand, the weapons arranged here according to type and geographical origin were displayed to impress visiting personages; on the other, they also served practical purposes. In the eighteenth century, the ruling family and court occasionally used some of the almost 2000 firearms collected here for hunting and target shooting.

Descriptions and travel reports attest to the keen interest in, and admiration for, the Firearms Gallery, which became part of the regular sightseeing programme of travellers to Dresden. After the Rüstkammer was moved to the Zwinger in 1832 and given the name Historical Museum, the first guides were published for the Firearms Gallery. When the Historical Museum returned to its original location in the New Stable Building (Johanneum) in 1877, it was possible for the Firearms Gallery to be directly connected to the museum for the first time. This also led to a certain degree of organisational and institutional integration between the two museums.

Following the transportation of the collections to the Soviet Union and the wartime destruction of the Long Corridor in 1945, it was anything but a foregone conclusion that the Firearms Gallery would be resurrected in the twenty-first century. The work of rebuilding the Residenzschloss began in 1986, and when the decision was made that the unique collections of the Rüstkammer, now restored to its original name, were to be accommodated in suitable rooms on the first and second floors of the palace, there was no question that the Long Corridor was also to be included. After extensive restoration and archival research, the gallery was recreated, incorporating the remnants of its original painting and with additional reconstructions, under the auspices of the Saxon State Office for Real Estate and Construction Management (SIB).

The installation of the museum (concept and realisation by Gernot Klatte, Stefano Rinaldi, and Bernhard Roosens) was completed in September 2021, under the directorship of Dirk Syndram. Up to 2024, further original paintings and antlers, as well as Baroque copies of the ancestral paintings, were added. The installation of the Firearms Gallery was made possible thanks to the ongoing conservation work and extensive restoration measures under the direction of Andreas Frauendorf.

Today, the Long Corridor is again one of the most impressive interiors of Dresden's Residenzschloss, in which different historical phases are intertwined. The exhibition provides an overview of the history of firearms while showcasing the sumptuous opulence of princely luxury weapons in a unique way. In addition, their technological and functional aspects are explained – thanks to close cooperation with Markus Wacker and students from the Dresden University of Applied Sciences (HTW) – in the form of animated videos. At the same time, dialogue situations and artistic interventions are used to critically question the overwhelming stock of weapons and to reflect on their historical significance and impact in the present day.

The architectural history of the Long Corridor

GERNOT KLATTE

In June 1586, just a few months after his accession to power, the young Elector Christian I laid the foundation stone for an illustrious edifice: the Electoral Stable Building. It contained rooms of eminent importance for a princely court: the ground floor provided stalls for the Elector's 128 personal horses, while halls on the upper floor accommodated the weapons of the Rüstkammer and were furnished as prestigious guest suites. The exterior of the Electoral Stable Building was completed in 1588 and cost the enormous sum of 130,000 gulden.

This structure formed the outer boundary of the palace complex on the eastern side. On the southern side, the Electoral Chancellery Building had already been built. In order to create an enclosed, integrated ensemble, however, it was necessary to construct the Long Corridor on the north side. Construction began in 1588 and lasted until 1590. The resulting Stable Courtyard provided the Elector and his court with an ideal location for tournaments, tilting at the ring, pageants, and processions. At the same time, the Long Corridor served as a connecting passage between the Residenzschloss and the Stable Building, decorated with dynastic portraits of Wettin rulers (→ see p. 17).

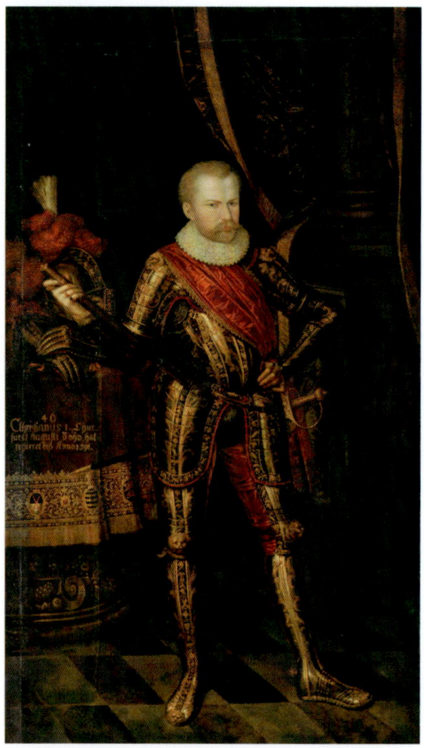

Zacharias Wehme, Elector Christian I of Saxony, Gemäldegalerie Alte Meister, Staatliche Kunstsammlungen Dresden

It is unlikely that it will ever be possible to clarify the exact contributions of individuals to the building's design and execution, although the participation of Paul Buchner is documented and it is generally accepted that Giovanni Maria Nosseni was involved. Paul Buchner (also known as Paulus Puchner), a screw maker from Nuremberg who had worked in the Netherlands and England in the 1550s, was summoned to the Dresden court by Elector August in 1558. There, he became Master of Ordnance at the Electoral arsenal and chief military architect for the fortresses. However, the basic concept of the Stable Courtyard complex is more likely

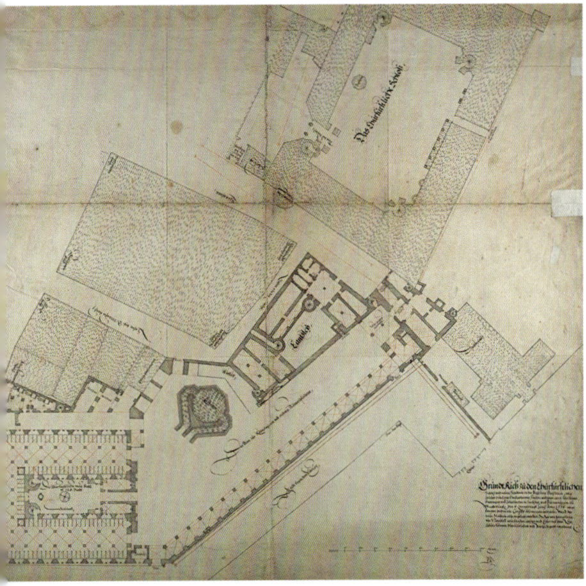

Paul Buchner, Floor plan of the Stable Building with the Stable Courtyard and adjacent buildings, 1586/1588, Sächsisches Staatsarchiv, Hauptstaatsarchiv Dresden

to derive from the Saxon court artist and 'artistic director' Giovanni Maria Nosseni, who must have been familiar with the Corridoio Vasariano in Florence, an elevated enclosed passage-way designed by Giorgio Vasari in 1565, as well as with the Uffizi Gallery. The design of the arched gallery with Tuscan columns may also have been conceived by Nosseni. In any case, Buchner's involvement is at least confirmed by his signature on the surviving floor plan dating from the construction period. Hans Irmisch is the third person sometimes associated with the construction of the Stable Building and Stable Courtyard. He had previously worked as a master bricklayer, and later as a master builder, on various electoral buildings such as the large Dresden arsenal (Albertinum).

While the Stable Building is very much in line with the stolid, transalpine German Renaissance style, the exterior and interior of the Long Corridor are much more elegant, streamlined, and Italianate. The building, which is almost exactly 100 metres long, is designed with arcade arches supported by columns in the Tuscan order. On the upper floor, the façade is divided up by coupled windows, each pair having a triangular pediment above it. The original roof had a curved cross-section. On the north and south sides, three wall dormers with gables were arranged symmetrically, between which small dormers also interrupted the roof surface. With its curved roof, the Long Corridor was similar in its structure and configuration to the Belvedere on the Jungfernbastei, which was also designed by Nosseni. This building was reminiscent of Queen Anne's Summer Palace in Prague (completed in 1563), with which Christian I, as well as Nosseni and Buchner, would have been familiar.

Along with the arcade architecture of the Small Courtyard in the Dresden Residenzschloss, which is evocative of the High Renaissance, as well as the aforementioned Belvedere and the Wettin burial chapel in Freiberg Cathedral, the Stable Building and the Long Corridor constitute the architectural legacy of Elector Christian I.

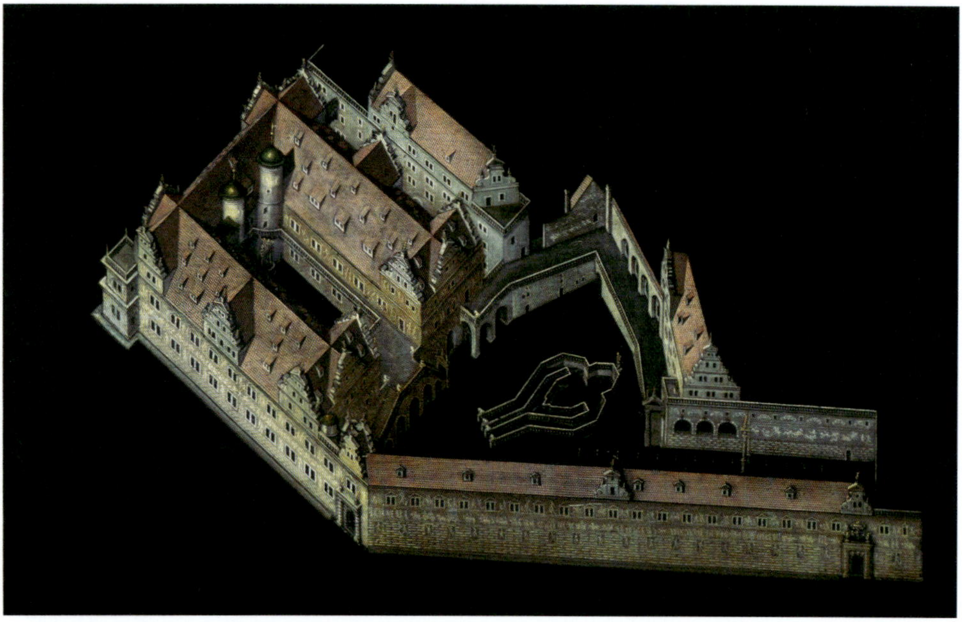

Andreas Vogel, The New Stable Building in Dresden, 1623, Rüstkammer, Staatliche Kunstsammlungen Dresden

Like the Stable Building itself, Nosseni and Buchner's edifice was decorated with grisaille paintings imitating the sgraffito technique, with a Roman triumphal procession being depicted on the north wall of the Long Corridor. The wall behind the arcades on the Stable Courtyard side was decorated with depictions of horses that could be covered over with wooden panels. The upper storey was decorated with scenes from the Labours of Hercules, with a sundial in the centre. Coats of arms of the Saxon hereditary lands were positioned in the spandrels, with alternating rams' horns and stag antlers below them.

The interior of the upper floor formed the actual corridor between the Georgenbau and the Stable Building. The passageway had a coffered ceiling decorated with projecting gilded wooden pegs. Three fireplaces provided a touch of warmth. The flues protruded obliquely into the room; similar Renaissance fireplaces have been preserved at Augustusburg Castle, for example.

The painter Heinrich Göding the Elder, a native of Braunschweig who had been a pupil of Lucas Cranach the Elder and who had already been summoned to the Dresden court by Elector August, was commissioned by Christian I to decorate the interior. Within just a short period, Göding and his assistants completed not only the painted ornamentation in the arched niches and on the coffered ceiling but, above all, the original 47 ancestral portraits – large-scale oil paintings on canvas – and 51 tournament paintings in oil on wood (→ cf. pp. 16–23).

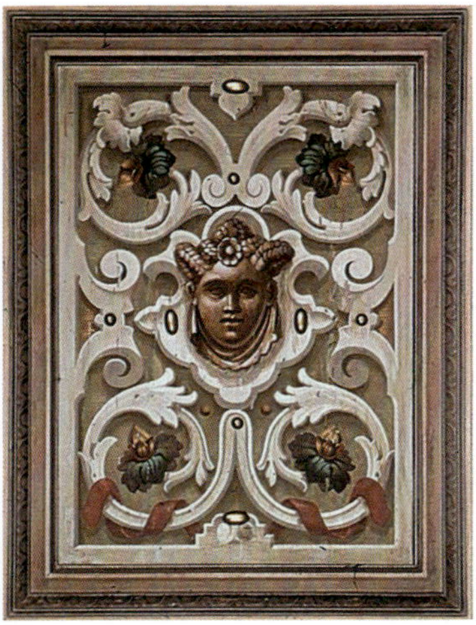

Heinrich Göding the Elder and workshop (repainted around 1860–61), Detail of the wooden ceiling in the Long Corridor, photo taken in 1943–44

The arched niches and 84 coffered panels were decorated with scrollwork ornaments, masks, and grotesques, as well as depictions of animals, plants, and allegories; the coffered panels also included male and female heads. The inside faces of the window surrounds featured medallions depicting Classical warrior heads.

The only changes made during the seventeenth century were the addition of further ancestral portraits (the Electors Christian II and the four Johann Georgs, I to IV). In the spring of 1733, the new Elector, Friedrich August II, decided to transfer the firearms collection to the Long Corridor and exhibit it there. Little is known about the construction work undertaken in converting the Long Corridor with the ancestral gallery into the "Royal Firearms Gallery at the Stables". This work was undoubtedly overseen by the Oberlandbauamt, whose director at the time was still Matthäus Daniel Pöppelmann. However, a brilliant architect was hardly needed: after all, it only involved bricking up every second window and painting mock windows in grisaille technique on the exterior walls. The window niches, which were bricked up alternately on either side of the corridor, were fitted with leaf-door wooden cabinets. These were used to display the firearms of the electoral-royal collection – in 1733 this comprised around 900 long guns and pistols. The remaining furnishings (the ancestral portraits and tournament paintings) were hardly affected. The character of the ancestral gallery was only disturbed by these installations in that the number of windows was halved, resulting in less harmonious lighting.

Heinrich Göding the Elder and workshop, Painted decoration of an arch over one of the windows in the Long Corridor (south side), photo taken in 1943–44

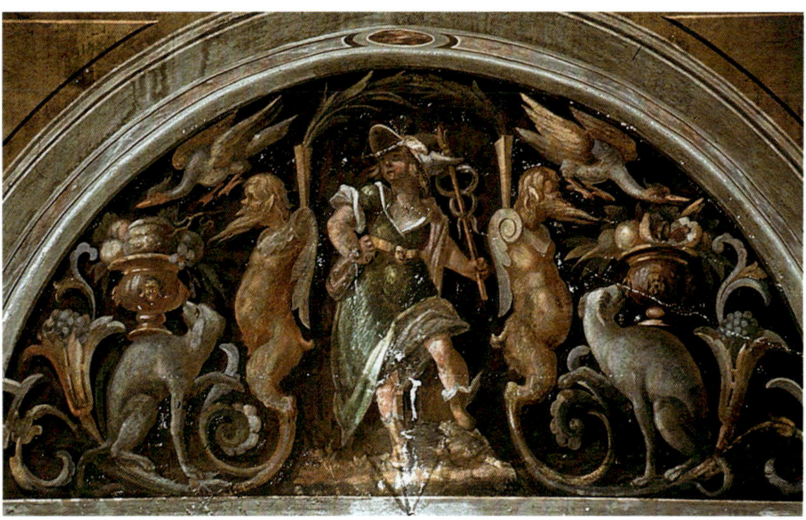

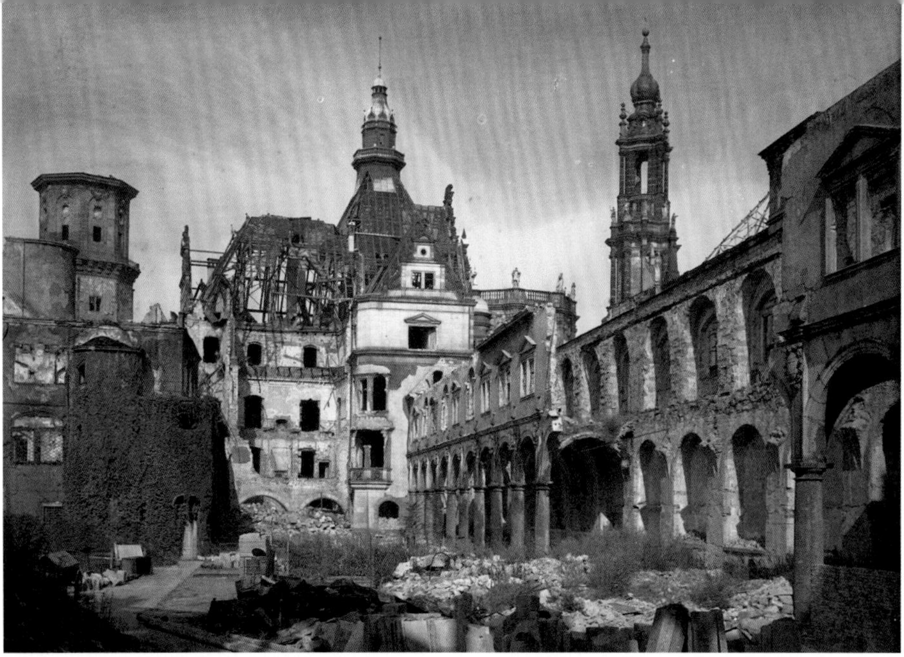

The Stable Courtyard in 1947. Westward view towards the Georgenbau of the Residenzschloss

An unrealised project devised by the court painter Johann Heinrich Schmidt for a completely repainted ancestral gallery would have led in about 1790 to the removal of the firearms gallery and the refurbishment of the Long Corridor in early Neo-classicist style.

In 1860–61, however, the entire building underwent extensive renovation, with the curved roof being replaced by a more easily maintained pitched roof, which required a completely new roof truss construction. The coffered ceiling – both its beam construction and its paintwork – was probably also replaced in the course of this construction work.

Just a few years later, between 1869 and 1876, the northern façade of the Long Corridor was decorated with an elaborate large-scale painting: the Procession of the Princes *(Fürstenzug)* by Wilhelm Walther. In contrast to Göding's ancestral gallery, Walther only depicted historically documented Wettin margraves, dukes, electors, and kings, including the four Ernestine electors who had been missing from the ancestral gallery. In 1907, the sgraffito painting of the Procession of the Princes was transferred, under Walther's supervision, onto Meissen porcelain tiles. Inside, the leaf doors of the gun cabinets were replaced by wooden roller shutters around 1900.

Starting in late summer 1939, all the exhibits were removed and put into storage due to the war. In 1943–44, the painted décor of the Long Corridor was documented in Agfacolor photographs as part of the campaign to record historic wall and ceiling paintings, known as the *Führerauftrag Monumentalmalerei*. During the bombing raid in February 1945, the Long Corridor suffered severe damage: the roof and the upper storey were completely burnt out; some axes of the south wall later collapsed into the Stable Courtyard, probably in July 1945. The north wall with the Procession of the Princes miraculously survived with little damage.

When the Stable Building, now called the Johanneum, and the Long Corridor were rebuilt for use as a transport museum in the 1950s, the three wall dormers with Renaissance gables on the Stable Courtyard side were omitted. Until 2016, the eastern end of the Long Corridor, adjacent to the Johanneum, was used for the Transport Museum's shipping exhibition, while the western third was used as a storage area.

In 1979, the Stable Courtyard – including the south façade of the Long Corridor – was the first part of the palace complex to be decorated with sgraffito painting modelled, albeit in simplified form, on historical precedents, omitting the depictions of the Labours of Hercules. Although rams' horns and stag antlers were again hung alternately in the spandrels, no attempt was made to reconstruct the horse pictures formerly present in the arcade.

Starting in 2016, the entrance to the Long Corridor via the new staircase at the Jagdtor (Hunting Gate) was created as part of a construction project carried out by the architecture firm Heine Mildner Architekten (Dresden) on behalf of and under the supervision of the Dresden I branch of the Saxon State Office for Real Estate and Construction Management (SIB). Heine Mildner also designed 18 wall cabinets and four table display cases for the Rüstkammer's new exhibition.

Since the opening of the Firearms Gallery as a permanent exhibition in August 2021, this unique space has finally become accessible to the public once again, allowing visitors to appreciate the combination of authentic architecture, colourful painted décor, ancestral portraits, and tournament paintings, along with the Rüstkammer's historical collection of firearms in its original location.

The Long Corridor with the Procession of the Princes facing the Augustusstraße

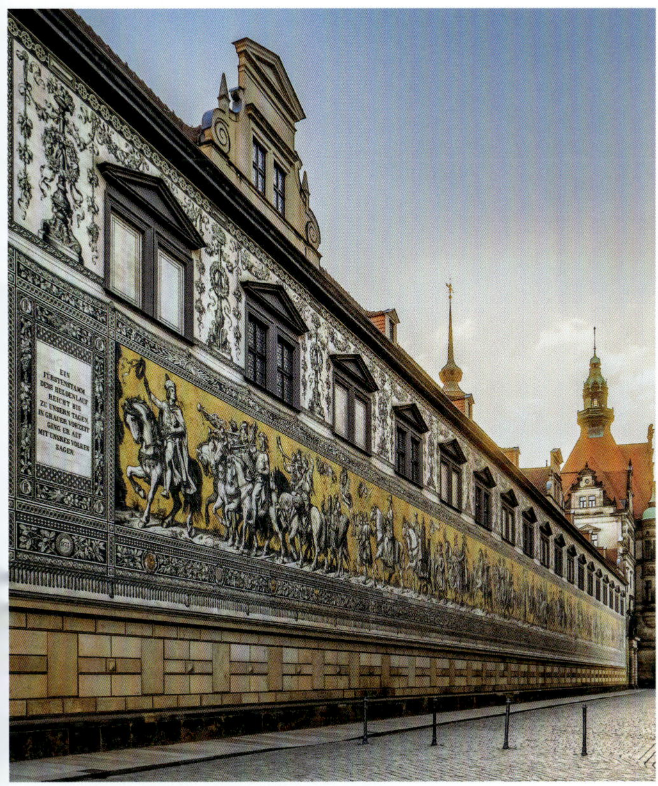

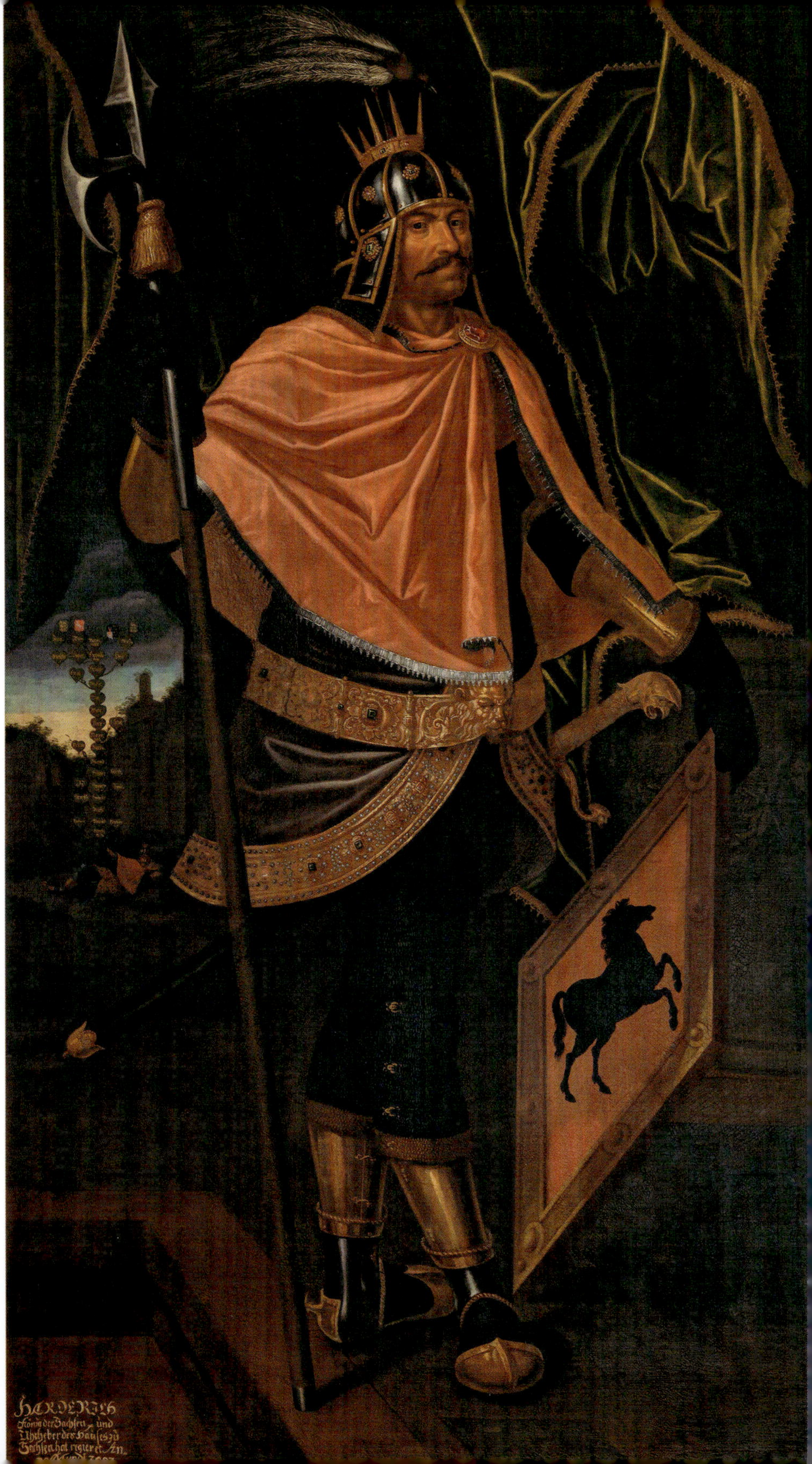
König der Sachsen und
Uhrheber des Hauses zu
Sachsen hat regieret An.

Ancestral gallery and depictions of tournaments: The paintings in the Long Corridor

STEFANO RINALDI

The Long Corridor functioned primarily as a connecting passage between the Residenzschloss and the Stable Building. It also served as an architectural complement to the Stable Courtyard, which was designed for court festivities and jousting tournaments. From the outset, however, it was also intended that the walls of the Long Corridor be used for displaying paintings. This idea, which was obviously influenced by Italian models, was probably the brainchild of the court artist Giovanni Maria Nosseni, who had been trained in Florence. Originally, Elector Christian I intended to assemble a series of portraits of famous personalities to be presented there. Such collections of so-called *uomini illustri* were particularly popular in humanist circles, not only in Italy. In 1588, however, the Elector changed his mind in favour of a series of dynastic portraits: an ancestral gallery that was intended to demonstrate the reigning Elector's descent from the Saxon tribe of late antiquity on the basis of forty-seven portraits of previous rulers. The partly fictitious dynastic succession was based on the genealogical research of the Saxon court scholar Petrus Albinus. The ancestral series began with King Harderich (1st century BCE) as the legendary founder of the House of Saxony and continued in a direct line to the electors of the Albertine branch of the House of Wettin – omitting the older Ernestine lineage of the family.

The oversized full-length portraits were created by the court painter Heinrich Göding the Elder and his workshop, and were delivered from 1589 onwards. The background of each one depicted an episode from the life of the respective prince. The monumental canvas paintings were presented in large ornamental frames decorated with carved and coloured appliqués. Below each picture, framed by Mannerist carved cartouches, was a small oval depiction of a heroic deed performed by the ancestor, along with his coat of arms and a calligraphic panel containing a short biography in German and a Latin couplet. This combination of a portrait with a caption (in this case supplemented by two history paintings) followed the basic principle of humanist portrait collections. After the death of Christian I, the series was extended by adding the portraits of his successors up to Elector Friedrich Christian (only August III was missing). One portrait (that of Duke Georg the Bearded) was removed at an unspecified date before 1873.

Heinrich Göding the Elder (copy after), Harderich, King of the Saxons, probably Dresden, before 1728, Rüstkammer, Staatliche Kunstsammlungen Dresden

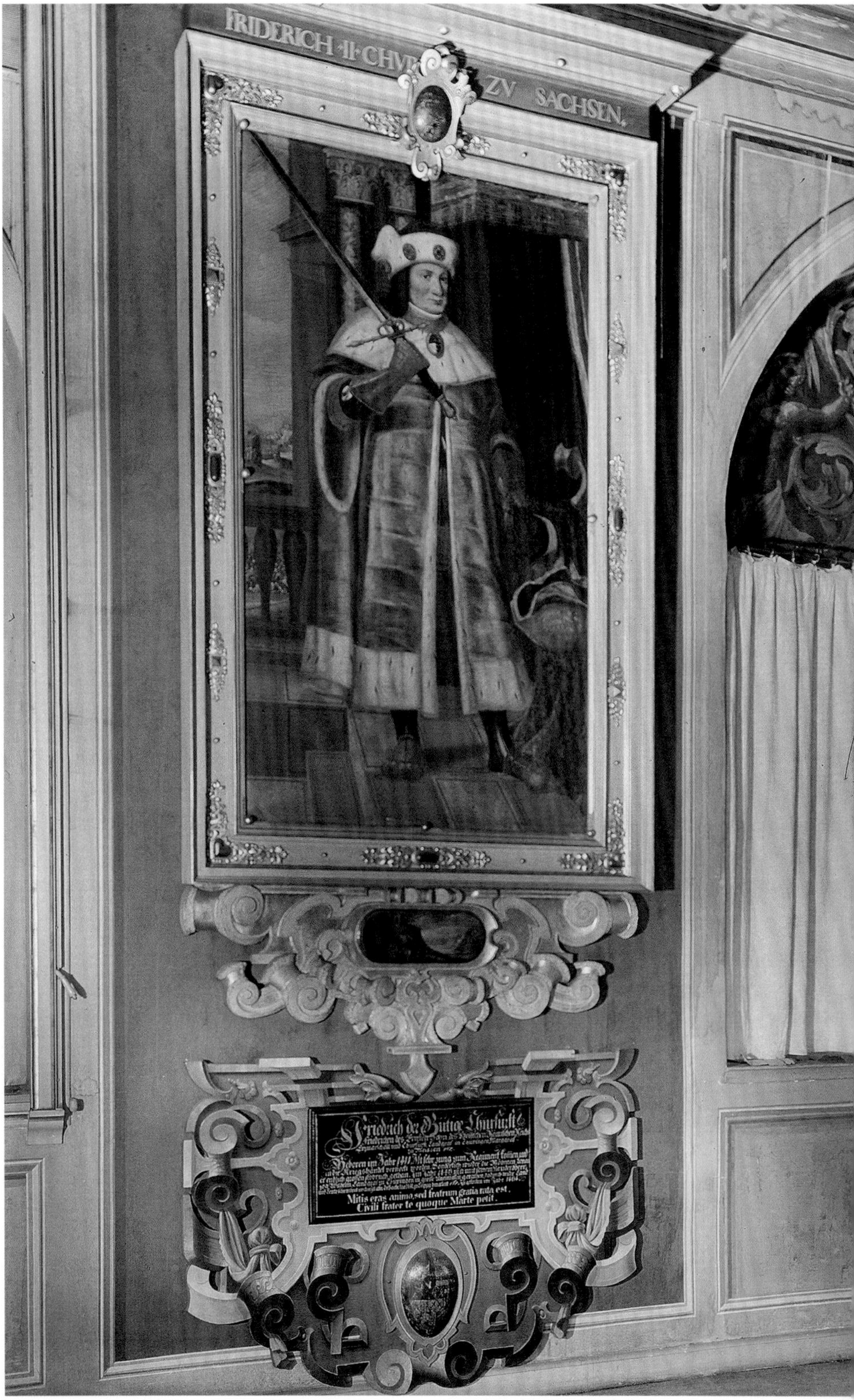
FRIDERICH · II · CHVR
ZV SACHSEN.
Friedrich der Gütige Churfürst
Mitis eras animo, sed fratrum gratia rata est.
Civili frater te quoque Marte petit.

Wall section of the Long Corridor with ancestral portrait of Elector Friedrich the Gentle, photo taken in 1943

Unfortunately, Göding's original ancestral gallery is one of Dresden's wartime losses; only some of the decorative frames and a single inscription panel with its cartouche have survived. The twenty portraits presented in the permanent exhibition are a series of copies in approximately the same format, which August the Strong commissioned for a room at Königstein Fortress in about 1728. The copies reliably reproduce Göding's originals; however, no text panels were included on the series made for Königstein – instead, a short version of the respective biography was integrated into the picture surface. The great vivacity of the lost ancestral portraits by Göding is clearly discernible in these high-quality reproductions – especially where the earlier, fictitious ancestors are concerned. With their curious weapons and exotic costumes, they represent an anticlassical Germanic ancestral myth, which almost seems to be in deliberate contrast to the Italianate architectural surroundings and the humanist concepts behind the collection. The baroque replicas of the ancestral portraits were restored in 2001–2005 with generous support from the Getty Foundation.

Göding's pictorial programme for the Long Corridor also included a second series of paintings. These were depictions of the tournaments in which Elector August, the father of Christian I, had participated. August had been a keen practitioner of this courtly sport in all its variants and had his total of 55 performances in jousting and tilting competitions documented in an illustrated tournament book (formerly held in the Saxon State Library in Dresden, wartime loss). Göding used this manuscript as the source for his images. The oil paintings on

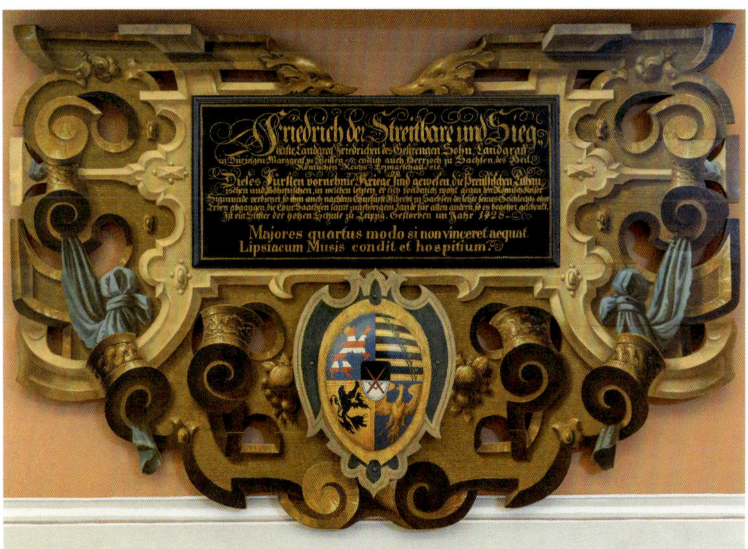

Inscription panel relating to Elector Friedrich the Belligerent, Heinrich Göding the Elder and workshop, c. 1589–1592, Rüstkammer, Staatliche Kunstsammlungen Dresden

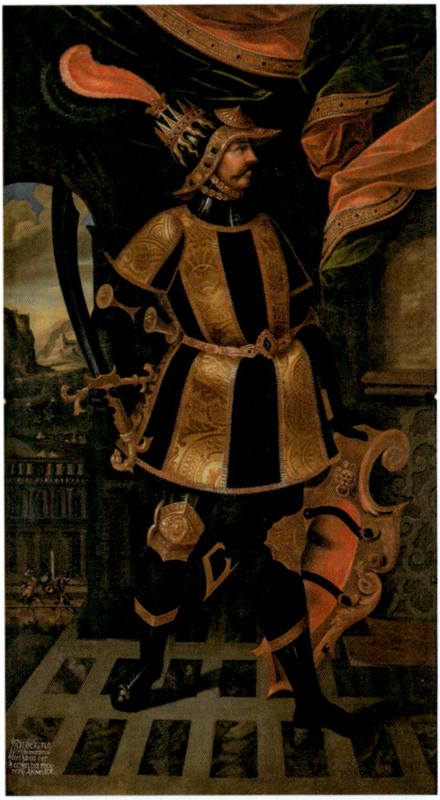

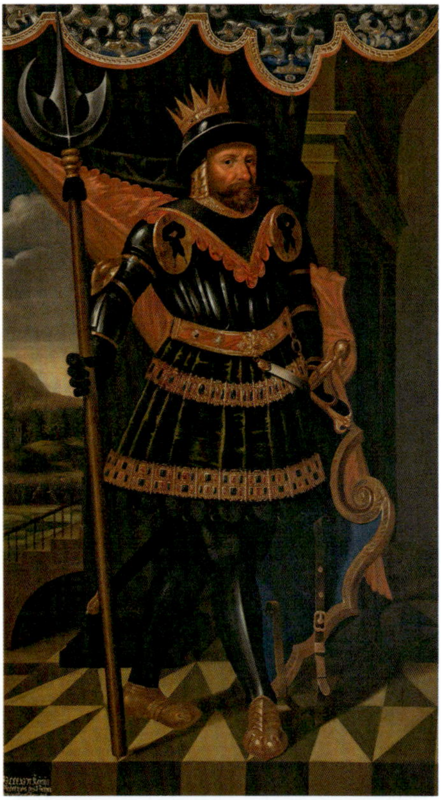

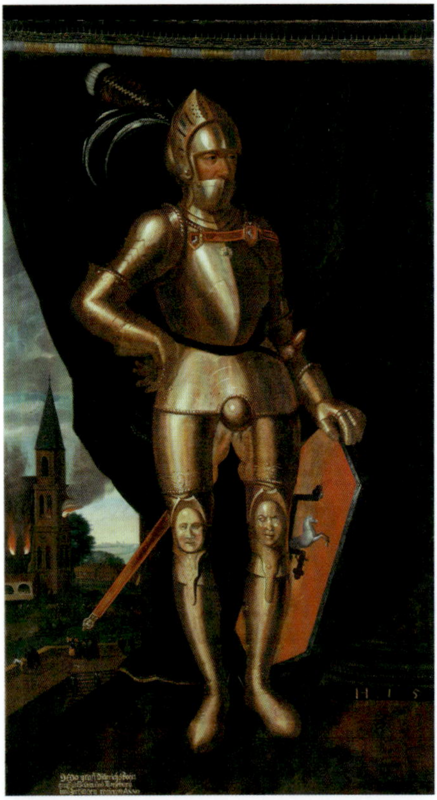

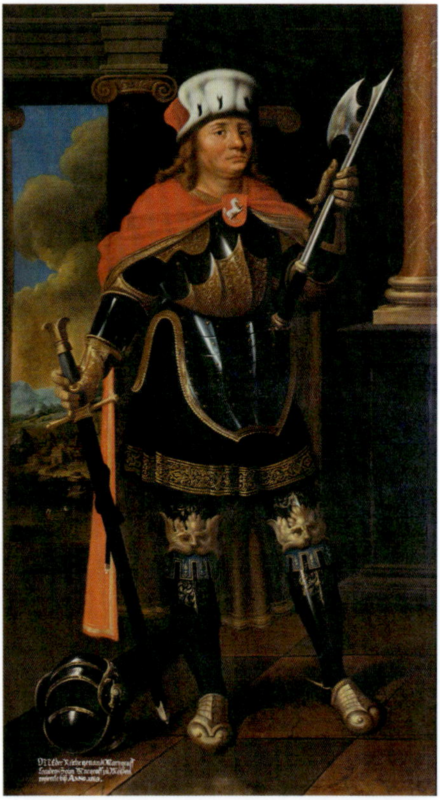

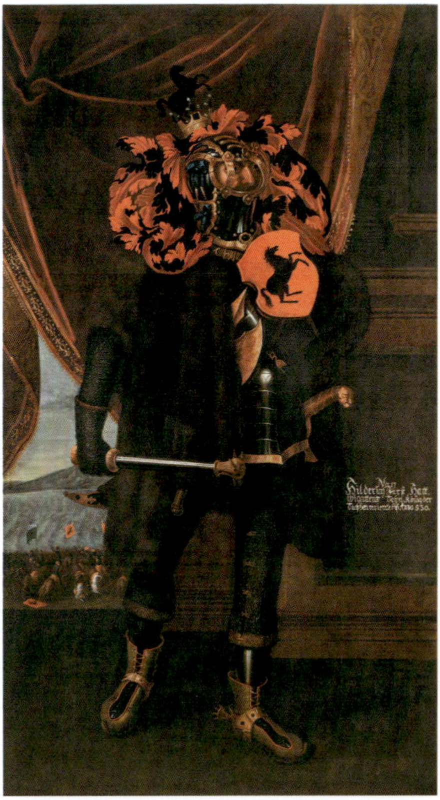

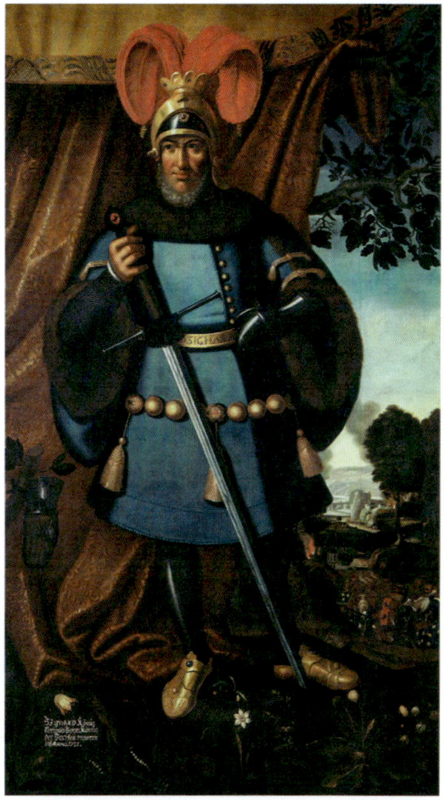

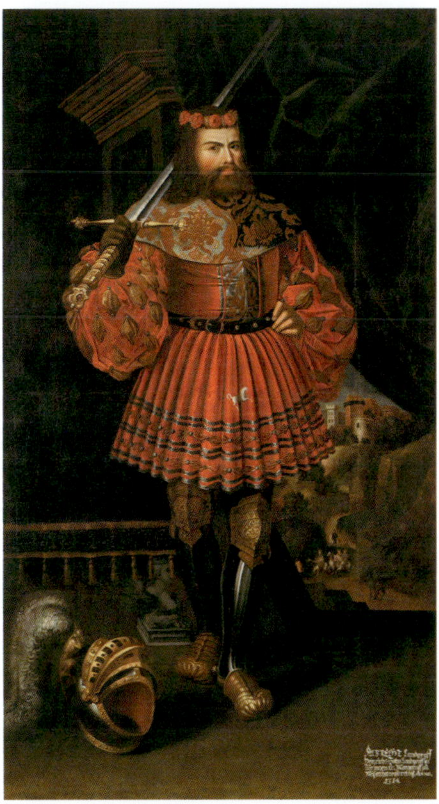

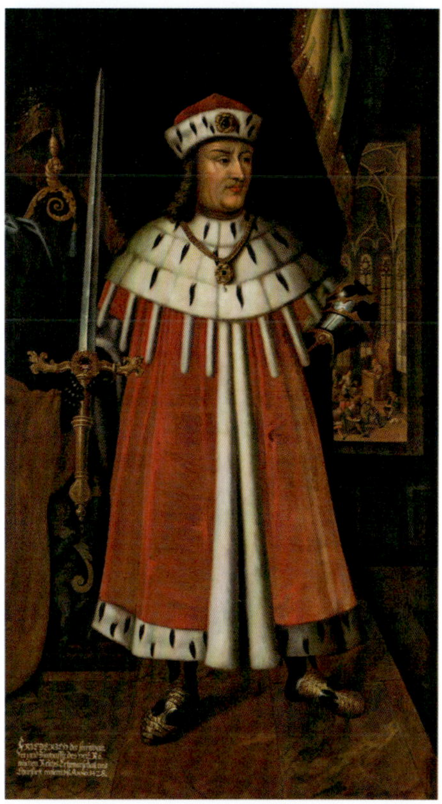

wood, in rectangular or oval horizontal format, were mounted on scrollwork cartouches similar to the text panels on the ancestral portraits. A caption, also copied from the tournament book, provided brief information on the type, year, and occasion of the respective tournament, the identity of the opponent, and the result – invariably a victory for the Duke and Elector of Saxony.

The tournament paintings occupied the only spaces on the wall in the Long Corridor that were not taken up by the ancestral gallery, namely the areas beneath the windows. The series was closely associated with the architecture, since these very windows (at least on the south side) afforded a privileged view of the Stable Courtyard. The past equestrian successes of Elector August could thus be seen in direct juxtaposition to the contemporary tournament performances of his son, Christian I.

Before the Second World War, there were 29 tournament paintings in the series; however, the chronicle compiled by Anton Weck (called the *Wecksche Chronik*), published in 1679, mentions 51 tournament depictions "under the windows in this gallery". If this description is to be believed, it must be assumed that under some of the windows, of which there were originally 36, two pictures were hung next to each other. It is possible that the conversion of the Long Corridor into the Firearms Gallery in 1733 prompted the removal of some of the tournament paintings. Ten of Göding's paintings – along with their cartouche frames – have survived down to the present day. Nine of them are on display in the Long Corridor.

→ pp. 20–21
Copies after the ancestral portraits by Heinrich Göding the Elder, probably Dresden, before 1728
From left to right, top row: Wiedekind I, Willekin, Hilderich, Sighard; bottom row: Dedo, Margrave Otto the Rich, Margrave Albrecht the Degenerate, Elector Friedrich the Belligerent. Rüstkammer, Staatliche Kunstsammlungen Dresden

Heinrich Göding the Elder, Three tournaments of Elector August, Dresden, c. 1589–1592:
vs Heinrich von Schönberg in Meißen, 1549;
vs Christoph von Wallwitz in Dresden, 1543;
vs Hans von Schönefeld in Merseburg, 1544.
Rüstkammer, Staatliche Kunstsammlungen Dresden

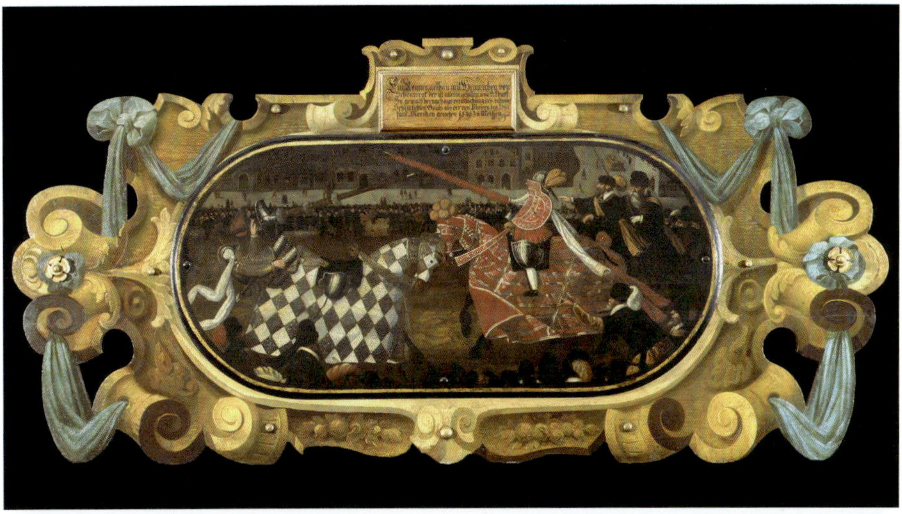

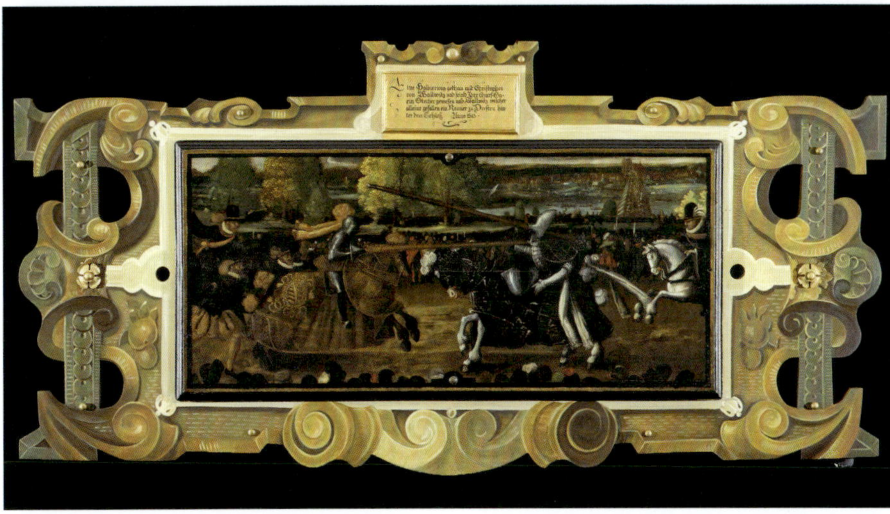

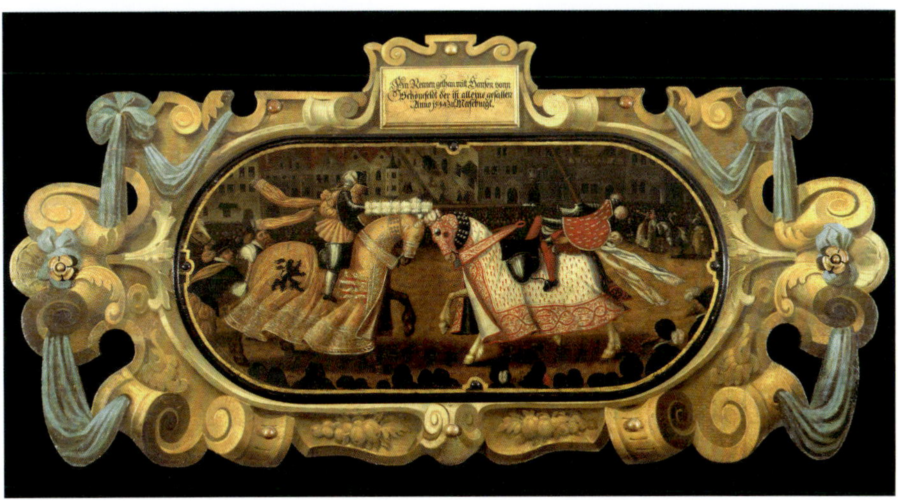

The history of the Firearms Gallery

STEFANO RINALDI

One of the first official acts of Elector Friedrich August II of Saxony (from 1734 also King August III of Poland) was to establish a museum that was unique in Europe. At the end of 1733, just a few months after his accession to power, the new Elector – who was a passionate hunter – had more than 900 hunting and luxury firearms put on display in the Long Corridor of Dresden's electoral and royal palace, the Residenzschloss. The collection consisted mainly of the personal arms (called *Leibgewehr*) that had belonged to his father, August the Strong, along with the new ruler's own collection of firearms, which he had assembled while still an electoral prince. Systematically organised and attractively presented, the collection soon became one of Dresden's most important places of interest for visitors. Organisationally, the Firearms Gallery constituted an independent museum institution.

Origins: The firearms collection in the Rüstkammer

By the late sixteenth century, the Rüstkammer (armoury) of the Saxon electors already contained numerous rifles and pistols. In addition to hunting and target shooting, these guns were used as prestigious display items and also as equipment for the Electoral Saxon Life Guards (*Trabantengarde*). Over the course of the seventeenth and early eighteenth centuries, the princes continued to accumulate firearms, adding considerable numbers of hunting, sporting, and luxury weapons to the existing collection. Weapons of war were not included in this collection – since 1563, these had been stored centrally in the Dresden arsenal (the building now known as the Albertinum).

Until the early eighteenth century, the firearms of the Electors were kept in various locations, primarily in the Stable Building (today's Johanneum), which was built in 1586–1588. The ground floor accommodated 128 stalls for horses, while the upper level and the two attic storeys housed the Rüstkammer, which served as a collection of equipment and accessories for festivals and masquerades, as well as being an illustrious museum collection. Most of the firearms were initially kept in rooms called the pistol chamber (*Pistolenkammer*) and the rifle chamber (*Büchsenkammer*) respectively; as the collection grew over the course of the seventeenth century, it became necessary to create a "second" and then a "third rifle chamber". Valuable small arms were also kept in the Residenzschloss; the *Ratsstube*

View of the Firearms Gallery from the east, photo taken before 1933

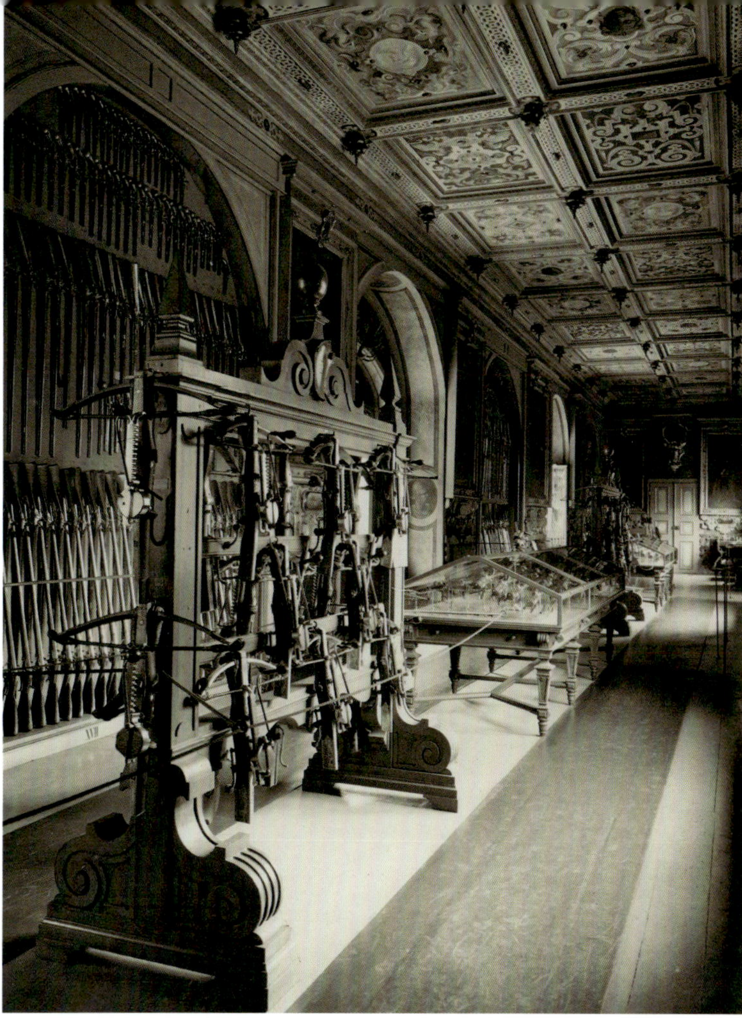

(council chamber), for example, contained several cabinets for storing particularly prestigious pieces, which were occasionally exhibited during state visits. In addition, from at least the second half of the seventeenth century onwards, the palace also incorporated one or even two "small rifle chambers" (*kleine Büchsenkammern*) for the personal firearms of the reigning elector and the electoral prince. When August the Strong was crowned King of Poland in 1697, a more complex collection topography emerged: around 1700 and in 1716, some groups of firearms were catalogued in Warsaw; and from the 1720s onwards, August's son kept parts of his personal firearms collection at his hunting lodge, Schloss Hubertusburg.

The *Leibgewehr* of August the Strong

The Firearms Gallery was created as part of the restructuring undertaken during the reign of August the Strong – a development that was to have an enduring impact on the Dresden collections. In 1722, it was decided to convert the Stable Building into an opulent guest residence. The neighbouring War Chancellery was chosen as the new home for the holdings of the Rüstkammer. Starting on 17 November 1722, the collection was transferred there, with the division into "chambers" for specific categories of equipment being retained: for example, the War Chancellery again included a "pistol chamber", although its contents were distributed among three small rooms. Certain groups of items in the collection were moved elsewhere, however. On 3, 5, and 8 December 1722, almost all the contents of the three "rifle chambers" (*Büchsenkammern*) were transferred to the Jägerhof, a hunting lodge on the right bank of the Elbe. There, the almost 1,000 guns formed a separate collection of firearms, which focussed on their practical use in hunting. This collection was limited to long guns, and instead of being administered by the Senior Court Equerry (*Oberhofstallmeister*) who remained responsible for the Rüstkammer until the early nineteenth century, it was now under the auspices of the Senior Court Master of the Hunt (*Oberhofjägermeister*), who was tasked with organising the court hunts. In the Jägerhof, the guns were kept in a room that was likewise called the *Büchsenkammer*. Those specifically responsible for the collection, which was known as the *königliches Leibgewehr* (king's personal arms), were the Head Custodian, Johann Christian Öttel, and the Keeper of the Rifles, Andreas Naumann. Under their supervision, the collection that had grown organically over the course of history was fundamentally reorganised, within a period of eight years, to become a modern collection of weapons intended for actual use. This involved rigorously selecting from among the older wheellock rifles dating from the sixteenth and early seventeenth centuries, in particular. At the same time, the collection was expanded by the addition of firearms from various Saxon hunting lodges and from Warsaw, as well as from the "small rifle chamber" in the Residenzschloss, which was apparently dissolved in 1729. This smaller collection of firearms had important features in common with the *Leibgewehr* in the Jägerhof, as it was a predominantly modern collection, the care of which was the responsibility of the Office of the Senior Court Master of the Hunt and which was organised along typological lines. It is therefore not surprising that in their inventory of the *Leibgewehr* in the Jägerhof, which they began in 1730, Öttel and Naumann emphasised its continuity with the "Rifle Chamber formerly in the Residenzschloss". This Jägerhof inventory presented the collection according

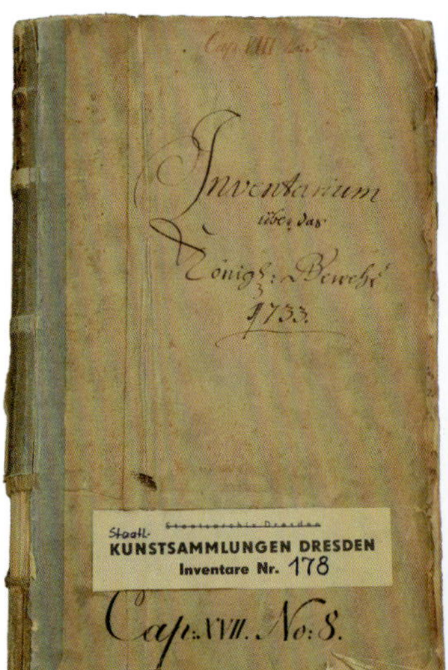

Inventory of the Rifle Chamber in the Jägerhof, 1730–1733

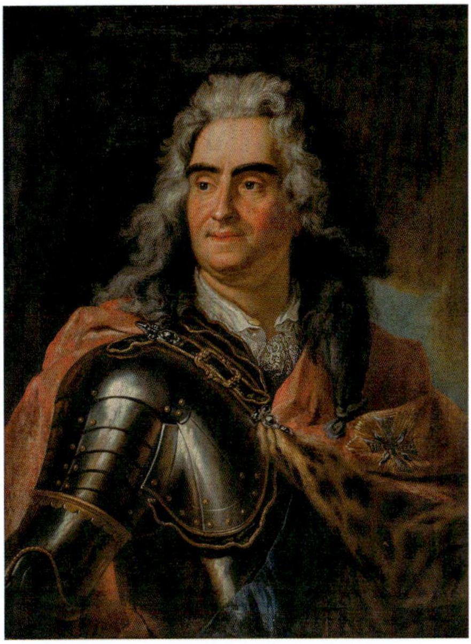

Louis de Silvestre (circle of), King August II of Poland, before 1733, Rüstkammer, Staatliche Kunstsammlungen Dresden

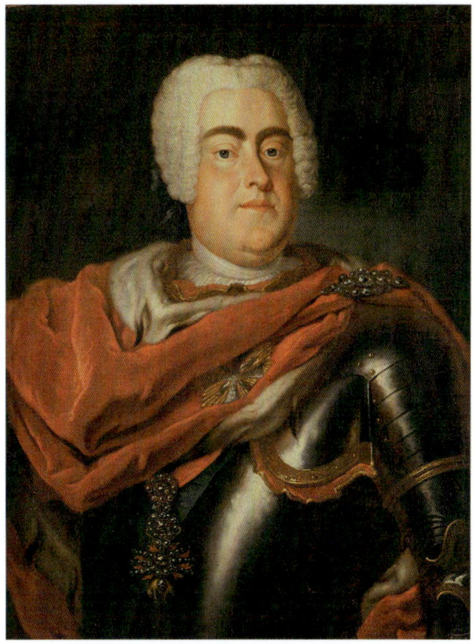

Louis de Silvestre (copy after), King August III of Poland, after 1733, Rüstkammer, Staatliche Kunstsammlungen Dresden

to its new form of organisation for the first time. The long guns were catalogued under 19 "chapters" according to their typology and origin, with the various categories differentiating between rifles and shotguns (i.e. guns with rifled or smoothbore barrels), wheellocks and flintlocks, as well as "short" and "long butts" (firearms with German or French-style stocks). Weapons with Middle Eastern barrels, as well as shotguns from France, Spain, and Italy were also listed separately. On the one hand, this new classification seems to reflect trends in collecting culture precipitated by the Enlightenment, but it also corresponded to the practical requirements of hunting.

August III and the *Leibgewehr* at the Gallery

On 30 January 1733, the Jägerhof inventory begun in 1730 was completed; two days later, August the Strong died. It is therefore questionable whether this ruler already had plans for displaying the *Leibgewehr* in the Long Corridor between the Residenzschloss and the Stable Building. Rather, the surviving sources suggest that the Firearms Gallery in its definitive form was an idea conceived by his son, Friedrich August II; the project was realised in its entirety during the first year of the latter's reign. Only minimal structural work was required, so that the installation of the new display could be completed in just a few months, between April and December 1733. For the presentation of the guns, every second window was bricked up and

17 large wooden cabinets were inserted in the respective niches. These cabinets were lined with green oilcloth and fitted with double-leaf doors. In order not to impair the lighting conditions too much, an alternating sequence was chosen, so that each cabinet faced a window. This presentation concept created sufficient room for the display without disturbing the harmonious character of the existing decoration. The ancestral portraits on the walls were not affected by the alterations, and on the south side even the tournament paintings beneath the windows could be retained, as the cabinet bases were at the height of the window sills. The much deeper niches on the north side, on the other hand, made it possible to place the cabinets in front of the window sills and thus utilise the entire available height. Although the grotesque painting in the lunettes was covered over, it was not destroyed. Overall, the Renaissance character of the room was largely preserved. The unique collection of weapons was substantially elevated in its status through the new display in the Long Corridor. Its harmonious integration into the historically preserved architectural and decorative setting heightened the collection's role as a prestige object. Travellers' reports show that the Firearms Gallery was open to visitors by 1741 at the latest. However, its utilitarian character was also preserved: the guns – now located in the immediate vicinity of the King's private quarters in the section of the palace known as the Georgenbau – were regularly taken out for hunting and target shooting.

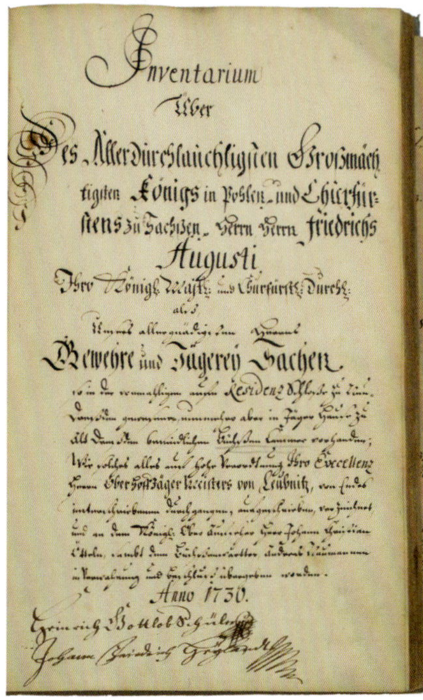
Inventarium
Anno 1730.

Inventory of the Firearms Gallery, 1733

Particularly in terms of the practical administration of the collection, it is not surprising that responsibility for the firearms remained with Head Custodian Öttel and the Keeper of the Rifles Naumann – although there was a change to the institutional structures in which these two officials worked. From 1733, the Hunting Department (*Jägerei*), to which they were both subordinate, was made part of the Chief Chamberlain's Office (*Oberkämmerei*), which was also responsible for the Cabinets of Curiosities (i.e. the art collections). Thus, the new administrative structure reflected the ambivalent nature of the Firearms Gallery as a collection that had both a utilitarian and a display function. It was probably Öttel who designed the presentation of the objects in the initially 17 cabinets. The attractiveness of the new display lay precisely in the consistency and clarity of its typological arrangement: the cabinets on the south side housed the (shorter) rifles, while the north side was reserved for the (longer) shotguns. This distinction also made optimum use of the space available, since structural reasons meant that the display capacity of the nine cabinets on the south side was smaller. At the same time, it resulted in a rudimentary geographical form of classification, as rifles were mainly produced in German-speaking countries, while most shotguns in the collection came from southern and western Europe. The more detailed categorisation resembled the typological-geographical classification system used at the Jägerhof, although the new cabinet names often placed greater emphasis on the function of the objects (for example with headings such as "stalking and target rifles" rather than "bullet rifles with short stocks and German locks"). In addition, the collection was enriched by a group of particularly lavish pistols from the Rüstkammer and the electoral prince's collection. These changes probably accorded with the king's specific preferences: an inventory from 1740 states that Öttel was to "keep the collection in good order, as favoured by His Royal Majesty himself".

Expansion in the reign of August III

The Firearms Gallery was not only the first museum founded by August III, he also succeeded in doubling the size of the collection during thirty years of enthusiastic collecting: according to a catalogue drawn up in 1767, the stock of firearms at the time totalled 1,996 objects. On the one hand, this increase was the result of gifts, commissions, and individual purchases. On the other hand, August was able to acquire significant collections of firearms *en bloc* through purchase or inheritance, for example from the estates of Duke Friedrich Ludwig von Württemberg-Winnental (1736) and Prince Günther I von Schwarzburg-Sondershausen (1741). The most important additions came from the Albertine secondary duchies of Saxe-Merseburg and Saxe-Weissenfels; these "hereditaments" came to Dresden after these Wettin collateral lines died out in 1738 and 1746 respectively.

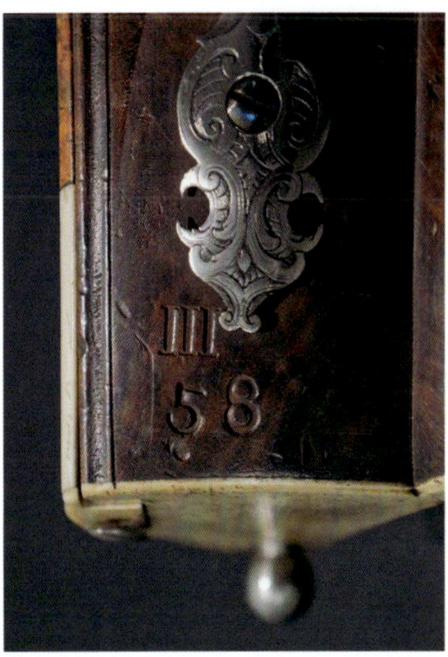

Butt stamp on a rifle from the Firearms Gallery

Owing to the new acquisitions, the original arrangement of the Firearms Gallery was no longer viable, and additional cabinets had to be installed. The initial seventeen cabinets had already proved insufficient when the gallery was first created in 1733, so that around 120 guns had had to be returned to the Jägerhof; now a further shotgun cabinet was installed in the last available position, and sixteen slim cabinets were fitted into the sides of the deep arched niches on the north side. The necessary capacity could only be achieved by displaying the guns in the cabinets in a particularly compact way. In addition, the passageway between the Long Corridor and the Stable Building served as a storeroom.

Over the course of the eighteenth century, each weapon was marked with a butt stamp indicating its precise location in the gallery. A Roman numeral from I to IX denoted the cabinet number and an Arabic numeral the position within the cabinet. These markings are still of decisive importance for identifying the objects today.

The Firearms Gallery from 1763 down to the present day

The heyday of the Firearms Gallery came to an end when August III died in 1763. Nevertheless, the following year a collection of weapons from the "electoral prince's gun chamber" that had belonged to August's short-lived successor, Elector Friedrich Christian, was added to the Gallery. This was followed in 1780 by a particularly high-quality collection of hunting firearms belonging to Friedrich Christian's widow, Maria Antonia of Bavaria. In the nineteenth and early twentieth centuries, the collection was further expanded by guns from the collections of deceased Saxon rulers; in particular, these included modern hunting weapons, such as two Henry repeating rifles – a breech-loading lever-action rifle which was the direct predecessor of the famous Winchester rifle.

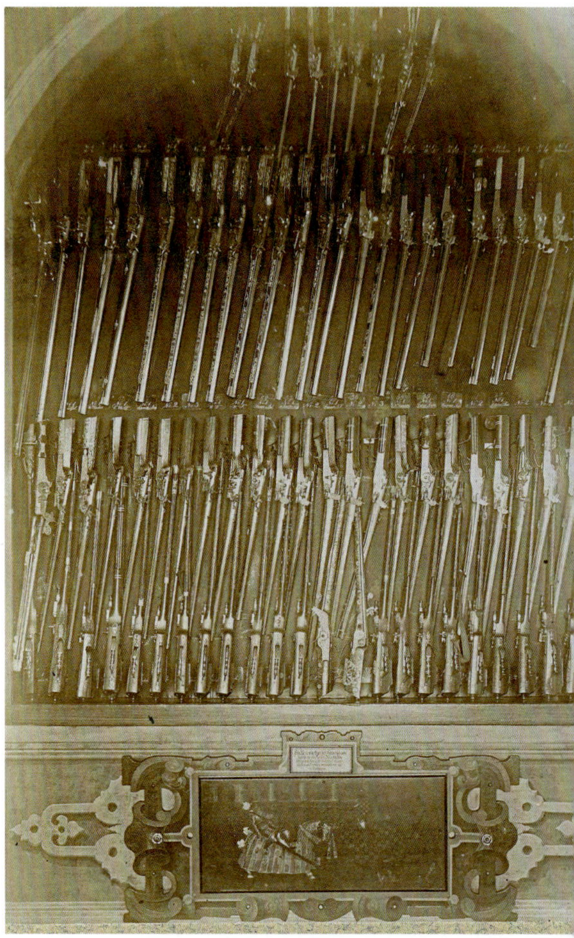

View of a gun cabinet on the south side of the Firearms Gallery, photo taken in the late 19th century (after 1865)

Institutionally, the Firearms Gallery was an independent museum within the Royal Art

Collections (*Königliche Kunstsammlungen*). The Rüstkammer (renamed the Royal Historical Museum in 1832) returned to its former location in the Johanneum in 1877. From 1887, the two museums, which were not only adjacent but were also closely related in terms of their holdings, were managed by a joint director. The original rationale behind the organisation of the Firearms Gallery was largely adhered to, although later additions made the exhibition less visually attractive. In the late nineteenth century, a row of display cases, crossbow stands, tables and two large sets of game scales stood in the central axis of the Long Corridor. In 1934, however, these extraneous items were transferred to the Historical Museum.

The removal of the collection for safekeeping during the Second World War and its transfer to the Soviet Union in 1945–46 marked the end of the history of the Firearms Gallery as an independent institution. When the firearms collection returned to Dresden in 1958 – complete except for one single object – it was made part of the Historical Museum (restored to its former name of Rüstkammer in 1992). Between 1959 and 2012 only a fraction of the collection could be displayed in the East Hall of the Semper Building at the Zwinger. The new permanent exhibition in the Long Corridor finally opened in summer 2021. There are now eighteen large wall display cases in the window niches, presenting around 500 small arms. Loosely based on the historical layout, the Central European gunmaking traditions are displayed on the south side (to the right of the entrance) and those of other European regions on the north side. In four tabletop display cases, technical and socio-historical issues are explored in greater depth with a broader theme-based focus. The three rear wall display cases are densely packed to give an impression of the original appearance. With the conserved fragments of Göding's grotesque painting, the reconstructed coffered ceiling, and the preserved elements of the interior décor, the Firearms Gallery is now a fascinating exhibition space in which its multi-faceted historical, artistic and institutional legacy are manifestly palpable.

Principal exhibits

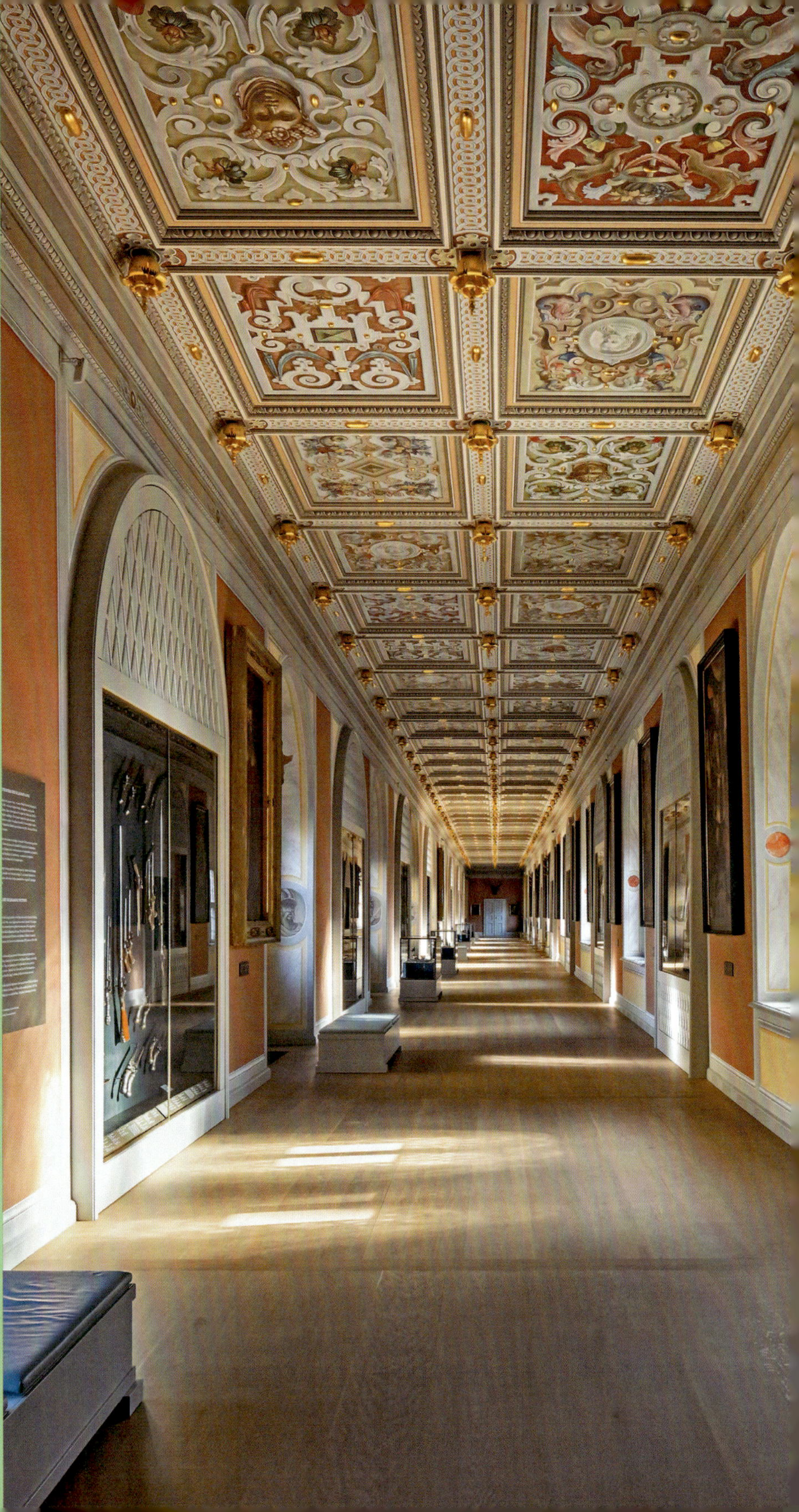

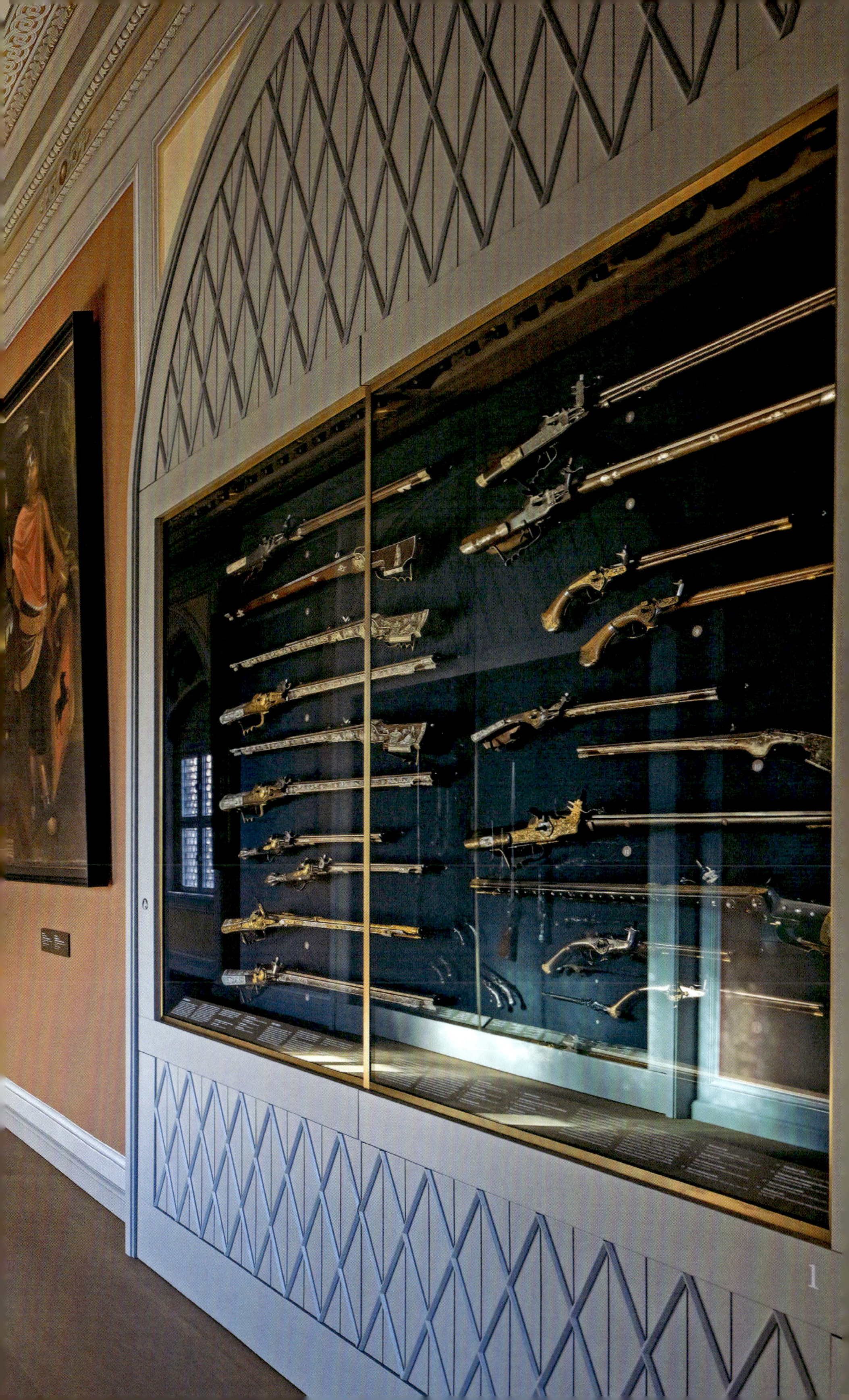

1

Dresden

Gunmakers are known to have been active in Dresden from the late fifteenth century onwards. The earliest examples of hand firearms manufactured in Dresden are dated 1567, these being a pair of wheel-lock pistols bearing the initials S S, produced by the gunmaker Stefan Schickradt for Elector August, which are still in the Rüstkammer today.

The history of Dresden's gunmakers in the early modern period is also a history of disputes between the court and the city, specifically between the electoral gunmakers and the gunmakers' guild. Gunmakers often worked for the court for years, or even decades, without a master's certificate, which they sometimes had to obtain later.

Masters such as Zacharias Herold, Anton, Abraham and Christoph Dreßler made hand firearms – pistols and rifles – on behalf of the court; for the Electors August, Christian I and Christian II, they created different versions of weapons, with varying forms of decoration. Of the wheellock rifles produced by Dresden gun manufacturers, however, only a few remain in the Rüstkammer, as large numbers were sold or discarded, especially in the eighteenth century and in some cases later, because they no longer met the high expectations or were so technically outdated that refurbishment no longer seemed worthwhile. Several early Dresden wheellock pistols – those with particularly ornate decoration – were, however, preserved in the Rüstkammer and are on display in the Residenzschloss. The exhibition also includes standardised pistols made in the late sixteenth and early seventeenth centuries for the Leibtrabanten (the Elector's personal bodyguards). Some of them originate from the workshop of the Dresden gunmaker Hans Stockmann and other court gunmakers such as Georg Geßler. In addition to the gunmakers known by name, who assembled the weapons and produced the lock, other craftsmen were involved in manufacturing the final product: barrelsmiths, gun-

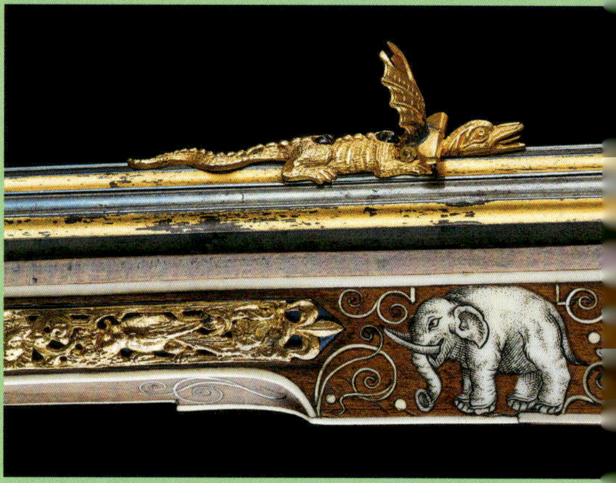

stockers, brassfounders, and engravers. Most of these individuals are not known by name, two exceptions being the gunmakers Hans Fleischer and Hans Frost, who signed their works HF.

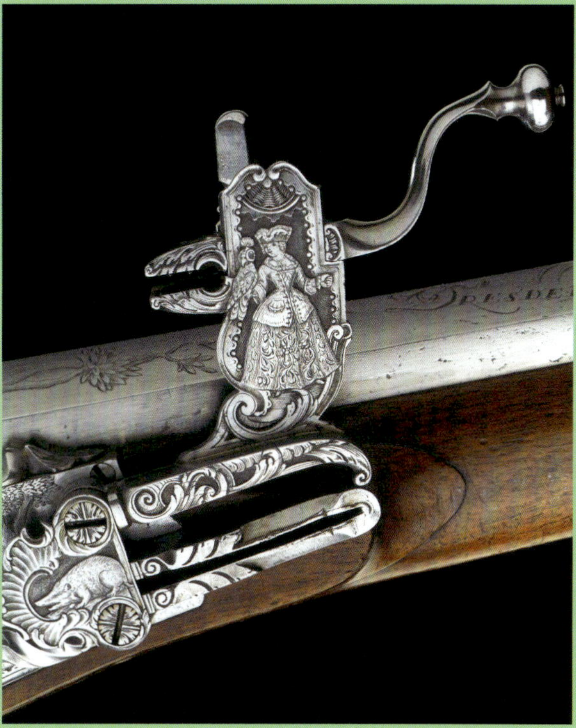

During the Thirty Years' War, only a few court firearms were produced in Dresden. Whereas Dresden gunmakers such as Martin Süssebecker and Nikolaus Fichtner, active in the mid-seventeenth century, left behind sound but not particularly lavish works, the leading Dresden gunmakers of the second half of the seventeenth century came from the Herold family. The father, Balthasar, and his sons Johann Georg and Christian are represented in the collection with wheellock weapons. From the 1690s onwards, flintlock shotguns and pistols were also manufactured in Dresden. Where rifles were concerned, the wheellock initially retained its dominance. Among the craftsmen who produced both wheellock guns and firearms with modern flintlocks ('French locks') were Valentin Rewer and Andreas Erttel, who worked for the court of August the Strong.

During the reigns of the Electors of Saxony and Kings of Poland, August the Strong and August III, the gunmaking trades enjoyed their last great heyday, which lasted until the Seven Years' War. These trades included gunmakers and barrelsmiths, as well as stockers, engravers, and decorators. Their interaction culminated in the exceptionally subtle and ornately decorated wheellock rifles for target shooting. A further activity that played an important role for Dresden masters in the 1730s to 1740s was the re-shafting and re-mounting of high-quality Ottoman barrels. GK

Four wheellock rifles

Hans Stockmann, Dresden, 1605
117.5/116.4/117.4/117.5 cm, Ø 15/16 mm, 4768/4404/4328/4786 g
Inv. nos. G 233, G 234, G 235, G 236

The leading and most productive Dresden gunmaker of the first two decades of the seventeenth century was Hans Stockmann. His birth and death dates are unknown; documents record the delivery of a shotgun made by him in 1590, and he is last mentioned in 1639. What is certain is that he worked at the Dresden arsenal from 1600, that he was appointed as a master of the guild in 1603 – at the Elector's behest and without producing a masterpiece – and that he was granted the status of a burgher in 1605. Stockmann worked primarily for the Elector's court, alternating between richly decorated hand firearms for the Elector and his entourage and more simply crafted wheellock pistols for the guards, the Leibtrabanten. A good 120 of Stockmann's firearms have been preserved in the Dresden Rüstkammer alone.

The four ornate rifles produced by Hans Stockmann for Christian II represent a high point of Dresden gunmaking prior to the Thirty Years' War. The butts of the four rifles depict the ancient legend of Pyramus and Thisbe, which was popular during the Renaissance and was first related in Ovid's Metamorphoses. Having found her lover Pyramus dead, Thisbe throws herself on his sword – a motif that was also used by Shakespeare around the same time: the tragedy of 'Romeo and Juliet' (1597) is a paraphrase of the ancient story. The theme of love – now in a marital union – is illustrated by the depiction of a young couple on the opposite side of the lock: perhaps they represent the young Elector Christian II and his newly wedded wife Hedwig, née Princess of Denmark, whom he married in 1604. The initials and coats of arms of the couple appear in several places on these richly decorated rifles: engraved and

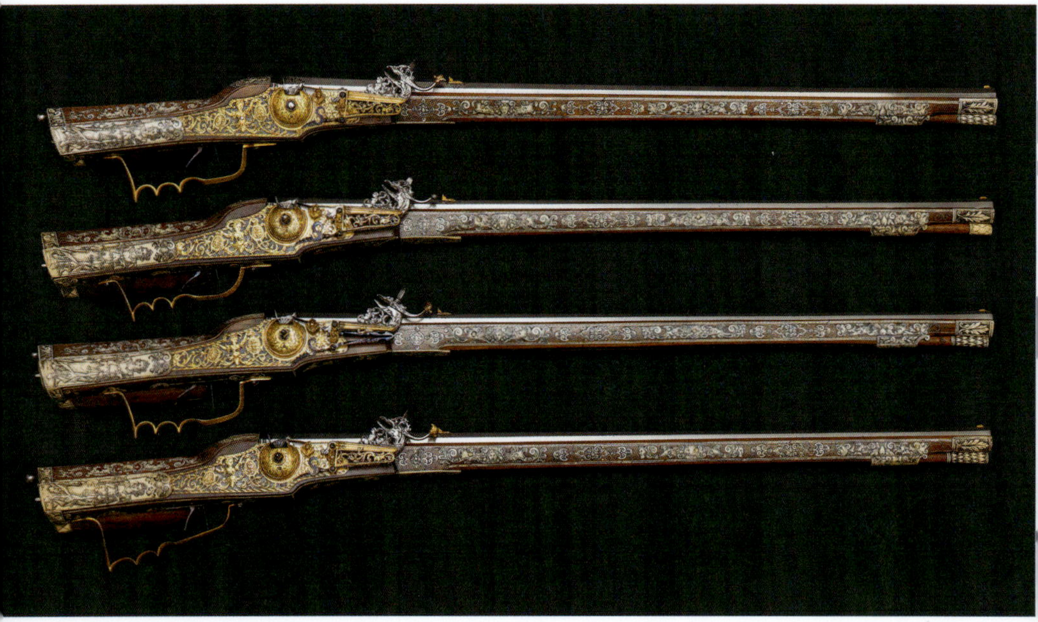

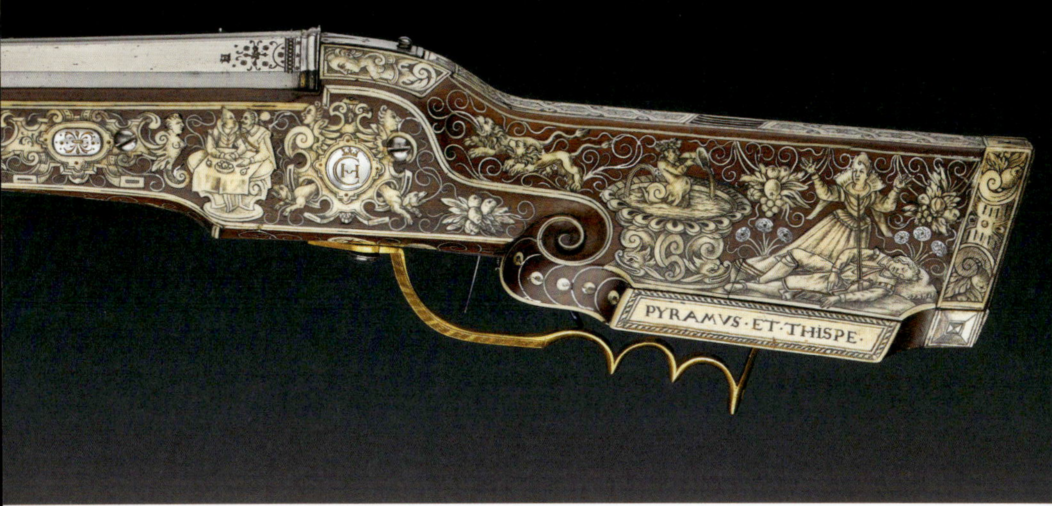

gilded on the brass lock plate (coat of arms); engraved on the butt plates (coat of arms of Electoral Saxony and that of Denmark with the three Danish lions) accompanied by initials; and the initials C and H engraved in mother-of-pearl on the opposite side to the lock. In addition to these heraldic motifs and the Pyramus and Thisbe image, there are depictions of animals, Leda and the swan, as well as grotesques, scrollwork, and a Justitia (without a blindfold) on each of the butt-trap cover plates.

The young Elector had this set of four guns made in 1605, one year after his younger brother Duke Johann Georg (later Elector Johann Georg I) had ordered a first set of luxurious wheellock rifles from Stockmann on the occasion of his marriage (in 1604) to Duchess Sibylla Elisabeth of Württemberg-Montbéliard. That set of four is also in the Rüstkammer collection (exhibited at Hartenfels Castle in Torgau). GK

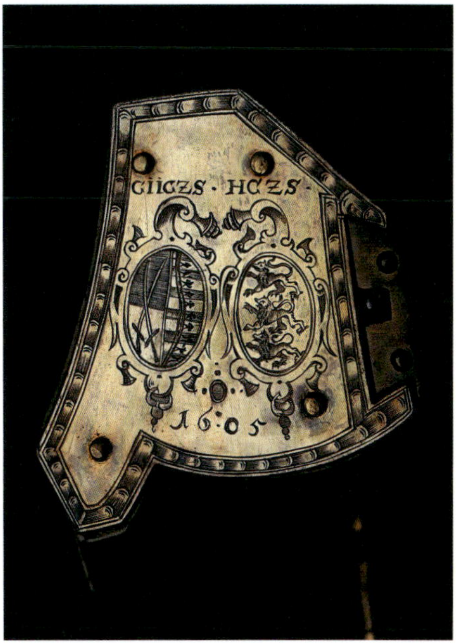

Dresden

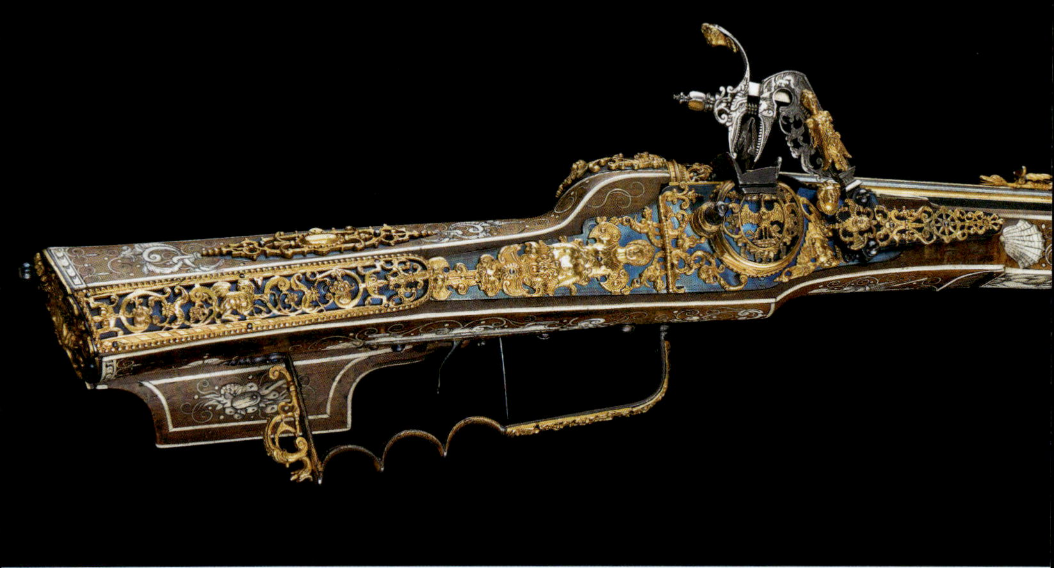

Wheellock rifle with indirect spanning axle and triple-rotating wheel

Georg Geßler, Dresden, 1611
112.8 cm, Ø 10 mm, 3352 g
Inv. no. G 237

In addition to Stockmann's works, the guns produced by Georg Geßler in the first two decades of the seventeenth century are also worthy of special attention. Geßler arrived in Dresden from his native Strasbourg around 1605, becoming a member of the guild in that year. Under Electors Christian II and Johann Georg I, he was a gunmaker "in the stables", i.e. in the Rüstkammer, which at that time was accommodated in the Electoral Stable Building. He mainly produced opulent and ornately decorated firearms for the Dresden court.

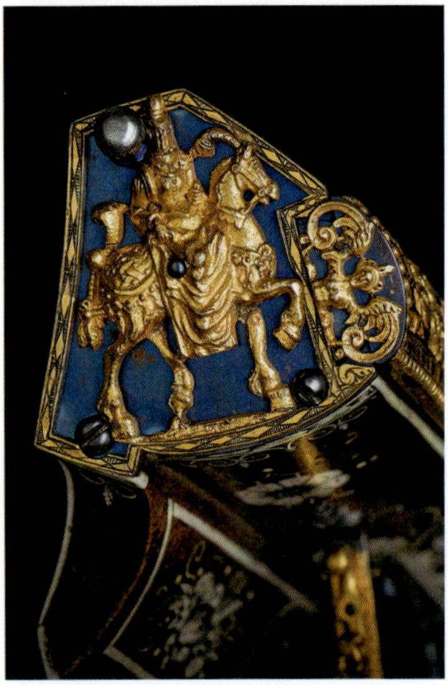

Of particularly exceptional quality is this wheellock rifle, which is designed as a so-called *Dreimalumschläger*, meaning that it has a triple-rotating wheel (→ cf. pp. 70–71). The muzzle and rear sight are in the form of dragons: the wings of the latter can be folded up and down in order to aim at different distances (→ cf. fig. p. 34). This magnificent rifle features a wide variety of decorative images: motifs from Christian iconography – such as the pelican with its young on the wheel cover; depictions of contemporary hunting scenes – a hunter with a hunting dog; exotic and native animals, such as the elephant and the stag; as well as a representation of an elegant lady on horseback on the butt plate, which can perhaps be interpreted as the

Elector's mother, Sophia. Those decorative features are executed in the form of gilded brass appliqués and engraved bone inlays. The picture of the hunter in the medallion on the butt is unusual: he is holding the lead of a dog which is positioned outside the medallion. The dragon motif, reflected in the scale-like surface of the barrel and the dragon-shaped muzzle and sight, can be traced back to older traditions: both hand firearms and prestigious bronze artillery pieces of the sixteenth century frequently featured the fire-breathing dragon as a fearsome symbol.

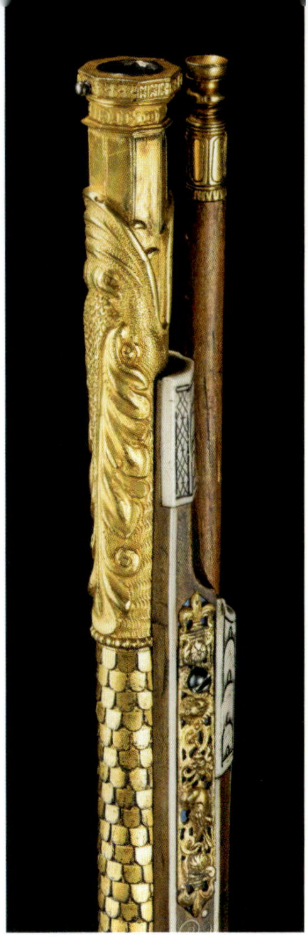

A surviving invoice in the Saxon State Archives describes "a beautiful gilt stalking rifle", which (Dowager) Electress Sophia ordered from Georg Geßler and gave as a gift "at holy Christmastide". It cost 62 gulden and 18 groschen. The name of the recipient is not entirely certain; it was probably Christian II or Johann Georg I. The rifle first appears in the 1667 Büchsenkammer inventory. There, it can be identified with a high degree of certainty on the basis of the remark that it is "dreimal umzuschlagen" (triple-rotating) and is a masterpiece by the gunmaker Georg Geßler. It is described as a gift from the Elector's mother to Elector Christian II. The date "1611" on the barrel is, however, problematic: Christian II died in June 1611. Perhaps it was given as a Christmas gift to his brother Johann Georg I, who succeeded him. GK

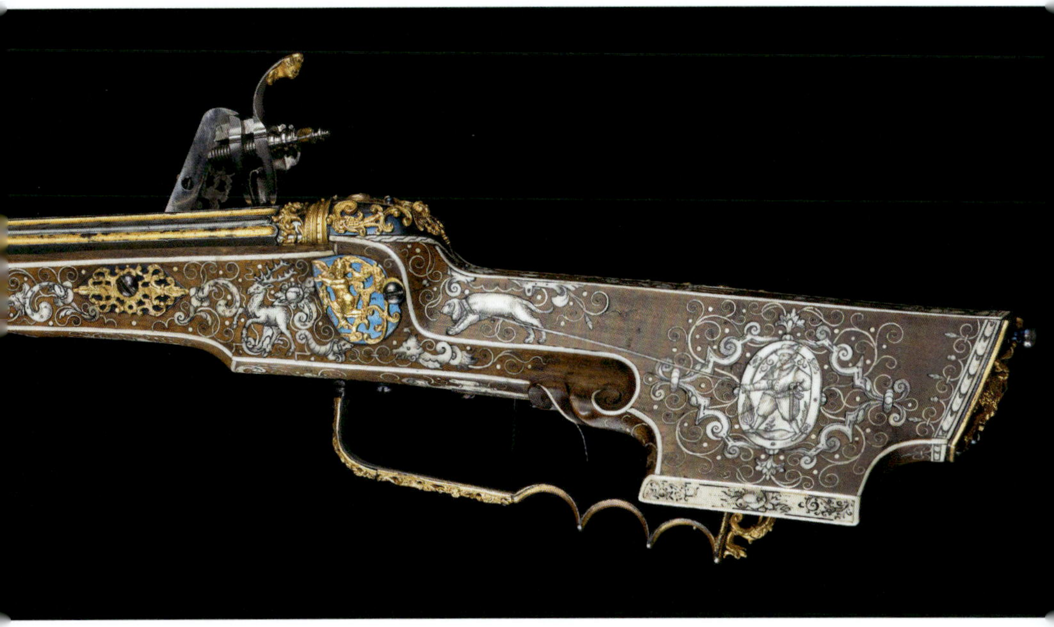

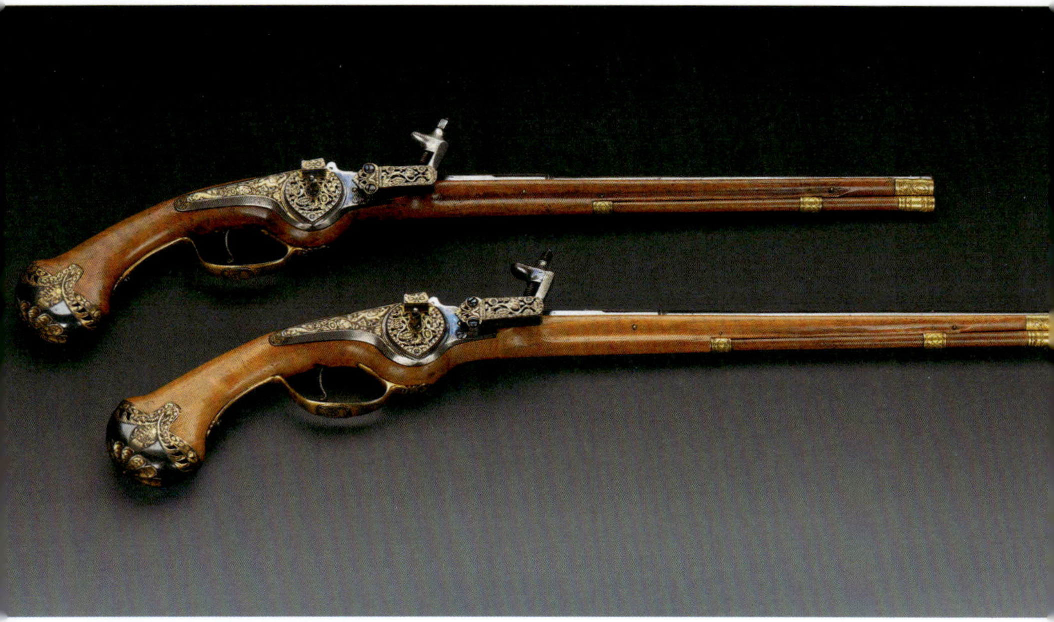

Pair of wheellock pistols

Christian Herold, Dresden, before 1663
64.8/64.6 cm, Ø 13 mm, 1255/1235 g
Inv. nos. J 491, J 492

The most important gunmaker in the Herold family was the younger son, Christian Herold, who made exclusive luxury weapons for the Electors Johann Georg II and III. Their opulent decoration can be seen on the gilded locks and mounts of this pair of wheellock pistols. Cornflowers and sunflowers are abundant among the early Baroque ornaments. These floral motifs may be based on engravings in pattern-books such as that of the French gunmaker François Marcou, which was published in Paris in 1657. The Electoral Saxon coat of arms in gold on the butt caps is particularly decorative against the dark blued background. The pistols stand out, in particular, due to their elegant overall shape and their sparing ornamentation.

Herold created an almost identical pair of pistols – also held in the Rüstkammer's collection – for the governor of Upper Lusatia and Chief Steward (*Oberhofmarschall*) of the Electorate of Saxony, Curt Reinicke I, Count Callenberg (the great-great-grandfather of Prince Hermann von Pückler-Muskau). Other wheellock pistols by this master, which likewise feature profusely gilded lock and barrel decorations, are modelled, in their general form, on slender Cieszyn (Teschen) rifles or on the latest contemporary French pistols. GK

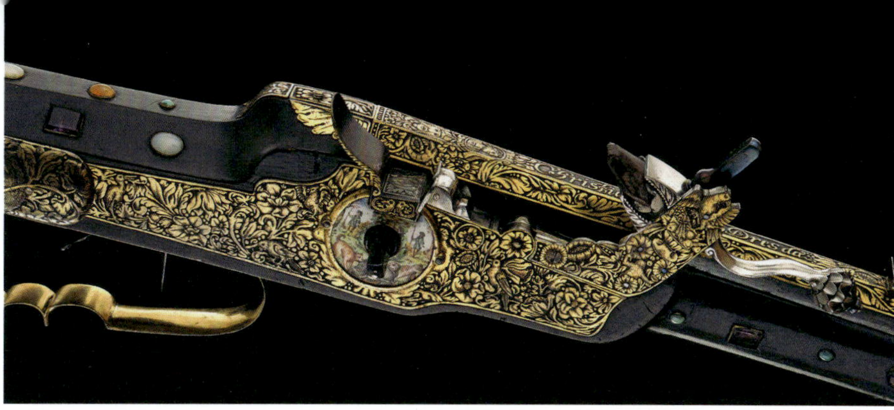

Wheellock rifle (one of a pair)

Christian Herold, Dresden, 1672
111.8 cm, Ø 16 mm, 4492 g
Inv. no. G 362

The pair of wheellock rifles, which were given as a gift by Master of the Hunt (*Landjägermeister*) Georg Carl von Carlowitz to Elector Johann Georg II in 1672, shows Christian Herold at the height of his creative prowess. The lock plates and barrels are completely covered with etched and engraved floral and plant decoration, lavishly gilded. One of the rifles is also set with precious stones, some in the form of rosettes: they consist of amethyst, rock crystal, topaz, and opal, some of which come from the Ore Mountains. Georg Carl von Carlowitz had his ancestral seat in Wolkenstein in the Ore Mountains, which explains why the rifle is decorated with (in part) local stones. Whether the topazes originate from Saxony is still unclear (the earliest confirmed finds in the Ore Mountains date from the beginning of the eighteenth century). The opals probably come from India and the garnets presumably from Bohemia.

The decorations are complemented by outstanding enamel paintings, which were probably produced in Augsburg especially for these rifles. On the butt there is a depiction of St George slaying the dragon. Other motifs on the enamel fittings include contemporary hunting scenes and a depiction of Diana.

A further pair of wheellock rifles by the same court artist dating from the same period – and almost identical in their basic form to this magnificent pair – were made in celebration of the admission of Elector Johann Georg II into the English Order of the Garter (1669). Christian Herold was also active as an etcher for armour made for the Electors Johann Georg II and III. Among other things, he decorated ceremonial parade gorgets with the insignia of the English Order of the Garter and the Danish Order of the Elephant. GK

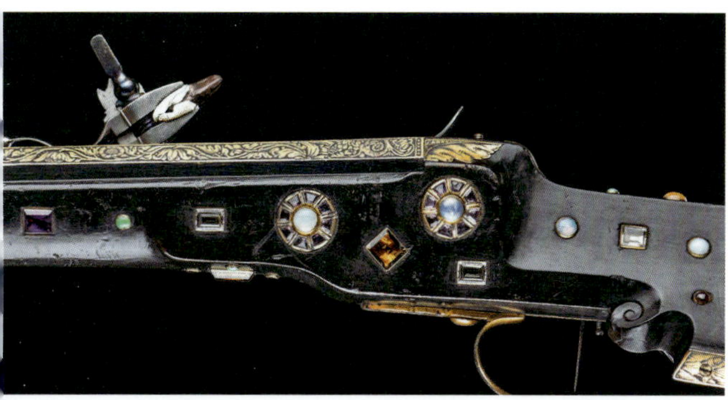

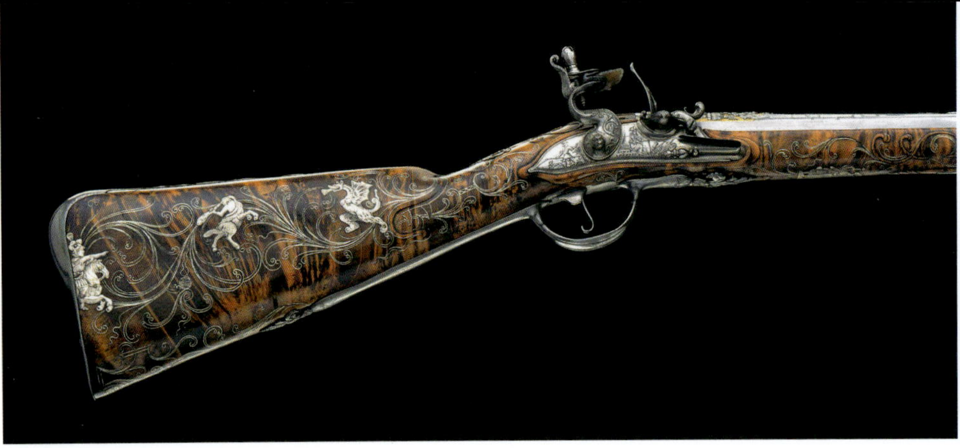

Flintlock shotgun

Valentin Rewer, Dresden, c. 1700
160 cm, Ø 17 mm, 3644 g
Inv. no. G 1562

Valentin Rewer, who was appointed as a gunmaker at the Dresden arsenal in 1695, created perhaps his most remarkable work with this long flintlock shotgun. The cambered lockplate suggests that it was probably made around 1700. Besides the chiselled iron décor on the barrel chamber depicting Mars, the god of war, along with trophies of arms, a further outstanding feature is the decorative stock made of flamed and stained birch wood. Silver wire inlays end in engraved sheet silver figures of a classical horseman, a centaur, and a fire-breathing dragon.

French luxury shotguns obviously played a role as possible models for the decoration of the shotgun, both in its technical design and in the motifs. With its picturesque and naïve engraved silver inlays, Rewer's work parodies the rigorously formalistic French precedents of Piraube and Languedoc (→ cf. p. 98). GK

Wheellock rifle

Andreas Erttel, Dresden, before 1707
117.6 cm, Ø 15 mm, 4705 g
Inv. no. G 583

Alongside Valentin Rewer, Andreas Erttel was the leading gunmaker of the 1690s and the first quarter of the eighteenth century in Dresden. Andreas Erttel's very heterogeneous body of works is evident in the various types of locks he produced: he designed wheellocks for target and hunting rifles, flintlocks for shotguns and pistols, but also snaplocks. The basic forms of his firearms, as well as the different styles of decoration he used, illustrate the transition from the somewhat rustic German to a more refined 'French' design vocabulary, thus demonstrating the 'simultaneity of the non-simultaneous'. While Erttel produced typical Central European wheellock rifles, he also created highly modern 'French' flintlock shotguns.

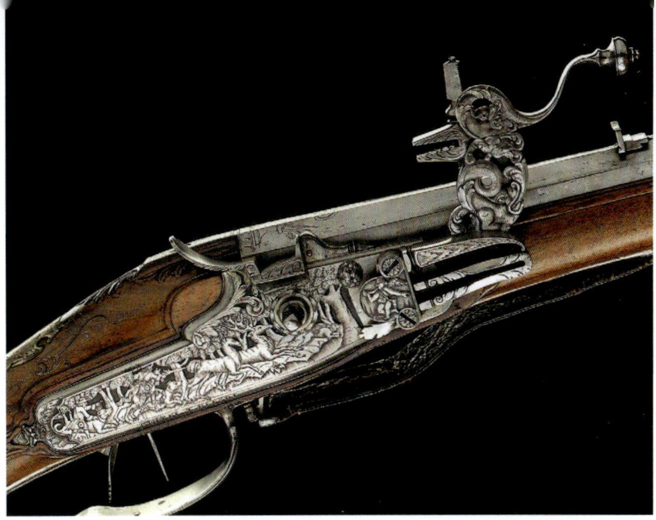

This wheellock rifle presents a mixture of both types of design. It combines a modern French butt featuring filigree patterns in inlaid silver wire with pictorial images on the lock plate, where there is an engraved depiction of a contemporary stag hunt. In June 1707 the rifle was given as a gift to the eleven-year-old Electoral Prince Friedrich August (II) by the Duke of Hollstein. This was probably Duke Philipp Ernst of Schleswig-Holstein-Sonderburg-Glücksburg, who was in Danish service and had a connection to the Saxon court. Alongside other gifts of weapons, this rifle formed the core of the electoral prince's *Gewehrkammer* (Gun Chamber). The many traces of use, including small nicks and dents in the stock, show that the rifle was used by the young prince, and also later after reaching adulthood. The leather carrying strap is original. GK

Flintlock pistol ('pepperbox')

Christian Salomon Rewer, Dresden, c. 1740
31.6 cm, Ø 8 mm, 2179 g
Inv. no. J 1327

Valentin Rewer's son Christian Salomon Rewer, who is mentioned as a journeyman gunmaker and master machinist at the Dresden arsenal, created this curious pistol with a six-shot barrel made of cast brass. Six shots, each from a separate bore, could be fired in quick succession by a single pull of the trigger. That is why this type of firearm is often called a pepperbox. The charges are fired in sequence, depending on the position of their respective ignition channels. The central bore is not a barrel, but serves to distribute the sparks to the ignition channels and to discharge smoke. Count Friedrich August Rutowski, son of August the Strong and his Turkish mistress Fatima (married name: Maria Aurora von Spiegel), gave this extraordinary weapon to his half-brother King August III in 1741. GK

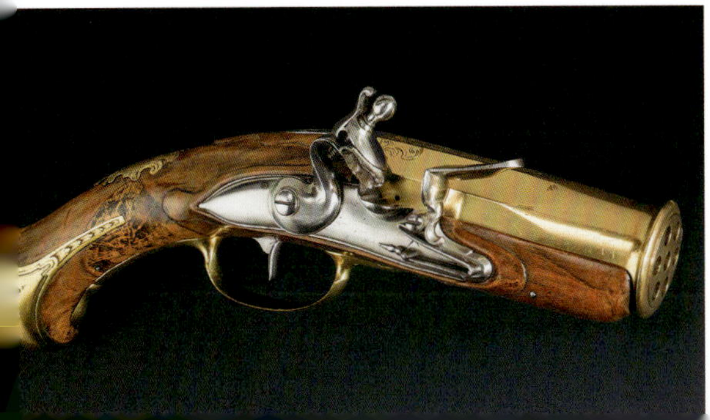

Flintlock gun with Ottoman barrel

Barrel: Husain
Rifling, stock: Georg Tobias Klette, Dresden, c. 1740
164 cm, Ø 20 mm, 5200 g
Inv. no. G 1170

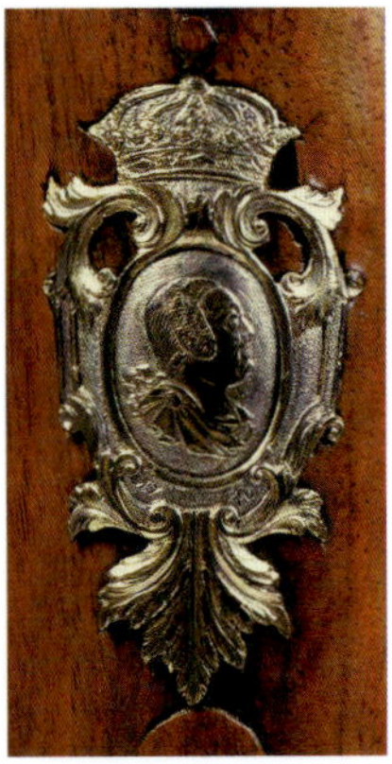

This rifle, restocked by Georg Tobias Klette, was probably a favourite weapon of King August III, whose engraved and punch-marked profile portrait appears in a silver-gilt medallion, topped by a royal crown, on the thumb plate. The barrel is known to have been in the Türckische Cammer of the Rüstkammer in 1717, at that time still in an Ottoman stock.

The opulent watered steel barrel, which bears the barrelsmith's signature "Husain", is decorated with silver- and gold-inlaid ornaments mounted with corals and turquoises. The muzzle resembles the head of a fire-breathing dragon. The dragon motif of the Ottoman barrel is taken up in the Dresden-made stock: on the silver-gilt engraved and punch-marked butt cap is a depiction of St George slaying the dragon.

Klette had been a gunmaker at the arsenal since 1730 and was head of the Dresden gunmakers' guild from 1748 onwards. He is represented in the collection with six of his own works, as well as eight rifled Ottoman barrels. GK

Flintlock gun with Ottoman barrel

Barrel: Mustafa Uskuli
Rifling, stock: Johann Christian Martini, Dresden, 1740
149.6 cm, Ø 17 mm, 3838 g
Inv. no. G 1652

Another Ottoman gun barrel restocked during the reign of August III is a work by the barrelsmith Mustafa Uskuli. The gun from which the barrel originates was a gift from the Ottoman envoy to the king in 1737. It was presented in the western Polish town of Wschowa/Fraustadt. The barrelsmith's mark is visible in a cartouche on the barrel. In 1740, the barrel was rifled and mounted in a new stock – featuring intricate carved décor around the tang, including a mascaron – by the Dresden gunsmith Johann Christian Martini. He also fitted it with a flintlock, which bears his signature. Besides more than twenty works made entirely by Martini (wheellock and flintlock firearms), a further three Ottoman barrels and three Italian barrels restocked by him have survived. GK

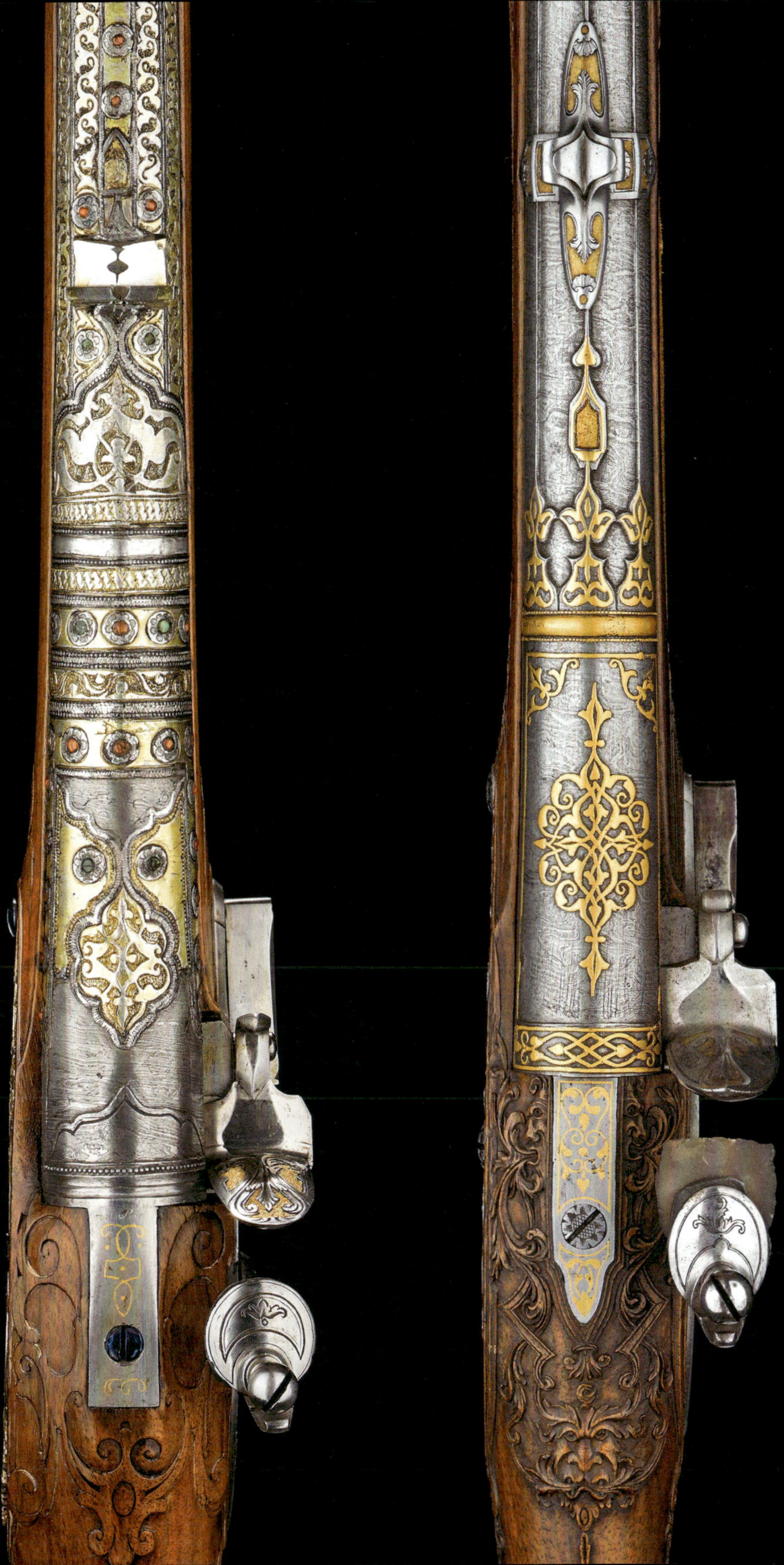

Pair of wheellock rifles

Johann Georg Erttel, Dresden, c. 1750
117.3/117.5 cm, Ø 15/16 mm, 6170/6090 g
Inv. nos. G 529, G 530

Heavy wheellock target rifles from the 1750s show Dresden gunmakers such as Johann Leopold Milotta, Johann Joseph Futter, Philipp Müller, Johann Christoph Dörries and Johann Georg Erttel at the height of their craftsmanship and artistic finesse. Weighing around 4.5 to 7 kg, these rifles for the court of King August III were used for target shooting, in which the royal family engaged with great enthusiasm, both as part of courtly festivities and for private pleasure.

This pair of target rifles manufactured by Johann Georg Erttel constitute what is probably the most important example of this type of weapon. The lock plates are harmoniously decorated by an as yet unidentified engraver. One depicts Venus, the goddess of love, bathing in the sea, surrounded by nymphs, a cupid sitting on a swan, and another small cupid. The other shows Diana, the goddess of the hunt, with two dogs in an expansive landscape with deer, wild boar, hares, ducks, a pheasant, and a capercaillie. The butt trap covers are particularly precious: they are made of ivory and decorated with rocaille cartouches of engraved mother-of-pearl.

These and other luxurious rifles can be regarded as the pinnacle and end point of the development of the wheellock rifle – not only in the superb quality of their technical components (barrel, lock) but also in their masterly embellishment and the meticulous elaboration of the rococo details. GK

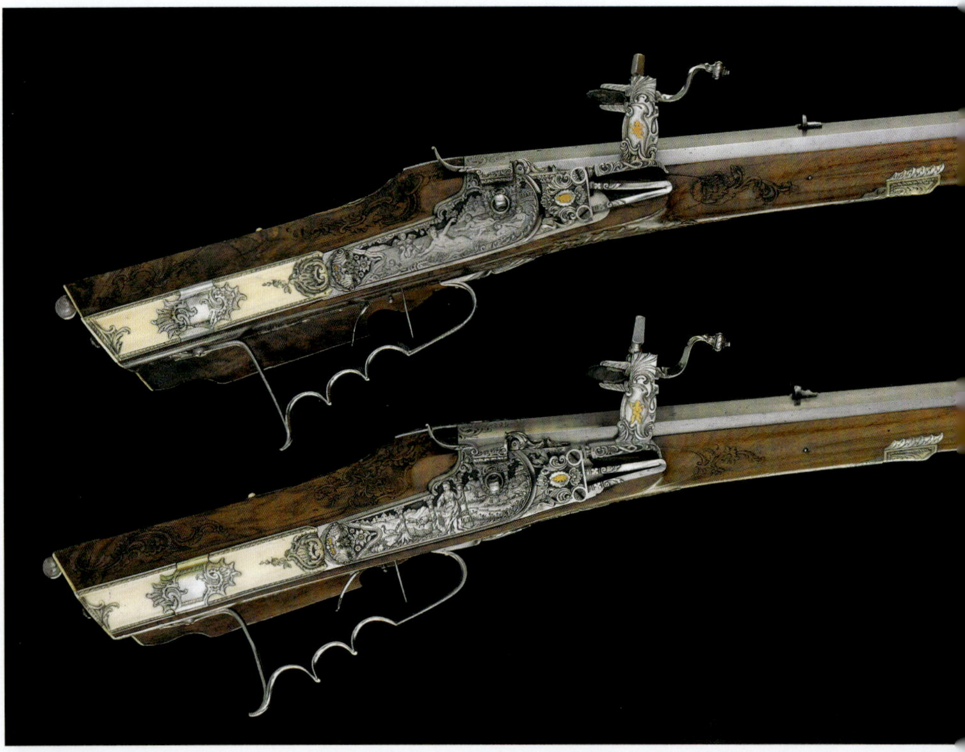

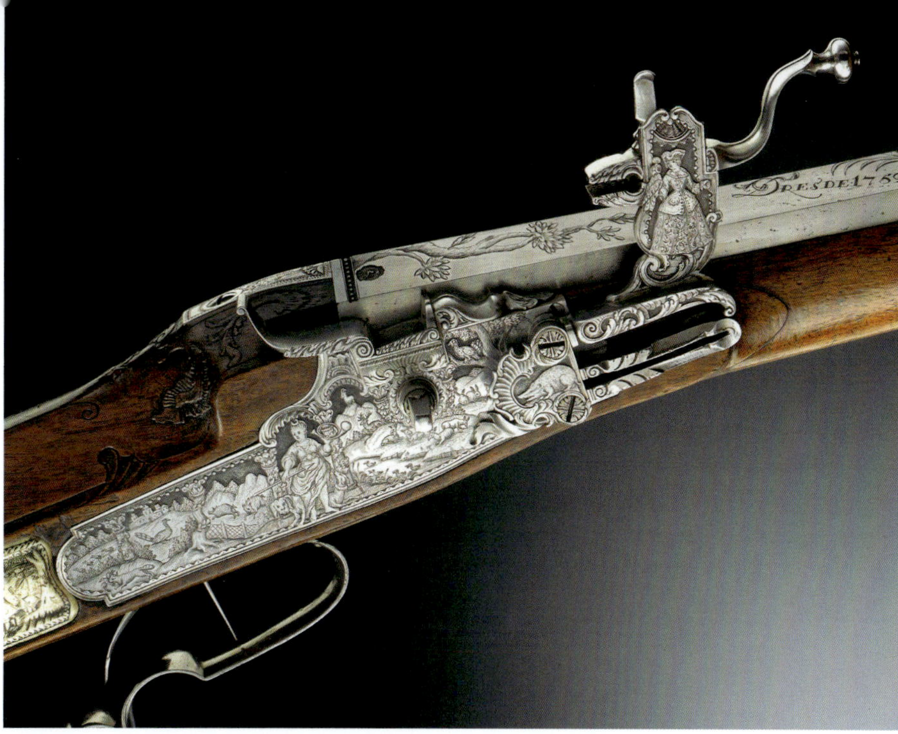

Wheellock rifle

Johann Leopold Milotta, Dresden, 1752
117.9 cm, Ø 17 mm, 6430 g
Inv. no. G 531

Heavy target rifles with a 'hog's back' barrel are exceptionally rare. In those guns, the octagonal barrel has been rotated by 22.5° so that the top is not a flat surface but an edge. This served as a sighting line. The rifle shown here, by Johann Leopold Milotta, has another special feature: the hog's back is not straight, but instead follows a wavy line. This is of no practical use but demonstrates the mastery of the barrelsmith.

The wheellock of this rifle has been decorated with meticulous attention to detail. The dog is covered with a plate bearing a depiction of a contemporary female falconer (→ cf. fig. p. 35). The engraving on the lock plate showing the hunting goddess Diana in a landscape with animals is almost identical to the lock of the rifle, inv. no. G 530, by Johann Georg Erttel (→ cf. fig. p. 46). The authorship of these particularly finely crafted engravings is still unclear. Evidently, some decorators worked for multiple gunmakers. As is the case on many other firearms, the motif depicted on this lock plate does not correspond with the weapon's intended use: even target rifles often feature images relating to hunting and Classical mythology, with Diana as the goddess of the hunt being most frequently represented. GK

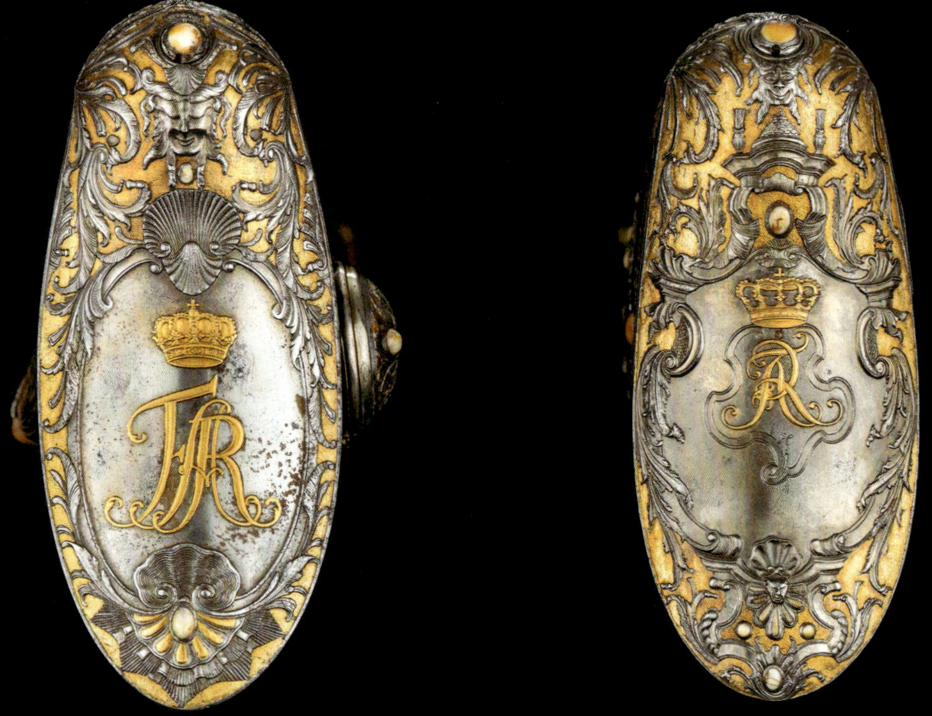

Showcase 7

Suhl

Suhl, a town in the Thuringian Forest, was already a metal processing centre in the Middle Ages. Iron ore was mined in the surrounding tunnels and smelted nearby. The existence of hammer forges is documented from as early as 1365. Like the neighbouring towns of Heidersbach and Zella-Mehlis (at that time Zella), Suhl belonged to the territories held by the counts of Henneberg. After the male line of the House of Henneberg became extinct in 1583–84, these territories fell to the Wettin dynasty and were divided between the Albertine Electorate of Saxony and the Ernestine duchies in Thuringia.

The Saxon electors and dukes, later the Brandenburg electors and Swedish troops, all commissioned Suhl gunsmiths to equip them with muskets and pistols. Military edged weapons were also produced there.

In the seventeenth century, Suhl was primarily renowned for producing armaments for military purposes, but some luxury weapons were also made there in the late sixteenth and early seventeenth centuries. A first high point in the manufacture of artistically sophisticated hand firearms in Suhl are pairs of wheellock pistols dating from the period shortly after 1600, several of which are in the Dresden Rüstkammer. They are characterised by the homogeneous iron-cut decoration of the barrel and lock, and a stock with similar carved design in fruitwood. Here, as elsewhere, this development was greatly disrupted by the Thirty Years' War.

Later, starting in the late seventeenth century, and increasingly from the 1720s onwards, outstanding firearms were finished by decorators and gunstockers in Suhl. The focus was mainly on prestigious hunting guns. Among the leading master craftsmen and decorators were the Stockmar family (father and two sons), who created magnificent sets of weapons for the Dresden court in the 1730s and 1740s. During the same period, the Suhl masters Johann Gottfried Kolb and the as yet unidentified masters GM and II K produced excellent hand firearms. Later, Johann Stephan Seeber and Johann Wilhelm Spangenberg worked for the court, lastly for Electress Maria Antonia. Of all international museums, the Dresden Rüstkammer holds the largest collection of such exceptional luxury weapons. Further magnificent firearms from Suhl can be found in the Royal Collection in Windsor and in Gatchina Palace near St. Petersburg, whose holdings include precious items from the estate of Count Heinrich von Brühl.

In the eighteenth and nineteenth centuries, military weapons were once again manufactured in Suhl, including for Prussia. However, the production of luxurious hunting rifles continued and still flourishes today. GK

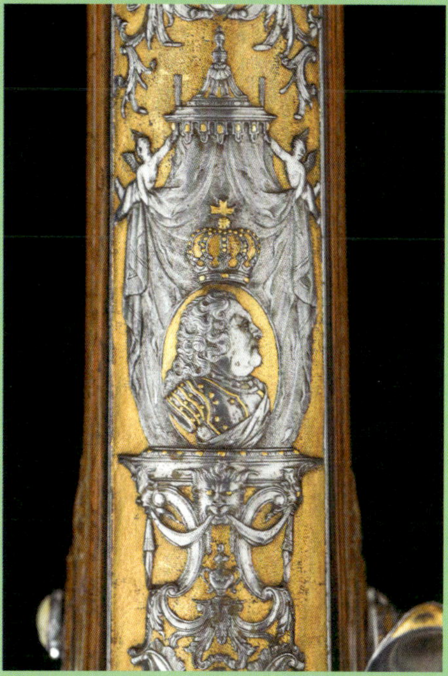

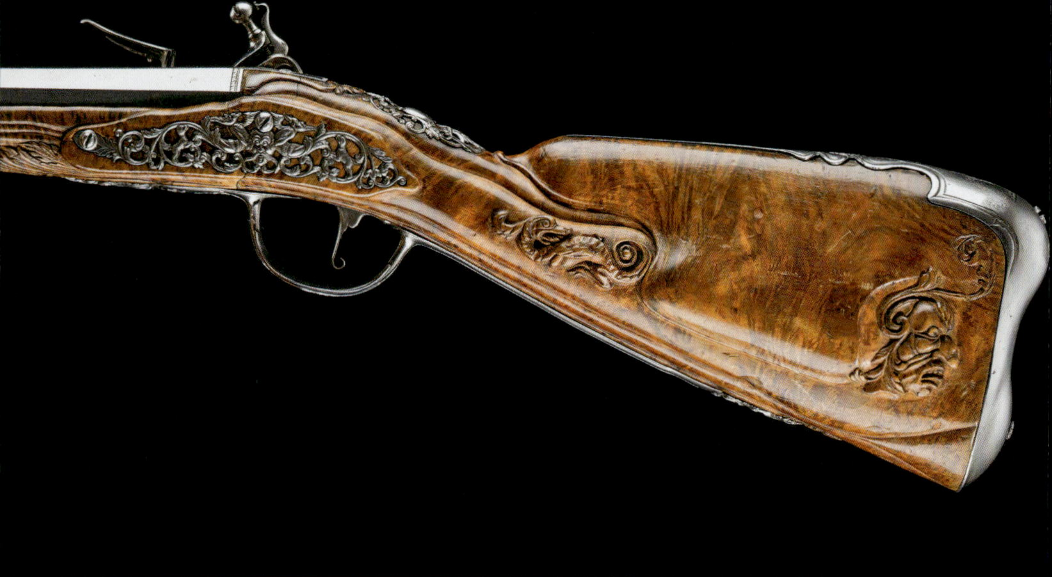

Flintlock rifle

Johann Matthias Hofmann, Suhl, 1697
121.3 cm, Ø 15 mm, 4735 g
Inv. no. G 812

An early example of a high-quality Suhl hunting gun is this flintlock rifle by Johann Matthias Hofmann. The focus here was on the fine-quality working of the wood. The design of the stock, with figural and wave-like carving in walnut, is highly original for a firearm and is reminiscent of contemporary furniture art, in which the decorative qualities of walnut burl wood had only recently become popular – also among the bourgeoisie. The carved ornaments on the butt, featuring a grimacing grotesque face and a mythical creature, are particularly whimsical. The finely crafted iron fittings – the lock plate, openwork side plate, and thumb plate – also demonstrate the outstanding skill of the master. GK

Set of flintlock firearms

Johann Nicolaus Stockmar, Johann Christoph Stockmar,
Heidersbach/Suhl, 1741–1744
Rifle: 102.5 cm, Ø 14 mm, 3753 g
Shotgun: 136 cm, Ø 15 mm, 3125 g
Pistols: 45.2/45 cm, Ø 14 mm, 1025/1001 g
Inv. nos. G 892, G 862, J 1400, J 1401

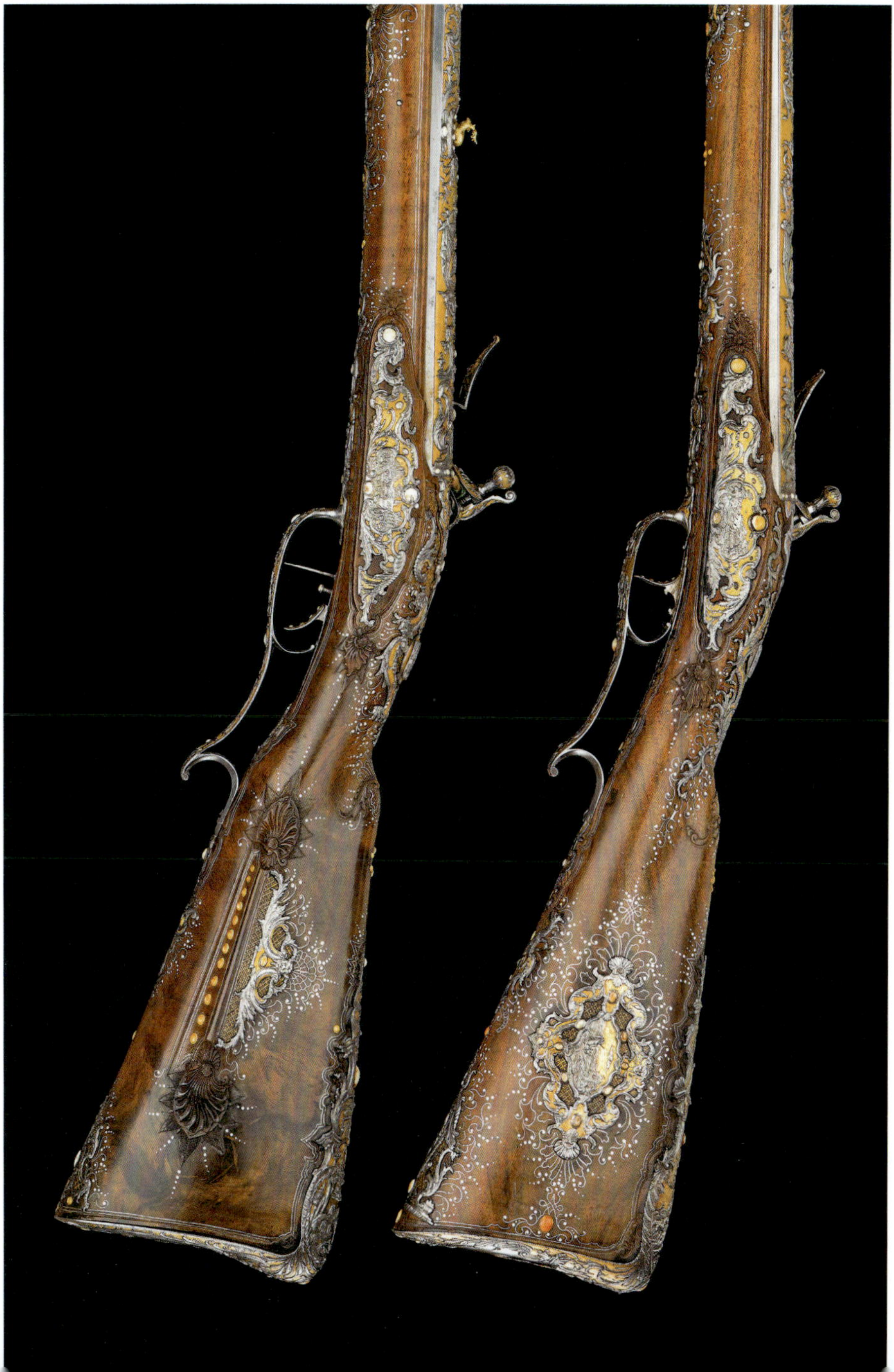

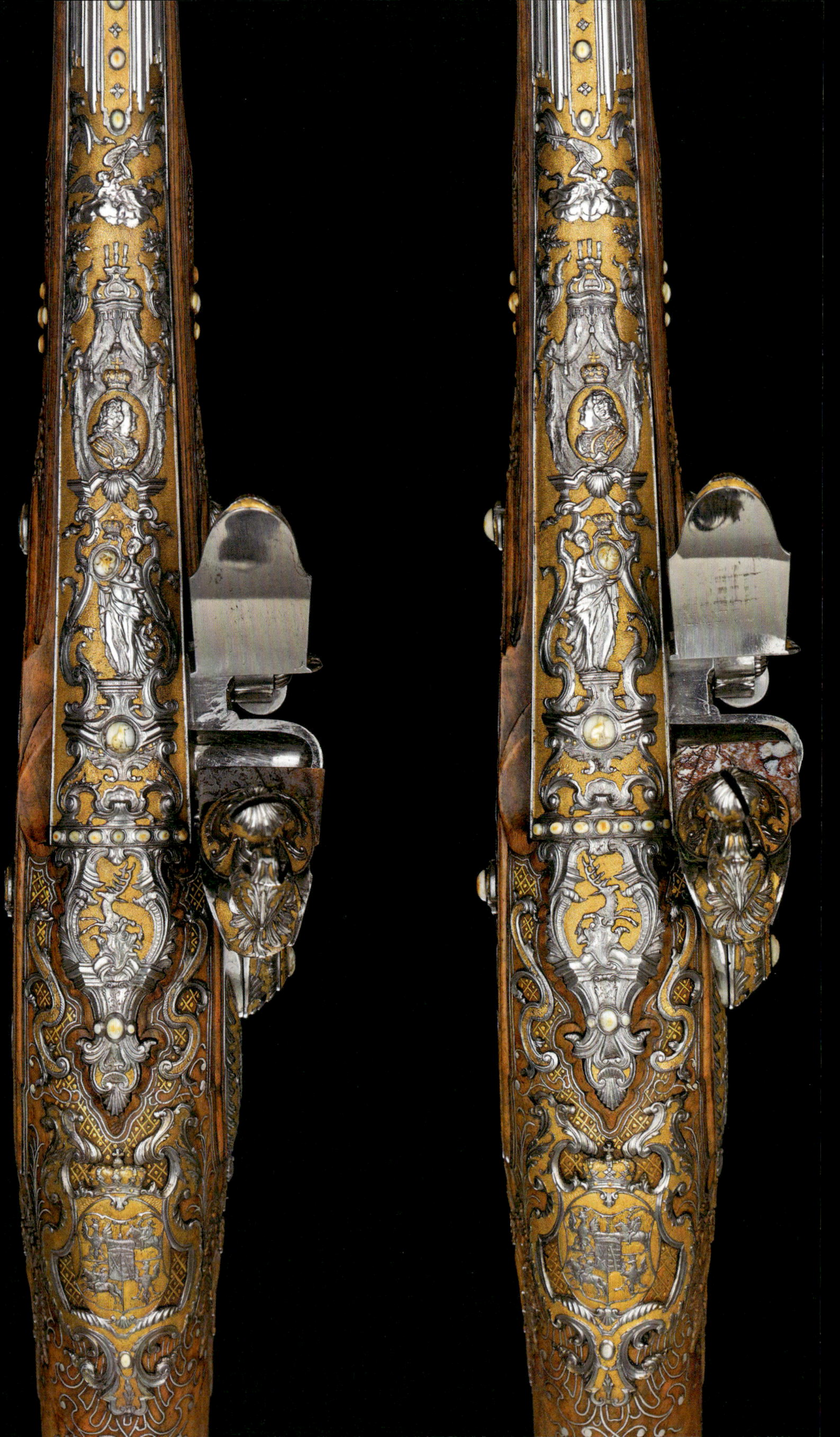

During the reign of August the Strong, the first of a total of nine magnificent Suhl flintlock sets came to Dresden as a gift from the Thuringian town to its sovereign, the elector of Saxony. Almost all of the sets consist of four firearms: a rifle, a shotgun, and a pair of pistols.

The majority of these splendid sets of Suhl firearms only entered the collection during the reign of Elector and King Friedrich August II/August III, however. The set manufactured by the Stockmar family marks the ultimate high point of rococo decoration on firearms: finely carved stocks with inlaid silver wire and with silver and gold-plated embossed mounts featuring rocailles and figural ornamentation. The luxurious fittings of the set also incorporate so-called stag burrs – the tips of deer antlers – as additional decoration, as well as cut agate and other gemstones instead of flints in the cocks.

The silver-gilt butt plates of the shotgun and the rifle bear the initials of the Elector and King – "FAR" for *Fridericus Augustus Rex* – in gold inlay (→ cf. fig. p. 48). Engraved iron ornaments with gilded details on the lock plates, side plates, barrel surfaces, and butt caps of the pistols depict contemporary hunting scenes: hunters on horseback in a *par force* hunt, stags and stag hunting, hounds chasing hares, and landscape motifs. Stag hunting is also reflected in an original detail: the rear sight of the rifle is designed as a miniature stag. All four firearms have thumb plates with the Polish-Saxon coat of arms as well as small crowned medallions containing a miniature profile portrait of the ruler, the quality of which is remarkable (→ cf. fig. p. 49).

The Stockmar firearms of the 1740s were not supplied as complete sets, but rather according to type: i.e. a number of rifles/shotguns/pistols from different sets were delivered together. They were assembled into sets in Dresden and then immediately presented separately in the Firearms Gallery, with rifles, shotguns, and pistols being displayed in different cabinets.

Two further flintlock sets in the splendid rococo style, this time by the Suhl master Kolb, were added to the collection in 1747 together with two pairs of rifles by the same master. The Rüstkammer also holds a similarly sumptuous set of firearms from an as yet unidentified master GM. GK

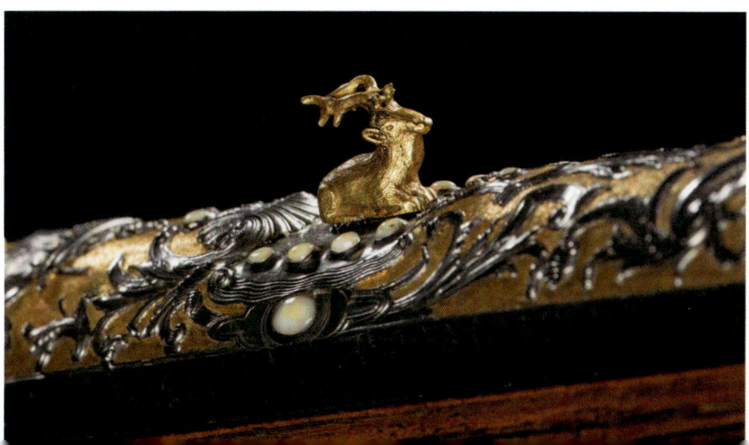

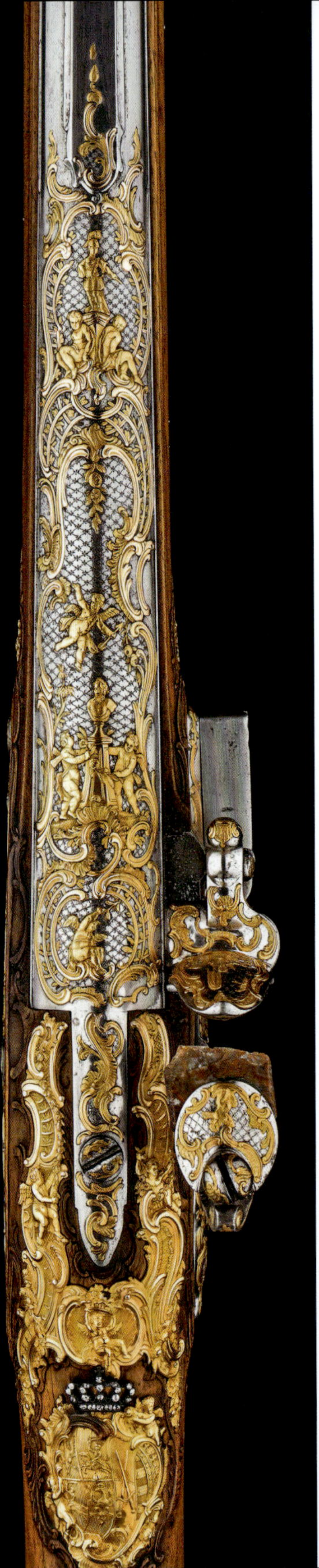

Flintlock shotgun

Johann Stephan Seeber, Suhl, 1750
143.5 cm, Ø 15 mm, 3175 g
Inv. no. G 899

This luxurious gun, made by the gunstocker and engraver Johann Stephan Seeber in 1750, represents a high point in the rococo decoration of Suhl luxury weapons. Delicately carved décor on the walnut stock, especially in the area around the tang and the small, as well as the top-quality gilded chiselled iron decorations and copper-gilt incrustations on the barrel, which show putti, a classical warrior, and an antique bust, culminate in a royal crown decorated with twenty brilliant-cut diamonds. This appears above the gilded thumb plate bearing the Polish-Lithuanian and Electoral Saxon coats of arms.

The butt cap of the shotgun has even more extravagantly rococo decoration in gold: surrounded by rocailles, festoons, and small putti stands the figure of a ruler in classical costume being crowned with the laurel wreath by Ares. It is presumably intended to represent King August III.

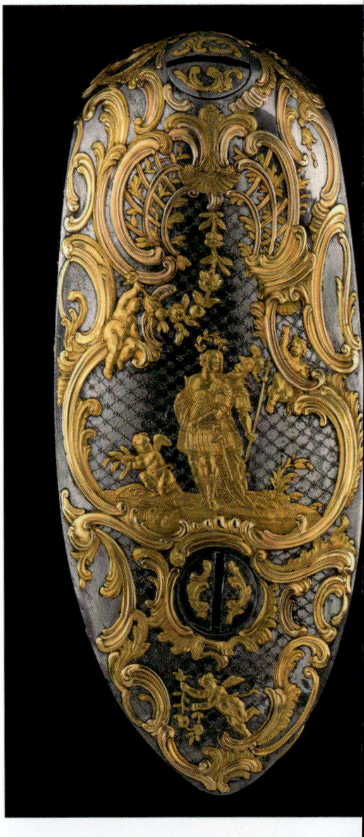

In his later years, Seeber worked as a court engraver in Dresden. GK

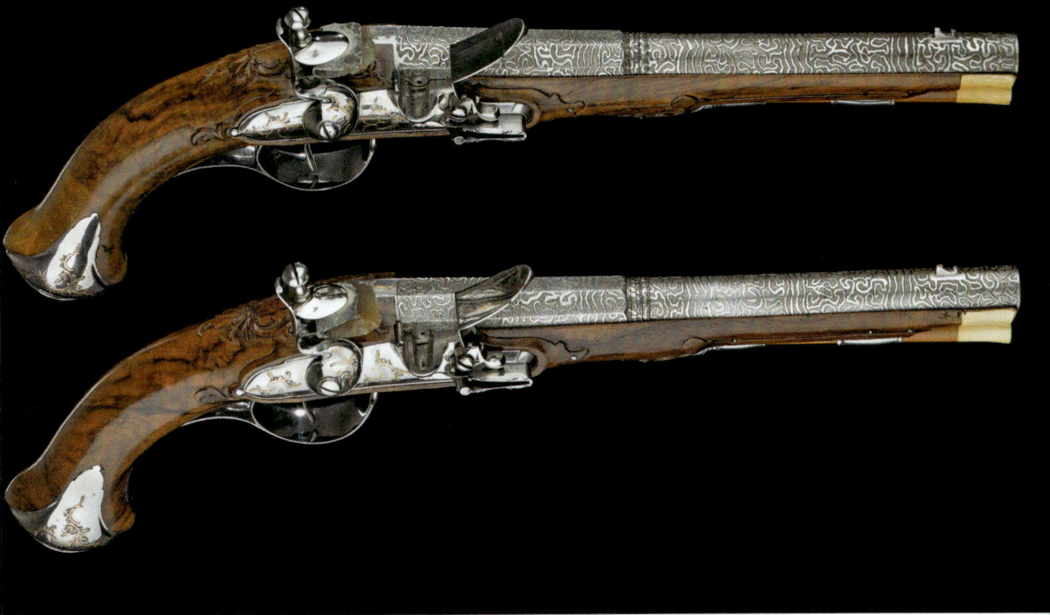

Pair of flintlock pistols, part of a set

Johann Wilhelm Spangenberg (attributed to), Suhl, c. 1755
38.4/38.4 cm, Ø 13 mm, 738/757 g
Inv. nos. J 862, J 863 (matching rifle: G 1569)

It was probably Johann Wilhelm Spangenberg who, around 1755, created a set of flintlock weapons consisting of a shotgun and a pair of pistols for Electoral Princess Maria Antonia, wife of the Electoral Prince and later Elector Friedrich Christian, and hence also daughter-in-law of August III. The polished locks and butt caps are embellished with inlays in yellow and reddish gold alloys depicting scrolling vines and, on the shotgun, intricate hunting scenes. In addition, the pistols have a distinctive form of decoration on the surface of the barrel, probably produced by etching, which is reminiscent of watered steel, as well as having beautifully grained walnut stocks.

After the death of the Dowager Electress in 1780, her small but important collection of firearms was incorporated into the Elector's *Leibgewehr*, i.e. the Firearms Gallery in the Long Corridor.

Other works by Spangenberg include a pair of wheellock rifles decorated in a similar rococo style (around 1760) and a flintlock double barrel rifle that was presented to August III by Count Brühl in Warsaw in 1762. GK

⊕ Courtly target shooting

Shooting competitions were an integral part of courtly festivities in the seventeenth and eighteenth centuries. During the reigns of August the Strong and August III, target shooting became a favourite pastime of the court and royal family, including the queen and electoral princess. Special target shooting rifles were used for this purpose (→ cf. fig. p. 46). Every detail of these heavy wheellock rifles was designed for precision: the rifled barrel increased accuracy, the weight of around 4 to 7 kg reduced recoil, the 'German' stock was designed to rest against the cheek, and the wheellock mechanism was suitable due to its smooth and relatively reliable action. The set trigger (*Stecher* system) allowed the trigger to be pulled (after releasing the safety notch) with only minimal pressure, without 'skewing'. The rifle could be positioned on a rest when firing; the distance to the target was usually 130 cubits (approx. 73 metres).

In many places, special buildings called *Schießhäuser* (literally: shooting houses) were constructed for this sport; in Dresden, it is known that competitions were also held in the Stableyard (Stallhof). Shooting ranges with pavilions were particularly popular architectural features in Baroque and Rococo gardens. The engraved lock plates of three target rifles give an impression of what these looked like. The first, made around 1733 (inv. no. G 250), shows a typical set-up, with an elegant pavilion and a shooting range lined with potted plants (fig. 1). The lock plate dating from 1743 (inv. no. G 514) depicts the shooting range in the Baroque Garden at Großsedlitz. The range is flanked by two water channels with fountains (fig. 3). From 1740, a major target shooting competition was held there every year at the beginning of August to celebrate the Order of the White Eagle. For this event, the shooting range was embellished with a painted rear wall (in 1742, for example, the theatre painter Giovanni Battista Grone was commissioned to produce the decorations). In this case, it is possible to discern an obelisk with the monogram of August III and the cross of the Order, as well as a river god, a nymph, a forest and two waterfalls.

The protagonists in a genteel scene set in the shooting house (inv. no. G 452, before 1756) are possibly to be interpreted as August III and Queen Maria

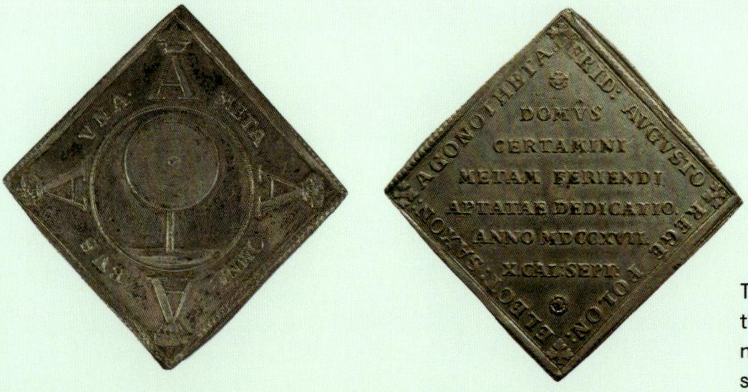

Taler klippe for the target shooting on the occasion of the dedication of the new shooting house in Dresden, 1717, silver, Münzkabinett, SKD

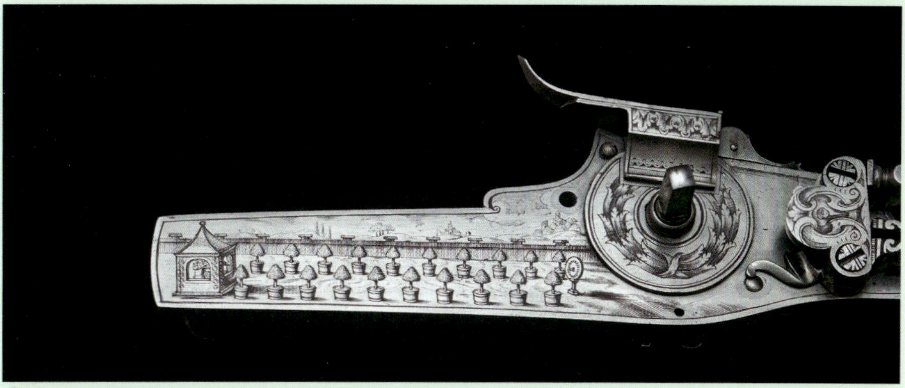

①

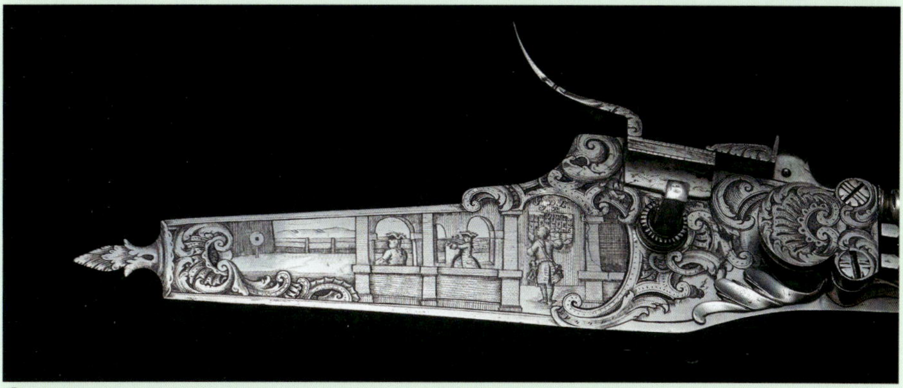

②

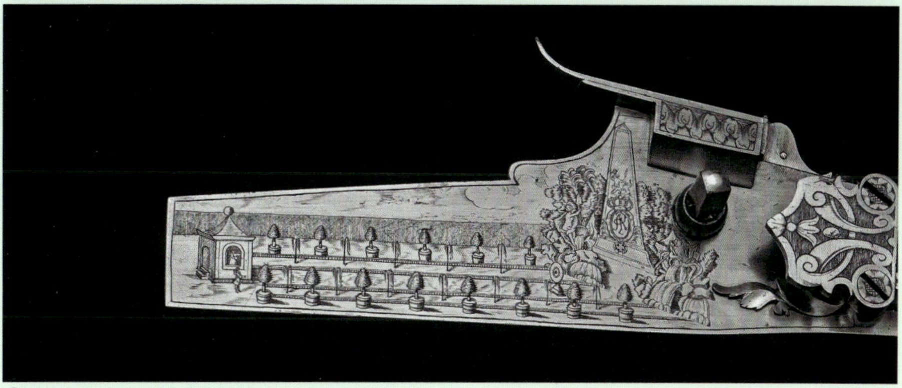

③

Josepha (fig. 2). A third figure is depicted recording the results of the shooting, with a bull's-eye scoring 12 points. Similar result tables for many courtly target shooting events have been preserved in the archives. The complex rules dictated that prizes be awarded not only for the overall score, but also for the best shot in each round. The prizes included medals and specially minted square commemorative coins called *Schießklippen*. The worst result (a 'long shot') was honoured with a jug of beer and a joke prize – such as a piece of cheese, a simple utility object, or even an elaborate *tableau vivant* of live animals dressed up in costumes. SR

Electoral Saxony and the Ernestine duchies

Outside the major gunmaking centres of Dresden and Suhl, the second half of the seventeenth century also saw the development of firearms production at various other locations in Electoral Saxony. In the Ore Mountains, gun manufacturing was particularly intensive and of high quality in the towns of Olbernhau and (Ober-)Wiesenthal on the Bohemian border. There, the gunmaking trade benefited from the presence of several ironworks and, in the case of Wiesenthal, from its close proximity to Karlovy Vary (known historically as Carlsbad). That famous spa town acted as a major stimulus for the production of luxury firearms, since it was frequented by a wealthy, mostly aristocratic, international clientele. In the period around 1700, a manufacturer like Georg Zöffel, probably the most important Wiesenthal gunsmith, was able to cater to this discerning demographic at the very highest level. His shotguns and rifles corresponded to the latest fashions in Germany, France, and Bohemia, and their quality was on a par with that of their international equivalents. A local gunmaking industry also developed in Upper Lusatia, which had been part of Electoral Saxony since 1635.

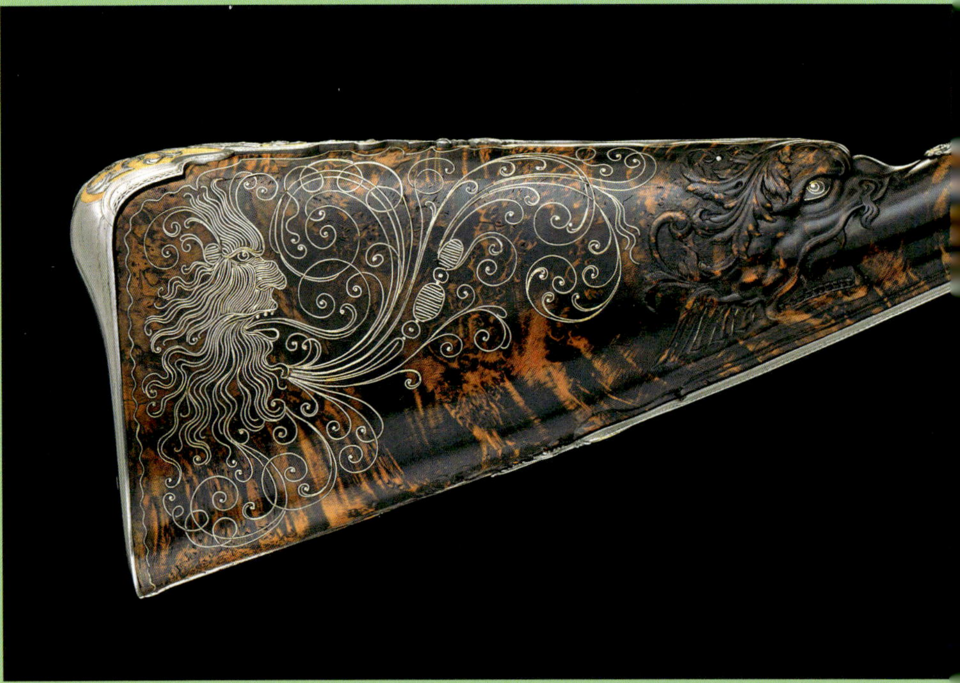

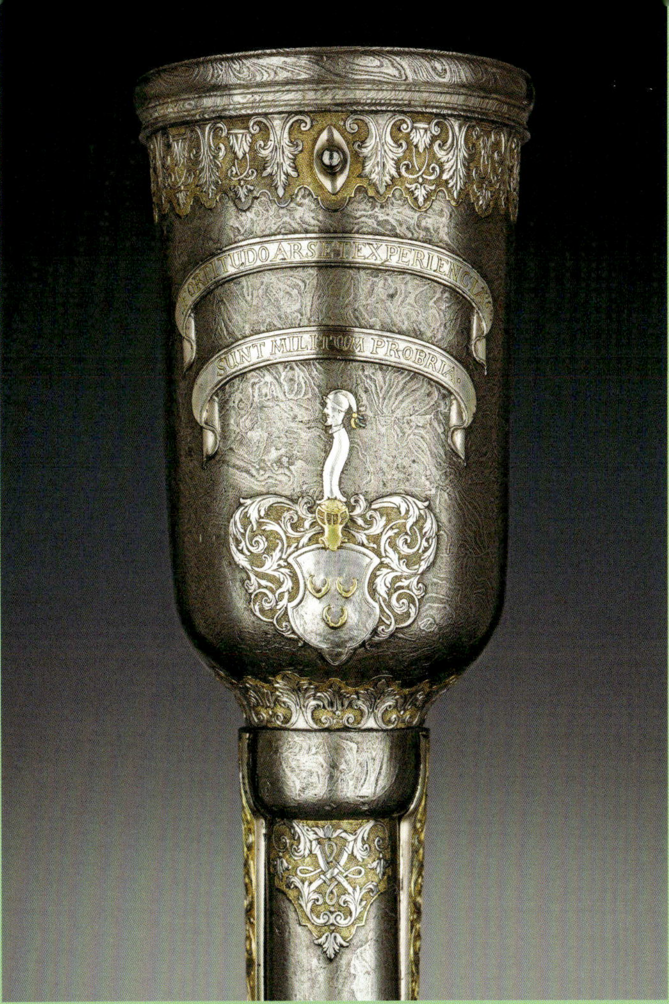

There, too, interesting international connections existed, not least thanks to journeyman migration.

Gunmakers were also active at the small courts of the secundogeniture duchies of Saxe-Weißenfels and Saxe-Merseburg, which were created in 1657. Of particular importance, however, was the zealous collecting activity of the dukes in these territories, since it resulted in the significant expansion of the Dresden Firearms Gallery after the extinction of these two collateral lines in 1746 and 1738 respectively. In addition, close contacts continued to be maintained between Dresden and the duchies of the Ernestine branch of the House of Wettin, which led to firearms being given as gifts. At the Gotha court, for example, the hand mortar described below was created in 1729, along with its accompanying support fork and hunting dagger. In terms of its typology, this spectacular luxury set is an exceptional case in the Firearms Gallery, as it is the prototype of a military invention. SR

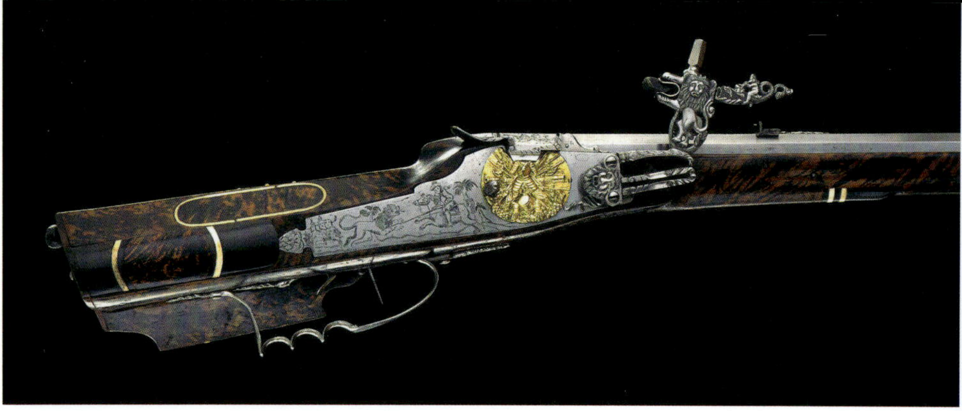

Wheellock rifle with indirect spanning axle and triple-rotating wheel

Hans Kutschera, Bautzen, late 17th century
118.3 cm, Ø 15 mm, 5365 g
Inv. no. G 291

The Kutschera family of gunmakers was active in Bautzen in the second half of the seventeenth century. A master's son, named "Johann Kutschera of Bautzen", is listed as a *Junger* (i.e. apprentice) in the register of the Vienna gunmakers' guild for 1688; he can probably be identified as the maker of this rifle signed "HANS KUTSCHERA". The rifle does indeed bear certain similarities to guns produced in Vienna towards the end of the century. For example, the elegant interplay of dark-stained burl wood, horn, and bone is reminiscent of a work by Caspar Zellner (→ cf. pp. 86–87) from around the same time. In contrast to the technically sophisticated spanning mechanism (→ cf. pp. 70–71), the decoration on the lock is rather provincial-looking. The iron dog cut in the form of a lion holding the pyrite between its paws is a particularly quaint feature. SR

Flintlock shotgun

Georg Zöffel, Wiesenthal, before 1705
157.3 cm, Ø 15 mm, 3347 g
Inv. no. G 1571

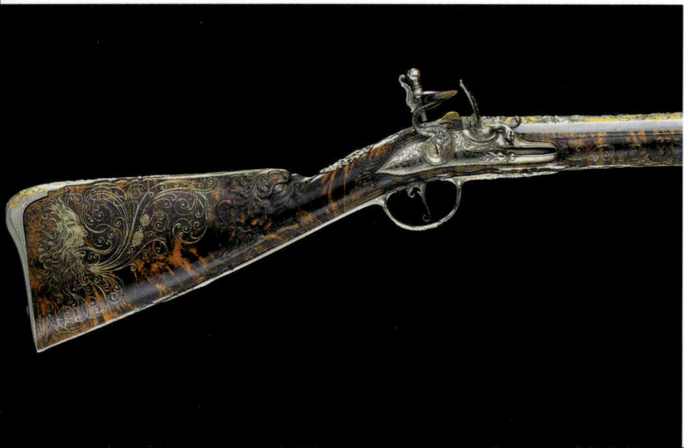

In June 1705, August the Strong (accompanied by his entire court) travelled to Carlsbad to take the waters. While there, he purchased this shotgun, which had been made in Wiesenthal (as carefully noted in the inventory). Since 1740, this unsigned

piece has been catalogued under the name of the local gunsmith Georg Zöffel – a very plausible attribution.

The design of this luxurious shotgun is based on French precedents – such as those by Piraube and especially Languedoc, whose decorative designs were also widely available in print. Zöffel modelled one detail of the carving on the butt, for example, on an engraving that was only published after 1702 – Parisian fashion was adopted quickly in the Ore Mountains. The choice of a fiery burl wood rather than walnut, which was favoured in France, however, testifies to a certain degree of artistic licence. The butt decoration is unique, seeming to deliberately parody Languedoc's inlaid silver wire ornaments (→ cf. figs. pp. 58 and 98). What at first appear to be scrolling vines turn out on closer inspection to emanate from the mouth of a bearded grotesque face! SR

Wheellock rifle

Georg Zöffel, Wiesenthal, 1708
132.6 cm, Ø 14 mm, 4642 g
Inv. no. G 201

Like many German gunmakers around 1700, Zöffel was proficient in two different stylistic idioms. While his shotguns corresponded to French taste, his wheellock rifles were in line with the domestic tradition in terms of both typology and design. Particularly outstanding on this piece is the decoration of the lock plate and the plate covering the dog, which depict an equestrian battle and a prisoner of war, respectively. The master personally executed the engravings, as evidenced by the signature "Zöffel fecit 1708" at the bottom edge of the image – a type of maker's mark that is otherwise customary in printmaking. The rifle was one of a pair, but its counterpart was auctioned off in 1919. SR

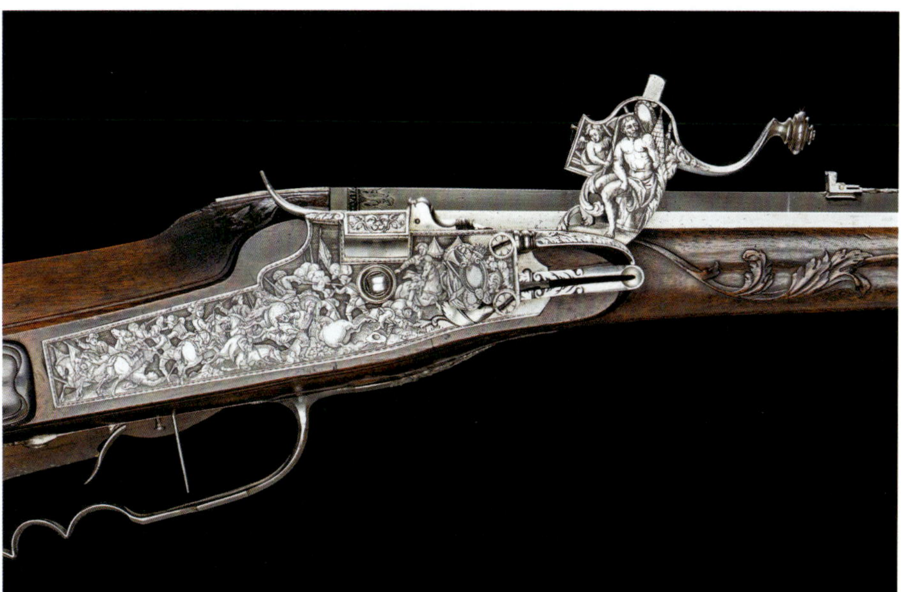

Luxury hand mortar with fork rest/halberd and hunting dagger

Tobias Gräfenstein after a design by Johann Wilhelm von Seebach, Gotha, 1729
Mortar: 80.2 cm, Ø cup 75 mm, 3322 g
Fork rest: 223 cm (with bayonet unfolded), 2269 g
Hunting dagger: 72 cm, 1170 g
Scabbard: 55 cm; ramrod: 53,5 cm
Inv. nos. G 1570, T 98, X 429, XI 199

This lavishly decorated ensemble, dated 1729, was the prototype of a military invention. The flintlock hand mortar (a grenade launcher or *bombarde*) was used to fire a hand grenade at long range. The grenade, which served primarily as an incendiary device, was placed in the large firing cup at the muzzle of the barrel. The gun has an elevation scale as an aiming aid. The raised rear sight in the shape of a dog's head with a heraldic shield on the back is aligned with the front sight on the rim of the cup. The accompanying polearm is an unusual combination of a halberd (with large folding bayonet) and a fork rest. A hook on the underside of the stock allows the hand mortar to rest on the fork, thus steadying the shot. There is no space beneath the barrel for the cleaning rod that is required for maintenance: instead, it is kept in the scabbard of an accompanying hunting dagger. Although hand mortars had been around since the Renaissance, this attachment of the firearm to a specially designed combination weapon was a new invention. The hunting dagger is of simple design, but the mortar and fork rest clearly constitute a prestigious luxury set: the barrel and cup are forged from fine watered steel and are extensively embellished with gold and silver inlays; the blade and bayonet of the fork rest are etched with scrollwork on a gilt ground. According to the inventory, August the Strong received the set in about 1730–1732 as a gift from Duke Friedrich II of Saxe-Gotha. The latter took part in the spectacular military exercise organised by August the Strong in June 1730 and known as the Zeithain Encampment. This would have been a fitting occasion for presenting such a gift.

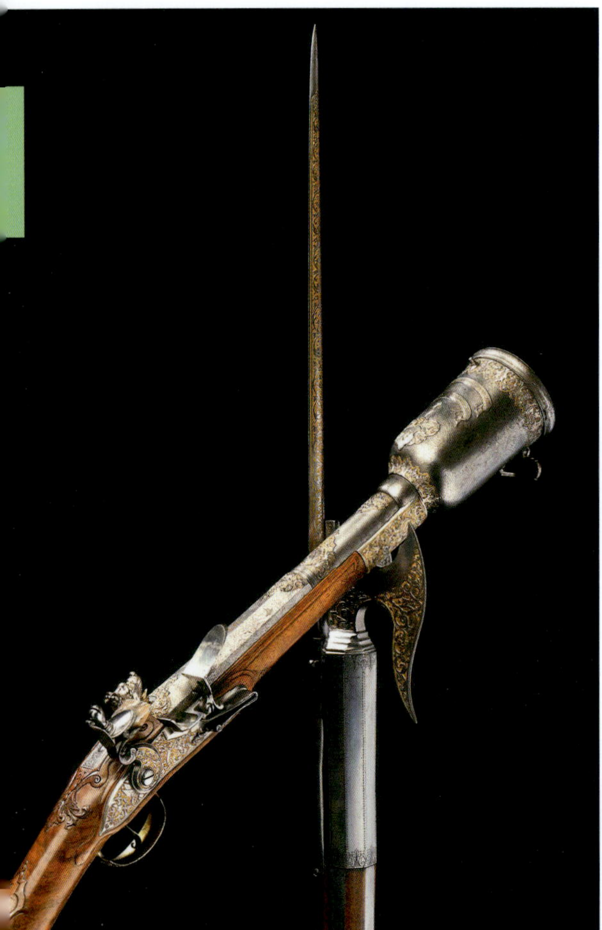

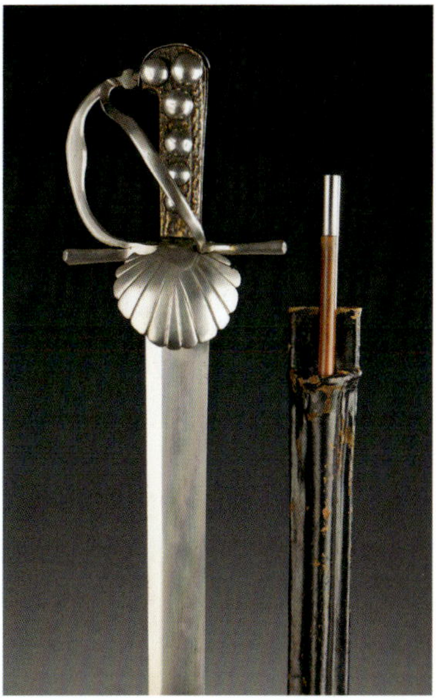

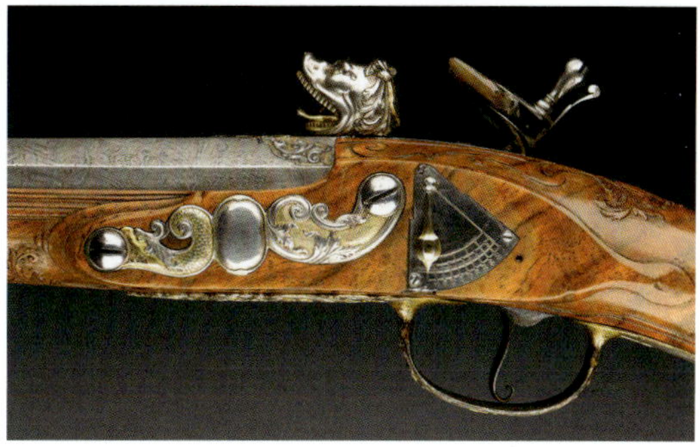

The lock is signed by Tobias Gräfenstein, a gunmaker who, from 1733, also worked as a die cutter at the Gotha mint. However, he was not the designer of this innovative set of weapons. Its inventor was Johann Wilhelm von Seebach, an artillery colonel in the service of Saxe-Gotha and commander of Friedenstein Fortress. His coat of arms is emblazoned on the firing cup (→ cf. fig. p. 59) and the rear sight, and his initials form a monogram in a medallion on the barrel. By presenting his invention in the form of such an opulent ensemble, he probably hoped to attract the attention of a princely collector and thus encourage its procurement for a standing army. Almost identical examples from 1731 and 1733 have been preserved in Munich and Coburg (albeit without the fork rest). If this concerted production of sumptuous showpieces was indeed a kind of publicity offensive by the colonel and the ruling duke, it was unsuccessful. In 1746, von Seebach made another attempt to arouse princely interest in his "newly invented bombard", this time in the much less expensive medium of a handwritten treatise. The manuscript has survived in three copies with different dedications: to Empress Maria Theresa of Austria, Empress Elizabeth of Russia, and the Dutch States General. Numerous pen and ink drawings illustrate the text, which serves both as a lavish advertising brochure and as an instruction manual. SR

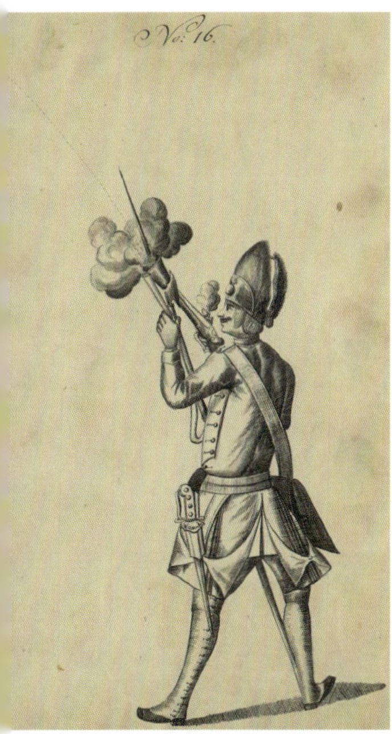

Illustration from: Johann Wilhelm von Seebach, *Beschreib- und Handlung einer neu erfundenen Bombarde*, 1746, Berlin State Library, Ms. germ. fol. 1232

Showcase 11

Germany

From the late Middle Ages onwards, there were several centres on the territory of the Holy Roman Empire which specialised in manufacturing weapons. While Solingen and Passau were famous for sword blades, the wealthy imperial cities of southern Germany, especially Nuremberg and Augsburg, as well as Regensburg, started producing handguns with wheellocks from at least the late 1520s. Munich, Braunschweig, and Dresden, and later Kassel and Berlin – all seats of their respective princely rulers – soon developed into further such centres. Other princely capitals followed suit. By contrast, some important trading cities had only small-scale firearms manufacturing, with comparatively few gunmakers known by name – although their products could be exquisite; these cities include Hamburg, Leipzig, Wrocław/Breslau, and Frankfurt am Main. On the other hand, Suhl, which is located in the Thuringian Forest, developed into a centre of weapons production from the late sixteenth century onwards thanks to its ore deposits and hammer mills; initially, the emphasis there was on military weapons, but later luxury hunting firearms were also manufactured (→ cf. pp. 48–55).

Especially from the late seventeenth century onwards, firearms were also increasingly produced in smaller princely capitals, mostly by a small number of court gunmakers who specialised in luxury handguns

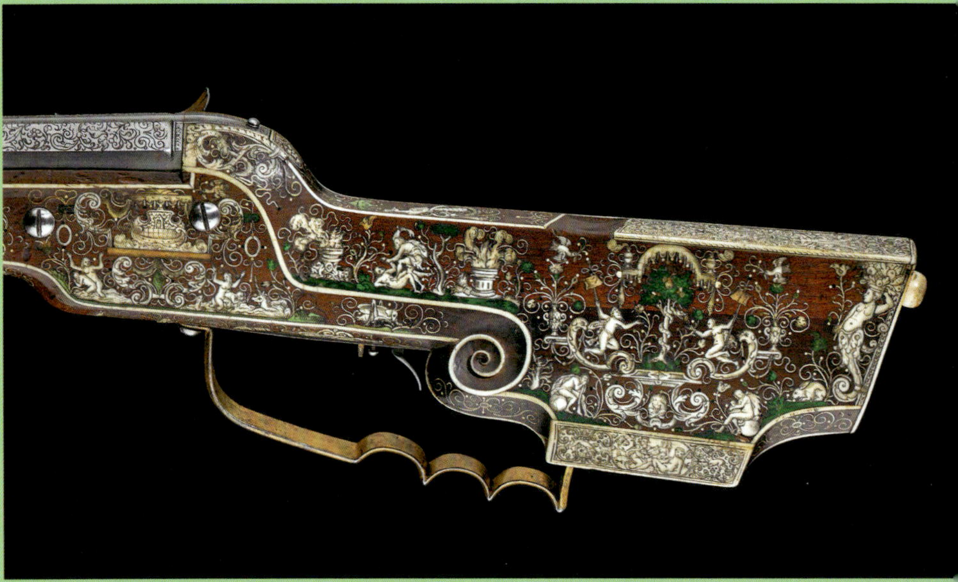

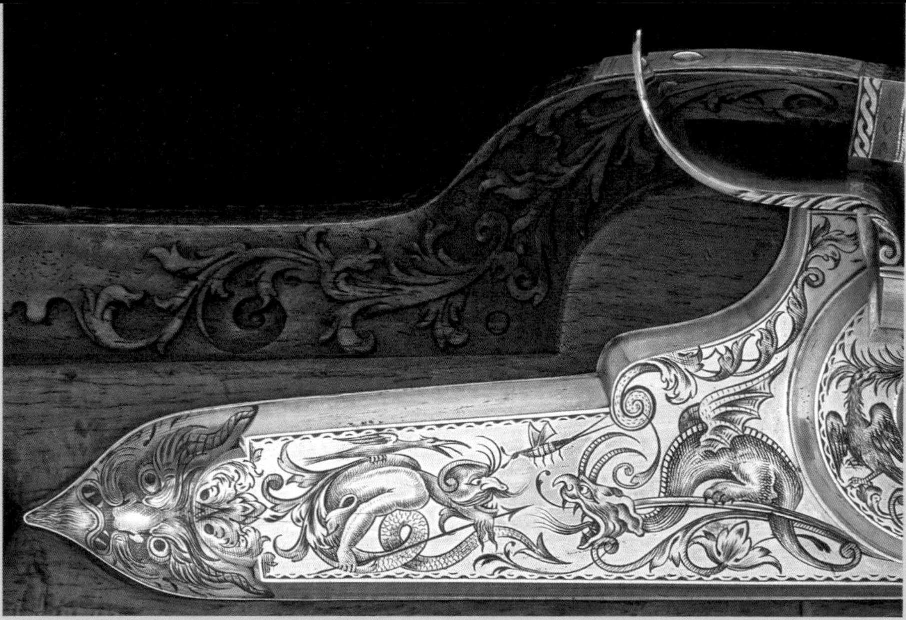

and collaborated with gun decorators, such as stockers and goldsmiths. This specialisation was something that the court gunmaking workshops had in common with the enterprises of an early capitalist character in the bourgeois urban centres, such as Nuremberg and Augsburg. Many craftsmen went on a journey – called the *Walz* – during which they often travelled to distant places and became acquainted with new ways of working, technical innovations, and different decorative styles. As journeymen, they often moved to other places and settled there to acquire a master craftsman's certificate and set up a workshop.

The Dresden collection contains handguns from many regions of the Holy Roman Empire, but especially from centres with which the electoral family maintained close ties: in the eighteenth century these included Munich, Darmstadt, and the capitals of the Thuringian principalities. From the capital of the rival state of Brandenburg-Prussia, a few – albeit very high-quality – works by the Berlin court gunmakers Lange and von der Fecht found their way into the collection of August III, for example as gifts from King Friedrich Wilhelm. Also of note is the firearms production of the small Thuringian principality of Schwarzburg-Sondershausen during the early eighteenth century. This was due to Prince Günther I's enthusiasm for hunting and the skills of his highly talented court gunmaker Johann Casimir Tanner, whose ornately decorated weapons were based on contemporary French models. He also created custom-made rifles with offset stock for the prince, who aimed with his left eye. GK

Flintlock rifle

Barrel: Wolf Danner, Nuremberg, c. 1540–1550
Stock, lock: German, before 1719
107 cm, Ø 14 mm, 2986 g
Inv. no. G 646

Electoral Prince Friedrich August (II) received this extraordinary weapon as a gift from the architect and Superintendent of the Royal Works, Matthäus Daniel Pöppelmann, on September 8, 1719 on the occasion of his marriage to Maria Josepha, daughter of the late Holy Roman Emperor. It is a hybrid consisting of an old barrel and a modern stock with a flintlock and set trigger. The particularly ornately etched and gilded barrel dating from the mid-sixteenth century bears the initials and serpent mark of the Nuremberg master Wolf Danner, a member of the famous tool- and gunmaking Danner family (Leonhard, Peter, Hans). Floral elements alternate with masks and wings; the coat of arms on a gold ground has not yet been deciphered.

The barrel is partially fluted on the outside and the rifling on the inside has 16 grooves: eight rounded and eight angled grooves. Dated rifled barrels are known from the 1540s onwards, but earlier guns with rifled barrels may have existed as early as 1500. A rifled barrel dated 1542, now held in the Krigsmuseet in Copenhagen, has 16 grooves like this one. This Danner barrel may be one of the earliest rifled barrels in existence.

The walnut stock corresponds to those found on *Müllerbüchse*-type rifles, which were popular in the early eighteenth century (→ cf. pp. 88–89). The delicate flintlock and butt cap are decorated with gold inlays (stars, leaves). This design suggests that it originates from the Baltic region, which also makes the entry in the inventory as a “Swedish rifle” more plausible. GK

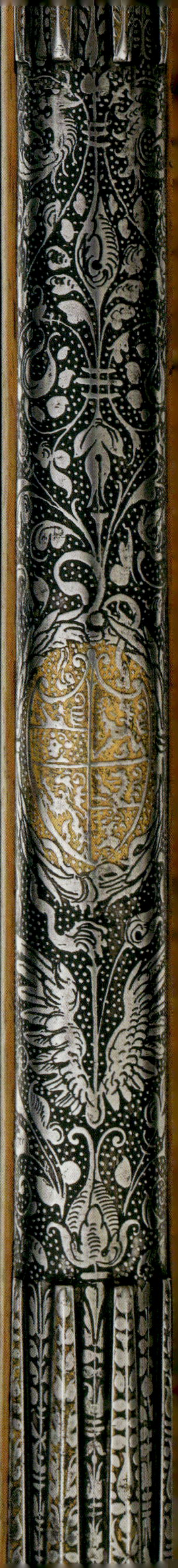

Wheellock rifle

Matthes Frosch
Stock: Master ES
Regensburg, c. 1610–1620
111.6 cm, Ø 14 mm, 3548 g
Inv. no. G 240

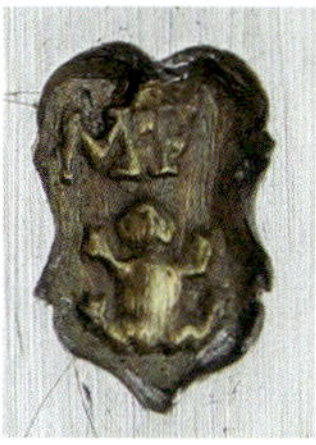

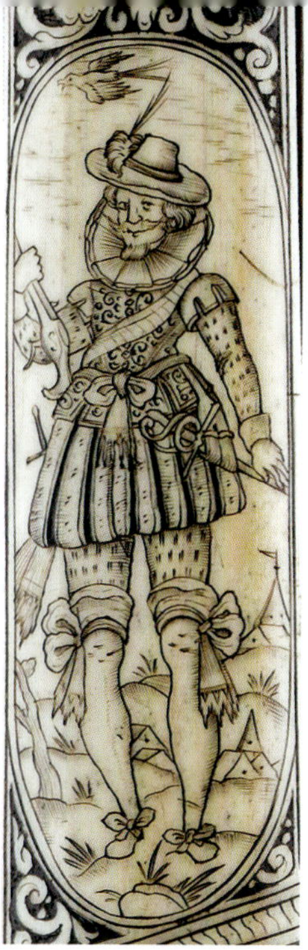

One of the most impressive works of South German gunmaking in the collection is the richly decorated wheellock rifle by the master using the maker's mark of a frog (German: *Frosch*), probably Matthes Frosch. The Frosch family was an important gun manufacturing dynasty in Regensburg from the late sixteenth century until around 1700.

In the seventeenth century, the rifle was kept in the still little-researched room called the *Ratskammer* (Council Chamber) in Dresden's Residenzschloss until Elector Johann Georg III had it moved to the *Kleine Büchsenkammer* (Small Rifle Chamber) in the area of the electoral apartments of the palace in 1687 – probably due to its particularly ornate decoration. From there, it was transferred first to the Jägerhof in 1722 and then to the Firearms Gallery in 1733; from 1740 onwards, it was kept in Gun Cabinet V on the south side, where the most precious rifles were displayed.

In addition to the floral engravings on the barrel and the gilt cast brass fittings – a wheel cover and an appliqué with a personification of abundance (*Abundantia*) – the highly artistic engraved bone inlays throughout the stock are particularly impressive. The biblical scenes from Genesis on the cheek piece are outstanding: beginning with the Garden of Eden, they show Adam, Eve, and the serpent in the Tree of Knowledge, then both at work, followed by Cain and Abel, Noah's Ark, and the Tower of Babel (→ cf. fig. p. 64).

The depictions of two contemporary cavaliers on the butt trap cover are interesting in terms of costume history. The two gentlemen present themselves in trunk hose, doublet, and cloak, with and without a hat – one holding a precious drinking bowl, the other a pistol. GK

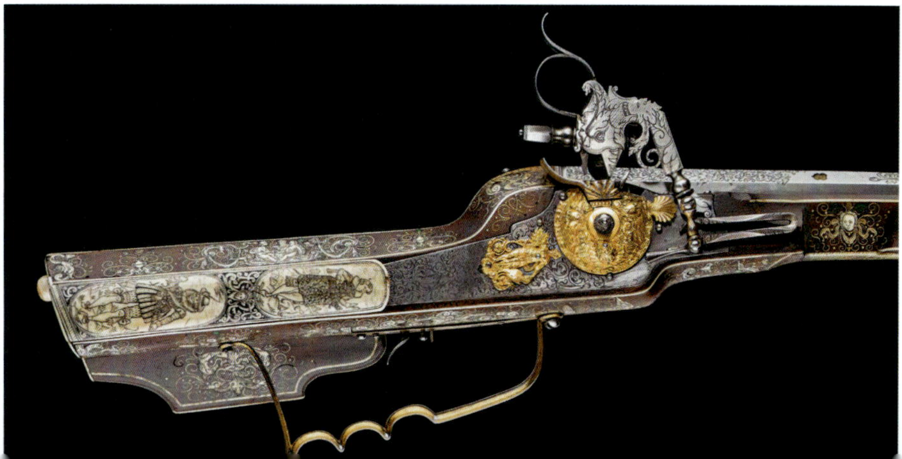

Germany

Flintlock shotgun

Johann Casimir Tanner, Sondershausen, 1726
138.5 cm, Ø 15 mm, 3300 g
Inv. no. G 887

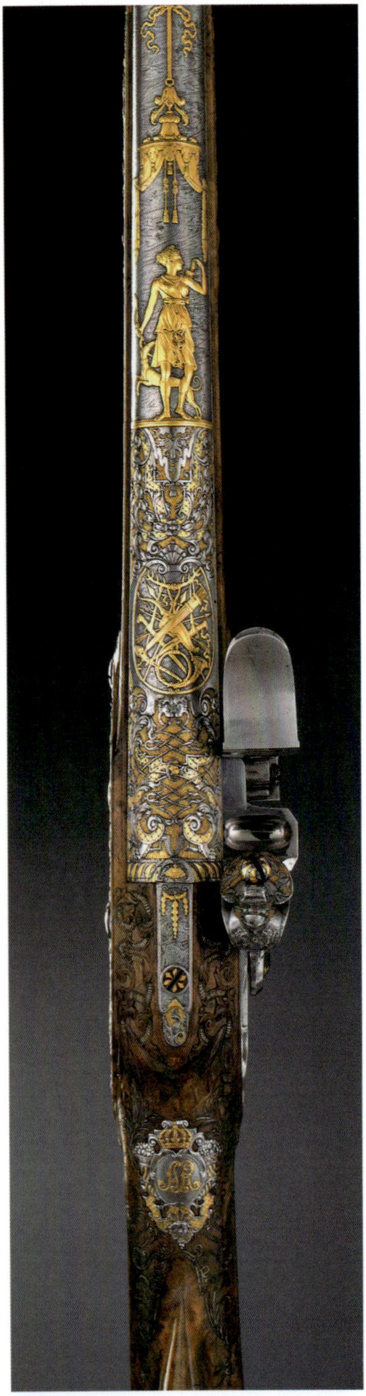

This lavishly decorated flintlock shotgun entered the collection in 1730. This weapon produced by the Schwarzburg-Sondershausen court gunmaker Johann Casimir Tanner, dated 1726, has a watered steel barrel with chiselled iron decoration and lavish gold inlays, with particularly fine bas-relief trophies of arms and a depiction of the goddess of the hunt, Diana, with a sighthound. The thumb plate features the monogram AR (*Augustus Rex*) beneath a royal crown. The finely carved walnut stock is already on the verge of rococo in its design. On the lock plate is an image of Hercules. August the Strong received a very similar luxury shotgun from the Tanner workshop at the Zeithain Encampment in 1730 as a gift from Prince Günther I of Schwarzburg-Sondershausen (inv. no. G 886). Both demonstrate a predilection for the French style and showcase the outstanding skills of the gunmakers and gun decorators in this Thuringian province.

In 1741, August III purchased further utility and luxury firearms from the estate of the late prince. As a keen hunter with an affinity for weapons, this prince had amassed an outstanding collection of small arms, which his widow was now selling. These acquisitions were among the most significant additions to the Firearms Gallery in the eighteenth century. Of the original 130 guns, 86 are still in the Rüstkammer today, as considerable numbers of weapons were already sold off in the eighteenth century and then especially in 1832. GK

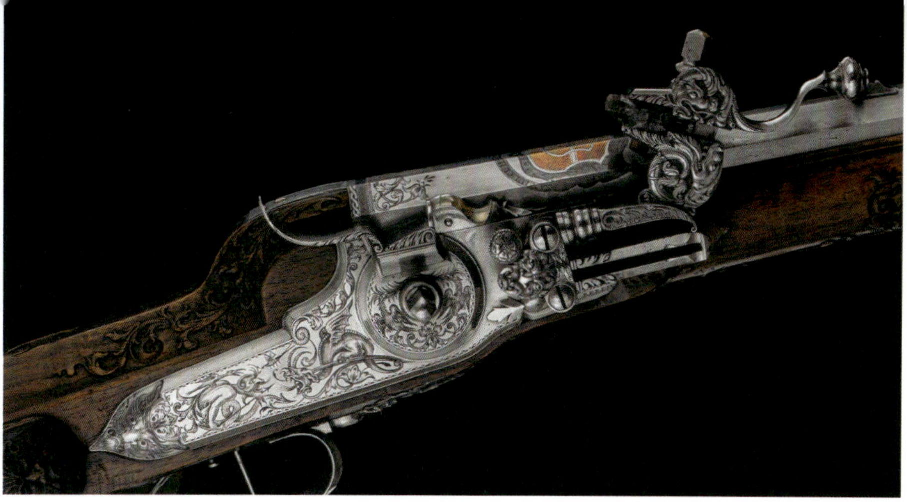

Wheellock rifle with square bore

J. Lange
Stock: Matthias Diemar
Berlin, before 1733
98.6 cm, Ø 14 mm, 4068 g
Inv. no. G 513

This unusual wheellock rifle with a square bore was manufactured by the Berlin gunmaker Lange (whose first name with initial J. has not yet been ascertained). Together with a very similarly decorated flintlock rifle by the royal Prussian court gunmaker Georg von der Fecht, it was a gift from the Prussian Soldier King Friedrich Wilhelm I for the Saxon ruler Friedrich August II on the occasion of his accession to power. The receipt of both rifles is recorded as an addendum in the inventory of the Electoral Prince's Rifle Chamber (begun in 1730): "given by His Majesty the King of Prussia to His Royal Highness and Serene Electoral Highness of Saxony on 10 May 1733". The barrel is inlaid with the Polish-Saxon alliance coat of arms in silver and copper, as well as a circumscription with the name and title of the recipient. The finely executed carving work by the Prussian royal court gunstocker Matthias Diemar is impressive, as are also the iron chiselling and intricate engravings on the lock plate, which depict a fight between a dragon and a mythical creature, supported by an insect and a bird respectively (→ cf. fig. p. 65). Two eagles are engraved on the wheel cover; the eagle motif is repeated on the chiselled iron side plate.

The butt trap contains a tool that corresponds to the square shape of the barrel bore and was intended for punching out leather ball patches. The rifle exemplifies the high technical and artistic standard of the court artists employed by the Soldier King on the threshold of the Frederician Rococo period. GK

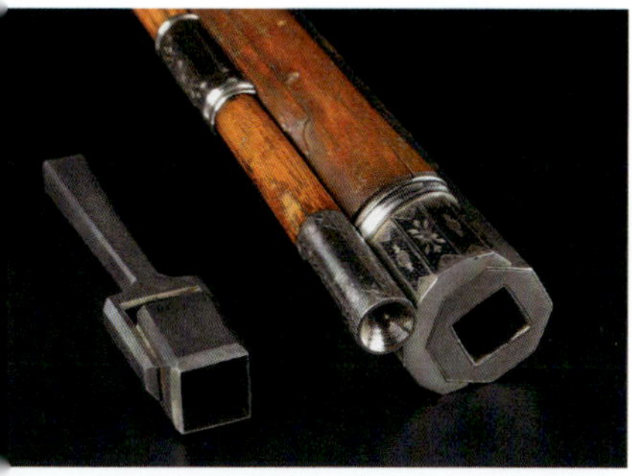

Germany

A triple-rotating wheellock rifle as a masterpiece

Some of the guns on display in the Firearms Gallery are masterpieces in the literal sense of the word: they were made in order to obtain the master's certificate of a gunmakers' guild. During the eighteenth century, these were systematically acquired for the Firearms Gallery.

Until well into the eighteenth century, prospective gunmakers in German-speaking countries were usually required to present a pair of wheellock rifles – probably due to the complexity of this type of lock. The most talented aspirants to the title of master craftsman opted to produce variants that were particularly technically challenging. A self-spanning wheellock (→ cf. pp. 83, 146), for example, could be spanned automatically by pulling down the dog, without the need for a separate wrench (or wheellock spanner).

Another popular special design was the *Dreimalumschläger*, so called because it has a triple-rotating wheel. As with a normal wheellock, it is spanned

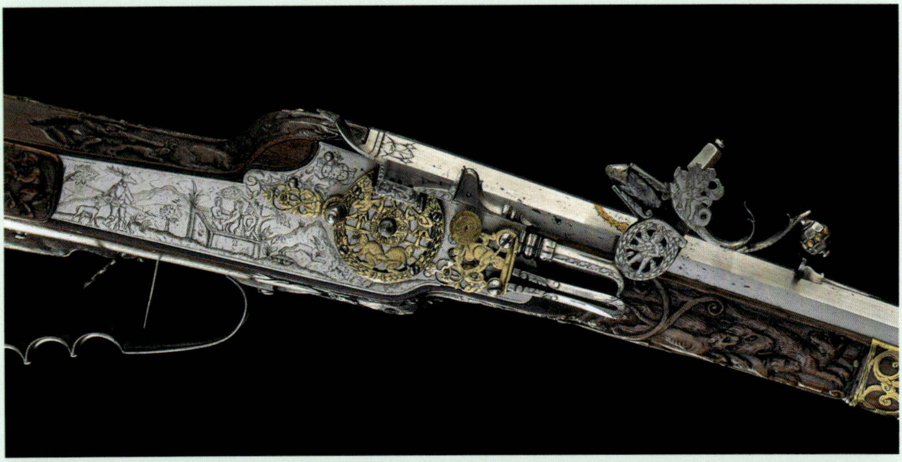

①

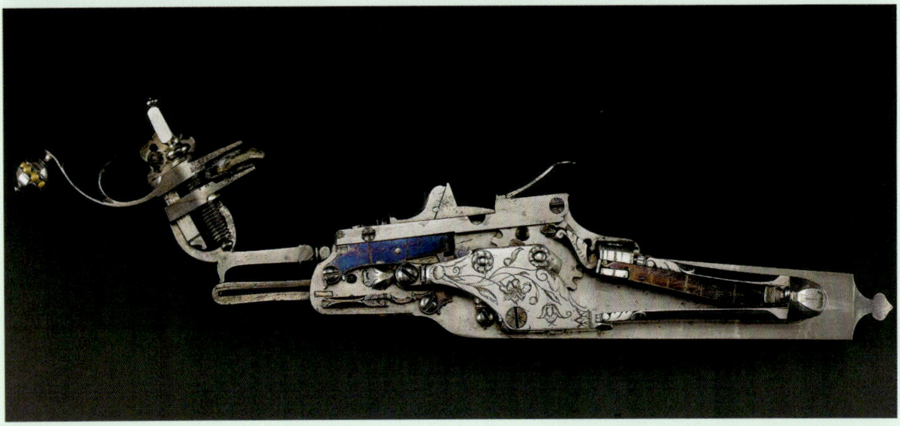

②

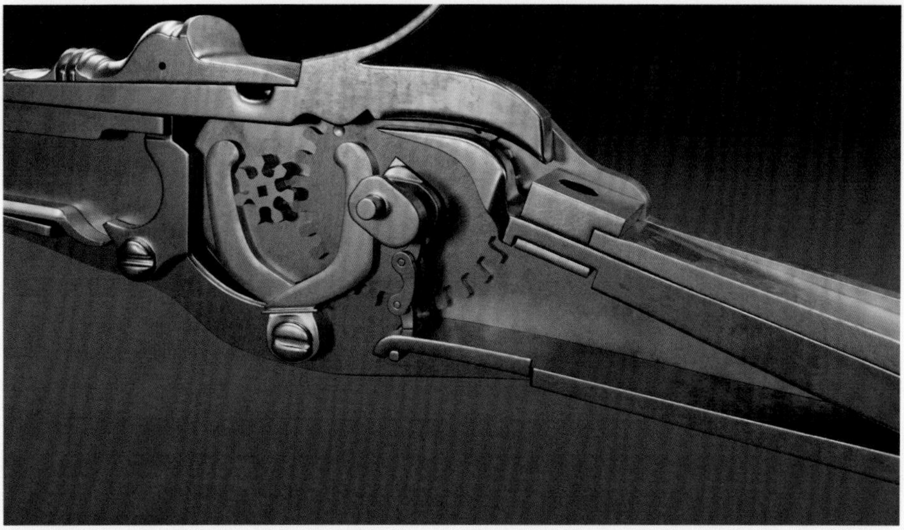

③

using a wrench, with the axle being rotated three quarters of a turn. The axle, however, is not positioned beneath the pan, but off-centre (fig. 1). In reality, it is not the friction wheel that is wound up in this way, but rather a separate spanning wheel that is connected to the friction wheel by a gear mechanism (fig. 3). Due to the transmission ratio of the two gearwheels, the friction wheel performs not just three-quarters of a rotation but three full rotations when it is released. This significantly reduces the risk of misfiring. In 2024–25, as part of a larger collaborative project, a digital video (see https://ruestkammer.skd.museum/ausstellungen/gewehrgalerie-im-langen-gang/) was produced in association with Dresden University of Applied Sciences (HTW) to explain how this rare type of lock works and how it is constructed.

Locks with such exclusive constructional features were often decorated with engravings not only on the outer face of the plate, but also on the reverse – even though this ornamentation only became visible when the lock was detached from the stock. One example of this is the *Dreimalumschläger* shown here, which was manufactured by the Durlach gunmaker Friedrich Bickel (inv. no. G 249, figs. 1, 2) and is dated 1663. According to the inventory of the Weißenfels *Büchsenkammer* (1739), "this rifle is to be considered a master piece", which could well be true. At any rate, in 1663 Bickel applied to become successor presumptive to the court gunmaker in the service of the Margrave of Baden-Durlach – this position was still held by his master at that time. SR

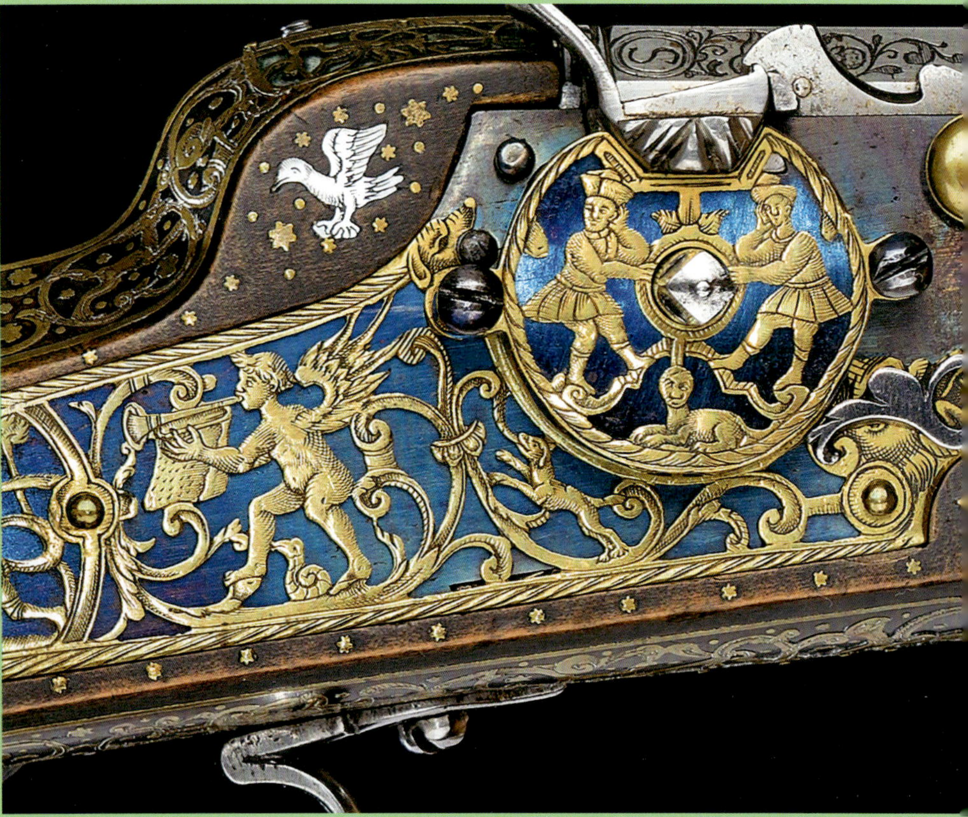

Showcase 13

Bohemia and Hungary

As a territory under Habsburg rule (since 1526), the Kingdom of Bohemia was historically part of the German cultural sphere of Central Europe. The gunmakers were mostly from among the German-speaking population. The most important centres of this craft were the capital city of Prague, the western Bohemian town of Cheb/Eger and the neighbouring spa town of Karlovy Vary/Carlsbad, which had been founded by Emperor Charles IV as early as the fourteenth century. Works in the Dresden collections show that in the seventeenth and eighteenth centuries hand firearms were also produced in the nearby towns of Ostrov nad Ohří/Schlackenwerth, Litoměřice/Leitmeritz, and České Hamry/Böhmisch Hammer, as well as in Loučná/Böhmisch Wiesenthal.

In terms of typology, seventeenth-century Bohemian wheellock weapons are similar to German products of the same period. A characteristic feature, however, is the more lavish decoration, including gilding. As in the other Central European gunmaking centres, the flintlock, which had been developed in France, gradually took over as the dominant firing mechanism towards the end of the seventeenth century. Initially, this mainly affected shotguns, which were also made with a French-style butt. Guns produced in Cheb/Eger typically have rustic-looking relief carvings on the stock and butt, usually depicting contemporary hunting scenes. This town in western Bohemia was a centre for the art of woodcarving – items featuring Cheb relief marquetry in boxwood and other woods were de rigueur in every contemporary *Kunstkammer*. The high nobility from all over Europe congregated in Karlovy Vary/Carlsbad. In the early eighteenth century, luxurious flintlock weapons were traded and manufactured specifically for this exclusive clientele. Typical features of Carlsbad firearms are exuberant décor and opulent gilding. In addition, elaborate engraved bone inlays with Christian, mythological, hunting, and other contemporary images were customary decorative motifs – as in the neighbouring territories of Saxony, Franconia, and the Upper Palatinate in Bavaria.

Košice/Kaschau, a town which is now in Slovakia but belonged to the Kingdom of Hungary (where it was called Kassa) until 1918, was home to gunmakers of German descent. Like their Bohemian colleagues, they manufactured their products in the Central European style. However, the decorations on these firearms also indicate that they were influenced by masters from north-eastern Europe. GK

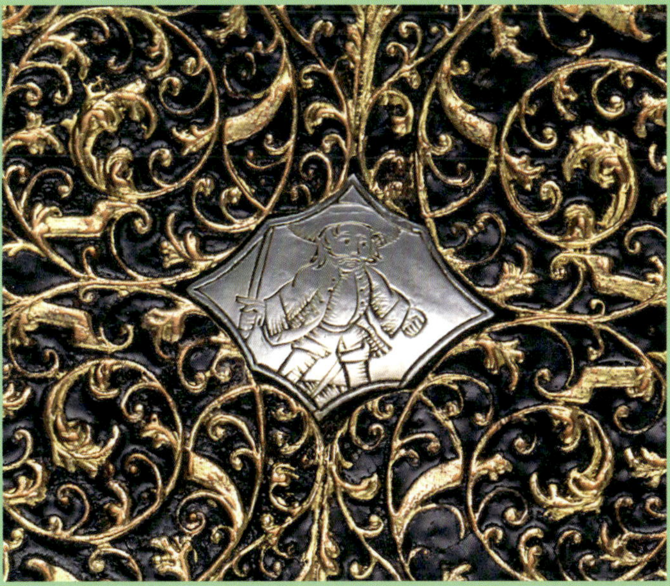

Wheellock rifle

Master CS, Kaschau/Košice/Kassa (?), 1618
143.1 cm, Ø 9 mm, 4589 g
Inv. no. G 245

This long and slender small-bore wheellock rifle with eight-groove barrel is one of the relatively few long guns in the Rüstkammer dating from the period before 1650, and it is probably the only example in Dresden of the art of Upper Hungarian gunmakers. It was purchased before 1733 from the "chief overseer and parforce hunter" Johann Andreas Ziegler. The somewhat eccentric, almost lattice-like brass decoration creates fascinating contrasts with the wood, mother-of-pearl, and blued steel (→ cf. fig. p. 72). With its naive, narrative motifs – including lovers, Orpheus with a harp, warrior scenes, animals, and musicians – and the intricacy of the brass and mother-of-pearl decoration, this rifle adheres to the traditional style of East-Central European masters. Consequently, it was incorrectly designated a "long *Tschinke*" in the old inventories (→ cf. pp. 80, 82). GK

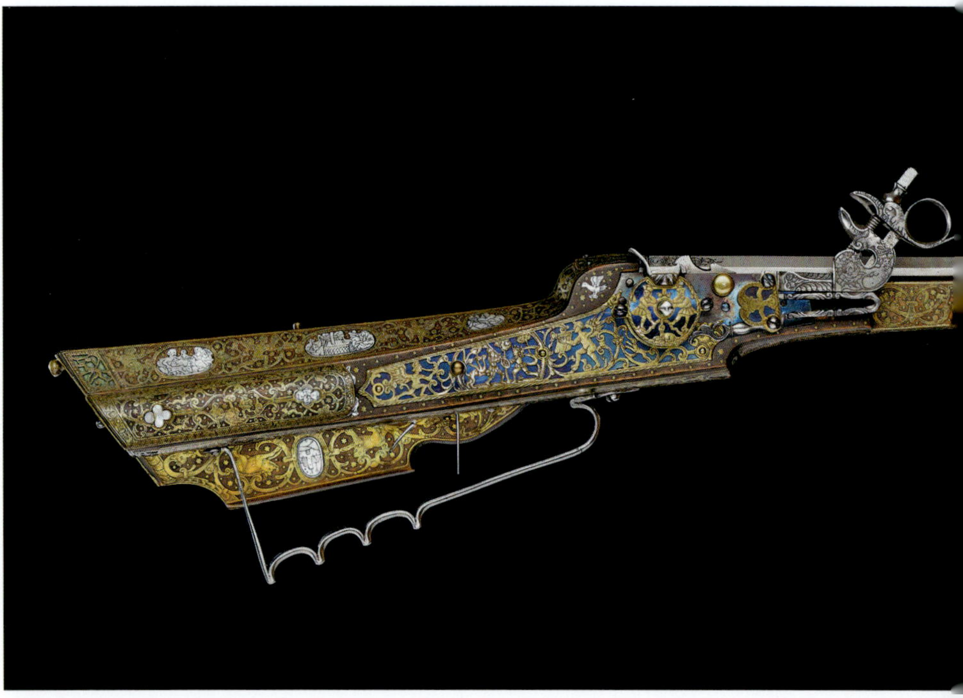

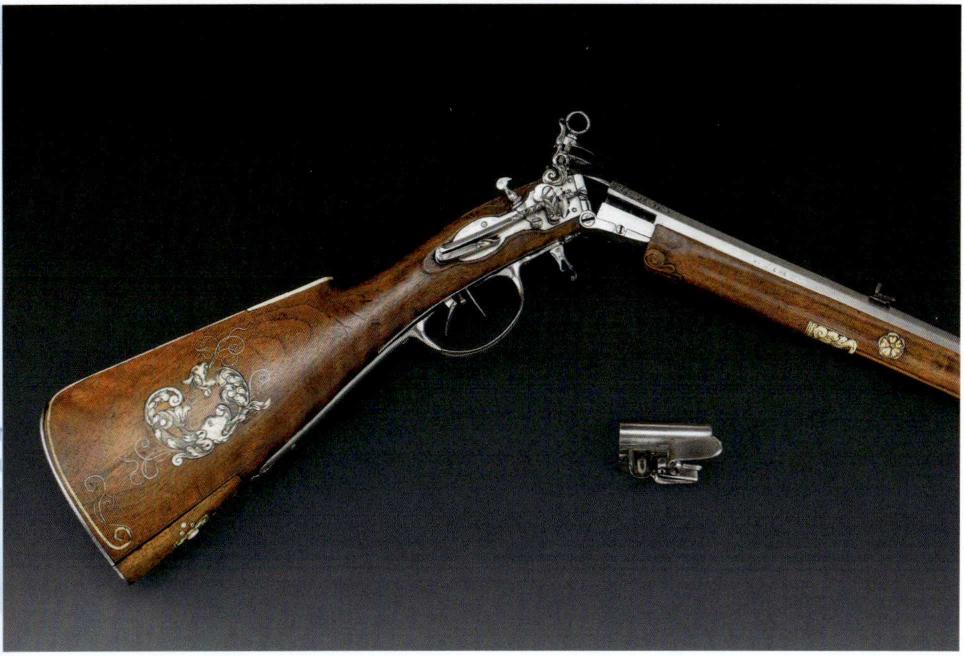

Breech-loading snaplock rifle

Johann Stifter, Prague, c. 1670
117 cm, Ø 14 mm, 3533 g
Inv. no. G 31

The most important gunmaker in Prague in the second half of the seventeenth century was probably Johann (Hans) Stifter, whose firearms have been preserved in many collections. The Dresden break action snaplock rifle is designed as a breech-loader. An iron cartridge containing a prepared charge of powder and lead could be inserted into the barrel chamber. Attached to this are the pan and the battery – the steel with the pan cover. The hook behind the cock serves as a safety catch. The 'modern' French butt features a grotesque ornament engraved in bone; on the opposite side is a contemporary horseman holding a commander's baton. An engraved Fortuna adorns the barrel tang. The butt-trap cover on the underside is unusual.

The rifle "that can be broken open at the back, with 3 cartridges" was acquired in 1740 from the estate of the Electorate of Saxony's chief forester and master huntsman Carl August von Carlowitz. Only one cartridge has survived. GK

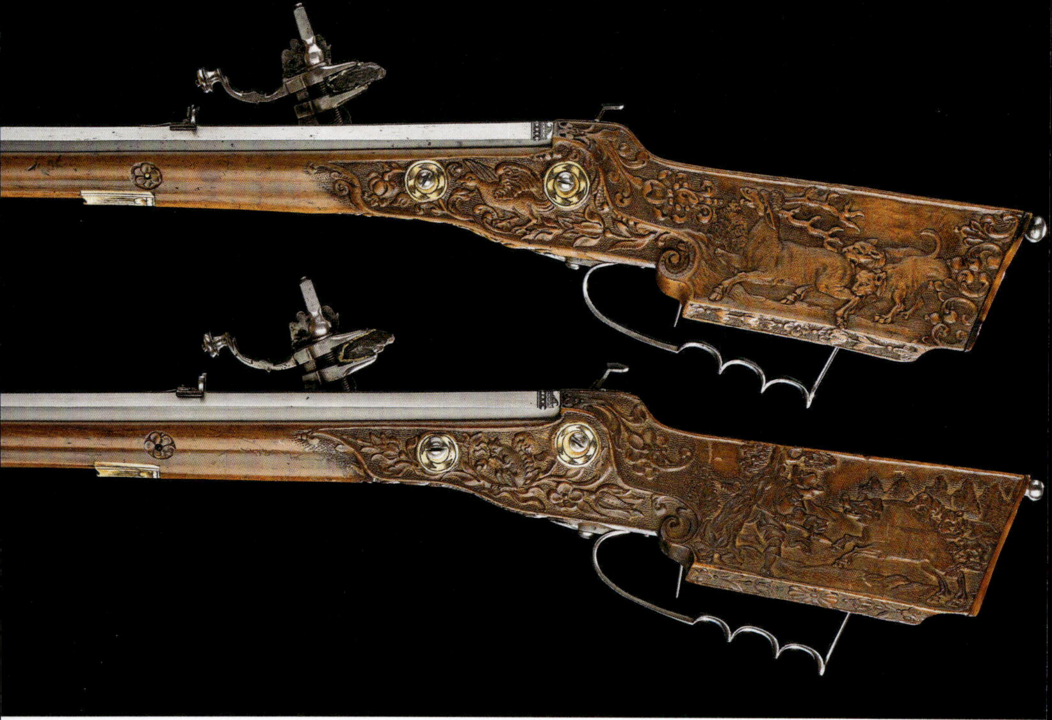

Pair of wheellock rifles

Hans Keiner, Cheb/Eger, c. 1665–1670
110.6/110.7 cm, Ø 11/13 mm, 4235/4383 g
Inv. nos. G 483, G 484

Members of the Keiner family were important gunmakers in Cheb during the second half of the seventeenth century: the father, Carl, and son Hans. Their descendants Hans Jacob, Johann Caspar, and Johann Conrad Ferdinand are known to have been active in Vienna, Kassel, Ludwigsburg, and Stockholm in the eighteenth century.

While the lock plates of this pair of rifles are elaborately engraved with war trophies, a hunting scene, birds, and flowers, the butts show two different hunting scenes carved relatively rustically in fruitwood: two dogs chasing a stag, and a wild boar hunt. The rifles originally belonged to Friedrich, Duke of Saxe-Gotha-Altenburg, a son-in-law of August, Duke of Saxe-Weissenfels. They came into the Dresden collection in 1746 after the Weissenfels secondary line died out. GK

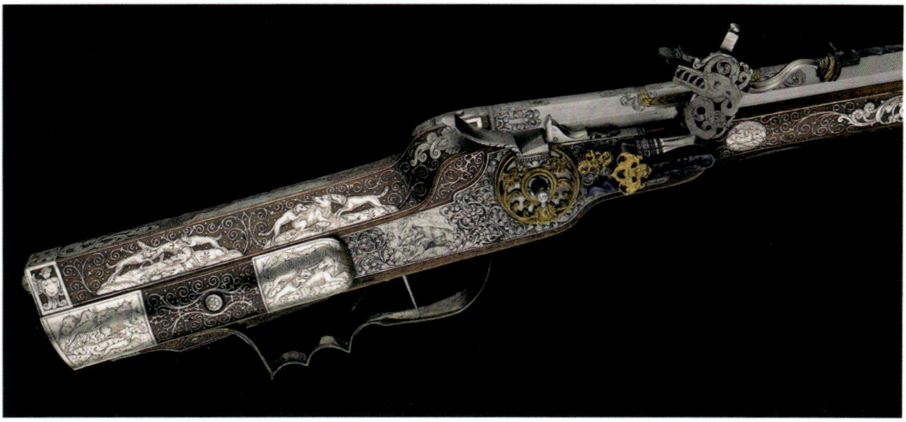

Set of wheellock firearms

Carl Keiner, Cheb/Eger, before 1680
Rifle: 111.2 cm, Ø 14 mm, 4645 g
Pistols: 51.5 cm, Ø 15 mm, 1389/1363 g
Inv. nos. G 365, J 521, J 1426

This set of wheellock firearms with silver mounts, which consists of a rifle and a pair of pistols, was manufactured by the Cheb-based gunmaker Carl Keiner, who was the leading master there in the late seventeenth century. The set was a gift from Moritz, Duke of Saxe-Zeitz to his elder brother, Elector Johann Georg II. The date 1680 can be found on the butt cap of the pistol J 1426 and on the large medallion on the cheek piece of the rifle. On the butt caps and on the medallion, the full heraldic achievement of the Electorate of Saxony is engraved in silver beneath a representation of the electoral hat, and on the rifle and the pistol J 1426 the name "Johann Georg Chur Furst Der II" is engraved around the edge. The crossed swords and the electoral hat are engraved on all the barrels. It is not known whether these precious weapons were actually received by the Elector. He had fled from Dresden, where the plague was raging, to Freiberg. He died there on 22 August 1680. Duke Moritz died the following year. There is no other comparable representation of the electoral dominions in heraldic form in the Dresden firearms collection: all of the territories belonging to Electoral Saxony are correctly depicted in the full achievement, both on the cheek piece of the rifle and on the pistol pommels. There is an abundance of other images on the rifle and pistols: from a Noah's Ark to various hunting scenes, animal baiting, a bear hunt, and a hunter with a rifle, as well as a scene depicting the fable of the wolf in sheep's clothing. GK

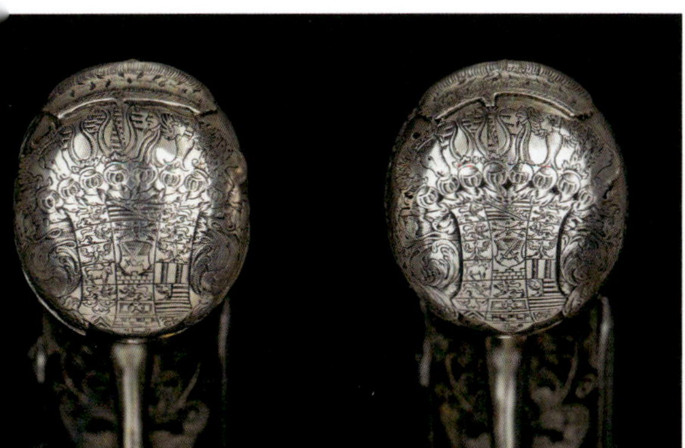

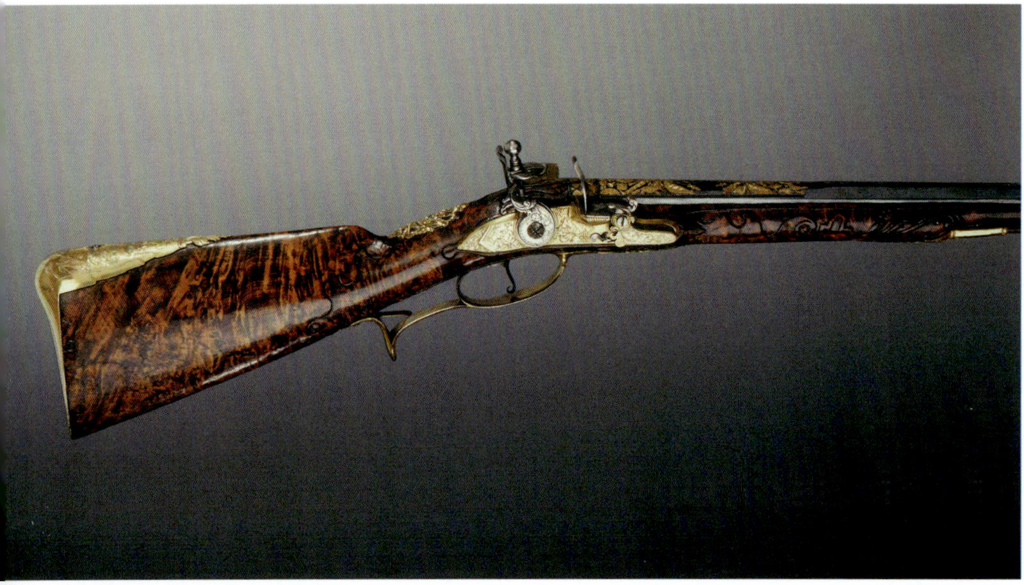

Flintlock shotgun

Master K (probably Johann Adam Knodt), Karlovy Vary/Carlsbad, c. 1710–1720
144.4 cm, Ø 15 mm, 3284 g
Inv. no. G 1567

This shotgun, purchased from the estate of Friedrich Ludwig, Duke of Württemberg-Winnental, who had for a time been in Saxon military service, is representative of luxurious firearms in the 'Carlsbad manner', with rich gilding on the brass fittings, such as the trigger guard, side plate, butt cap and thumb plate, as well as gold inlays on the barrel. In terms of motifs, the decoration on the lock plate, trigger guard, and openwork side plate follows French models, with designs referencing classical antiquity: the images depicted include a couple in classical attire, an ancient warrior (Mars?), and dogs on a stag hunt. The barrel is marked "K·C/B". The gunmaker was probably Johann Adam Knodt, who made luxury weapons for the European upper classes, many of whom 'took the waters' in Carlsbad. The gilding contrasts with the decorative, flamed wood of the stock and butt, which is probably dark-stained birch burl wood. GK

Pair of flintlock shotguns

Franz Anton Peret, Litoměřice/Leitmeritz, c. 1730
142/141.7 cm, Ø 16/17 mm, 2779/2780 g
Inv. nos. G 1741, G 1742

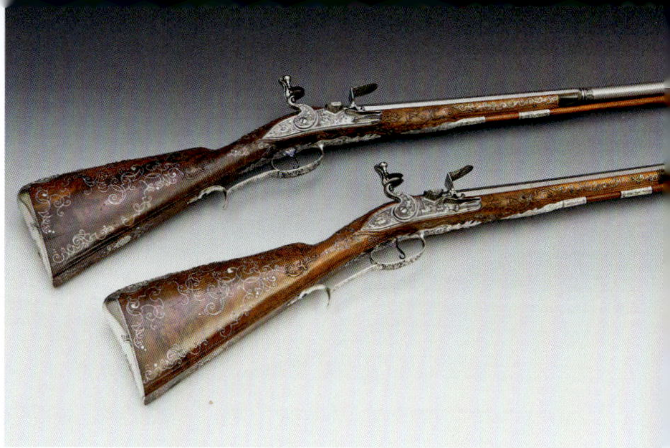

Gunmakers producing high-quality firearms also worked in Litoměřice/Leitmeritz, a town on the River Elbe. Their reputation must have reached the Dresden court, for in August 1732 the Electoral Princess Maria Josepha presented her husband Friedrich August (II) with a pair of flintlock shotguns made by the master Franz Anton Peret. The elegant half-stocked weapons are characterised above all by the silver fittings (trigger guard, side plate, butt cap, and ramrod pipe), which contrast with the beautifully flamed wood. The graceful silver wire inlays already reflect the influence of the early rococo. The marks inlaid in gold on the barrels are in the Spanish style, which was popular at the time.

August III ordered further firearms from the gunmaker Peret: two pairs of shotguns and two pairs of rifles. GK

Flintlock rifle (one of a pair)

Barrel: Carl Keiner, Cheb/Eger, before 1690
Lock, stock, mounts: probably Karlovy Vary/Carlsbad, around 1740–1750
113 cm, Ø 14 mm, 3755 g
Inv. no. G 800

This rifle is one of a pair presented in 1752 to his sovereign, King August III, by the court jester, postal courier, superintendent of hunting, and finally inspector of Ortenburg Castle in Bautzen, Gottfried Schmiedel, also known as Baron Schmiedel. The filigree mounts, with rich gilding and enamel ornaments, on the butt cheek piece and side plate, are remarkable and reflect the taste of the aristocratic circles who flocked to Carlsbad. The unknown decorator and engraver possibly used a print set by the Lorraine etcher Jacques Callot depicting little people (the *Varie Figure Gobbi*) as inspiration for the small mother-of-pearl inlays in the centre of the butt decoration (→ cf. fig. p. 73). The finely woven green carrying strap is notable. Such carrying straps have only very rarely survived. GK

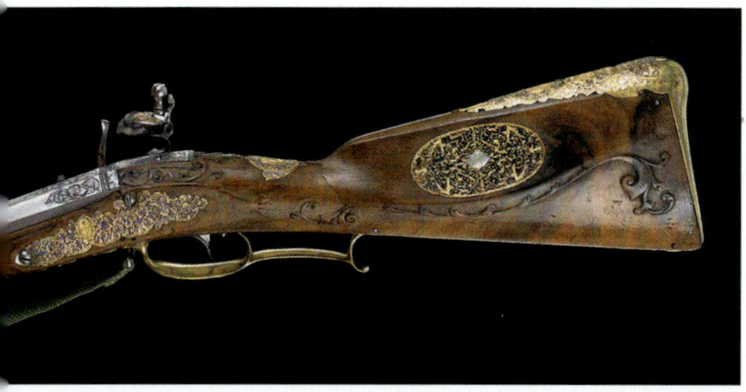

Silesia and Austria

In what is now the Polish-Czech twin town of Cieszyn (German name: Teschen) and Český Těšín – historically the capital of the Silesian Duchy of Teschen, a Bohemian fiefdom – unique small-calibre wheellock rifles were manufactured from the late sixteenth century onwards. These firearms, which soon enjoyed great popularity throughout Europe, were known as *Teschinken* (or *Tschinken*). Due to a misunderstanding arising from the fact that the type had been developed by a gunmaker named Kurland, or originating from Courland, these weapons were, and still are, often referred to as as Courland *Tschinken*.

The Silesian capital, Wrocław/Breslau, which had become prosperous and important primarily through trade, did not have a major gunmaking tradition. However, in the second half of the seventeenth and in the early eighteenth century, it produced a small number of technically spectacular masterpieces: wheellock rifles with insert barrels or with highly sophisticated locks. These were produced by a few masters known by name: Martin Scholz (sometimes spelled Schultz), Johann Balthasar, and members of the Nussbaum family.

In the Austrian heartlands of the Habsburg Monarchy, the capitals of Tyrol, Styria, and Upper Austria – Innsbruck, Graz, and Linz – as well as Ferlach in Carinthia and, of course, the imperial capital, Vienna,

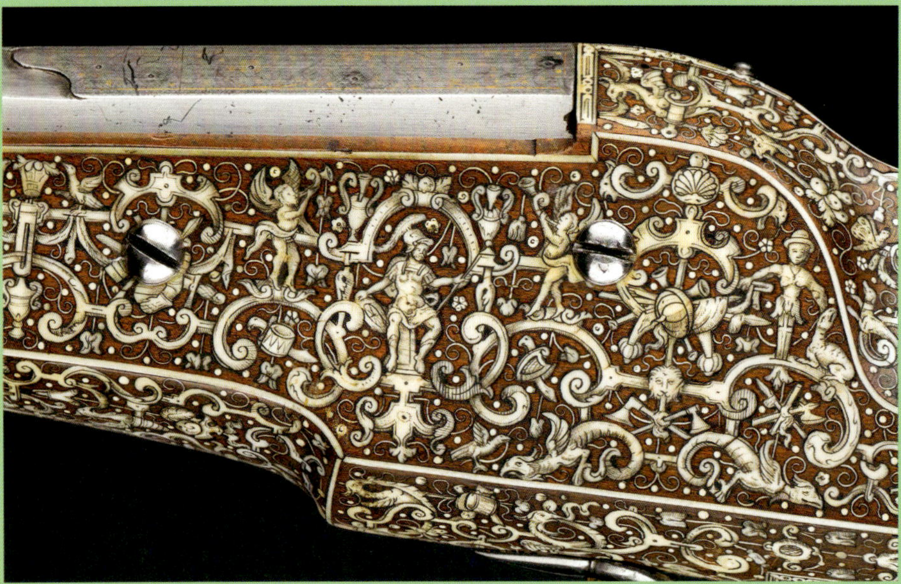

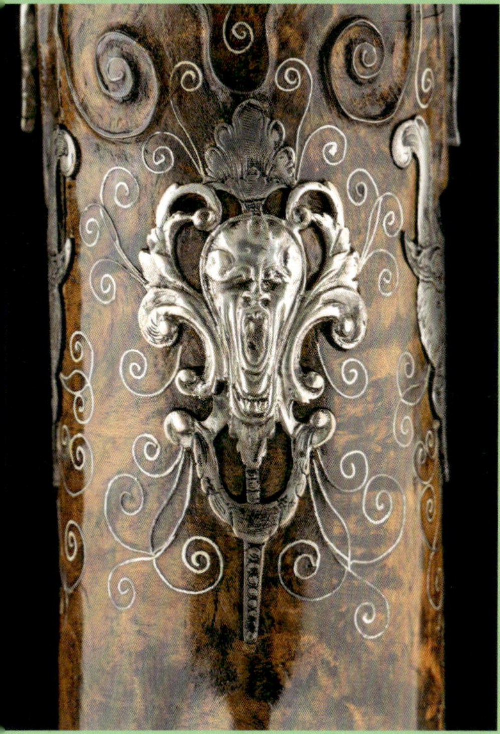

were all centres of the gunmaker's craft. In Graz, the holdings of the Landeszeughaus (Styrian Armoury), which is part of the Universalmuseum Johanneum, still testify to the large-scale production of armaments in that region, predominantly for military use.

Luxury firearms were primarily made in Vienna – for the imperial family as well as for Austrian, Hungarian, and Bohemian-Moravian magnates, such as the Houses of Schwarzenberg, Liechtenstein, Kinsky, Andrássy, Károlyi, Esterházy, and Lobkowitz. Leading Viennese masters in the later seventeenth and early eighteenth centuries were Michael Gull, members of the Zellner family, Felix Meier, and Joseph Hamerl. Some gun manufacturers, especially court gunmakers, were not members of the guild.

A typical feature of guns made in Vienna in the early eighteenth century is the combination of modern flintlocks with 'old-fashioned' German butts; this applies, in particular, to short rifles, known as *Stutzen*.

Starting in the late seventeenth century, pistols were made in Vienna on the basis of French models, displaying their typical butt shape and flintlocks. They were decorated, however, in the 'Viennese style', often with watered steel barrels, flat gold inlays, and Spanish-style barrel marks stamped in gold.

Both pistols and long guns often featured gilt-brass trigger guards and fittings. Vienna shared this predilection for gilding and exuberant décor with the Bohemian centres of luxury weapon production, notably Karlovy Vary (Carlsbad). GK

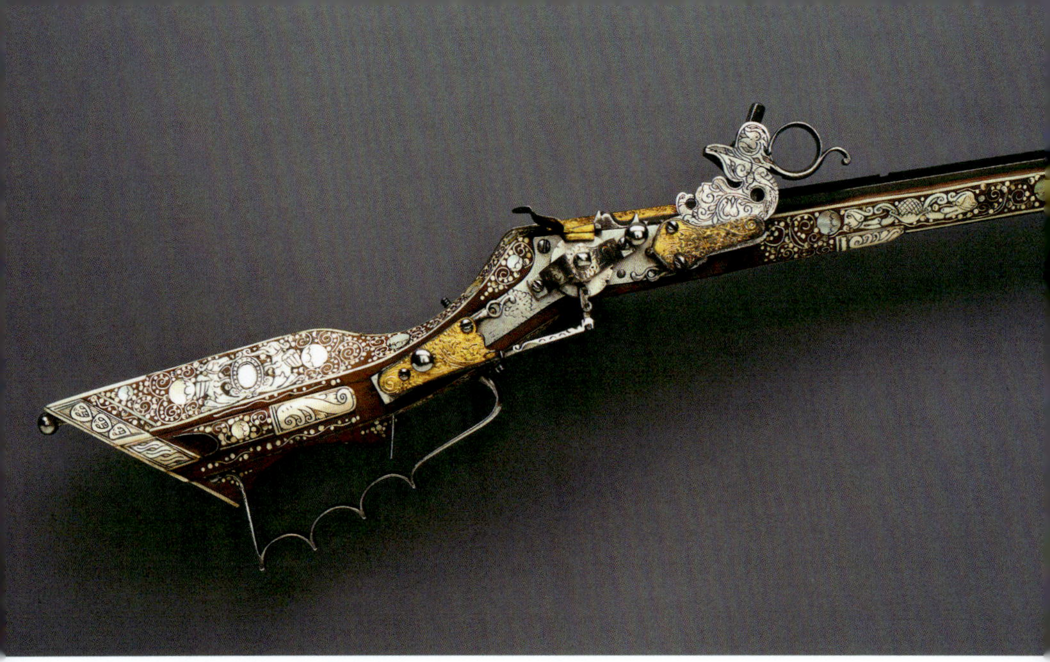

Wheellock rifle *(Tschinke)*

Cieszyn/Český Těšín, 1st half of the 17th century
116.9 cm, Ø 8 mm, 2724 g
Inv. no. G 224

This *Tschinke* by an unknown master is a typical weapon from Cieszyn from the first half of the seventeenth century. *Tschinken* – small rifles with an exposed wheel and chain, external dog spring and mainspring, and a distinctively shaped butt – were used particularly for shooting wildfowl.

The inexpensive, somewhat old-fashioned lock design with the mechanism visible from the outside allows for a slender stock shape. *Tschinken* are also characterised by the playful, unpretentious décor on their stocks. The motifs mostly derive from the realm of hunting: birds, hares, dogs, and huntsmen, but there are also floral and geometric ornaments, often in engraved bone and mother-of-pearl, sometimes with brass plates and inlaid wire. The metal parts, such as barrel surfaces and lock components, like the dog, are usually decorated with punch-marked and engraved ornaments, which were often gilded. This Cieszyn decorative art can also be found on pistols and rifles in south-eastern Central Europe.

This rifle, one of only four Cieszyn *Tschinken* rifles in the collection, entered the Dresden Firearms Gallery in 1746 from the gun collection of the recently deceased Johann Adolf II, Duke of Saxe-Weißenfels. GK

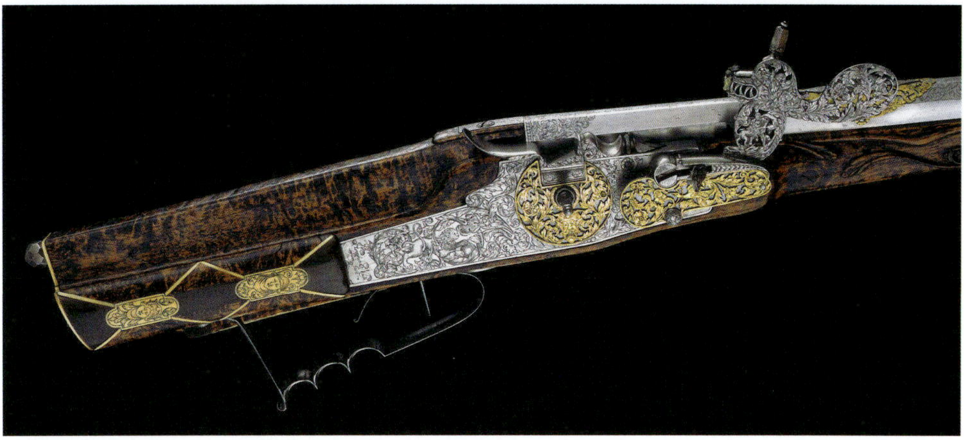

Self-spanning wheellock rifle with insert barrel

Heinrich Nussbaum, Wrocław/Breslau, c. 1700
119.5 cm, Ø 7/15 mm, 7952 g
Inv. no. G 431

This unusual rifle from Wrocław, a wheellock rifle with a so-called insert barrel, is one of the most technically sophisticated items in the Firearms Gallery. It is constructed in such a way that a small-bore barrel is inserted into a large-bore barrel which is mounted in the stock. The smaller barrel is adapted to the rifling and twist of the main barrel (which in this case has nine grooves) so as to allow a smooth insertion. Hence, the shooter has two different calibres available in a single weapon. This rifle, by master gunmaker Heinrich Nussbaum, was probably made as a masterpiece, which, considering the year of Nussbaum's birth (1663), puts it in the period between around 1690 and 1700 at the latest. It is signed and bears the Wrocław municipal coat of arms engraved in bone on the butt plate. Another special feature of the weapon is the design of the wheellock. It is a so-called self-spanning lock: when the user pulls down the dog, positioning it on the pan, the wheel is automatically spanned at the same time.

The collection also includes another wheellock rifle with an insert barrel and self-spanning mechanism, made in 1669 by the Wrocław master gunmaker Johann Balthasar and the stocker Caspar Sommerfeld. As masterpieces in the broader sense, these rifles with insert barrels are outstanding products of pre-industrial craftsmanship. There are only about a dozen of these rifles in the world, all of which were made in the second half of the seventeenth century or in the early eighteenth century. Most of them come from Wrocław, as does the piece that most closely resembles the Dresden specimens, a rifle by Martin Scholz in the weapons collection of Veste Coburg. GK

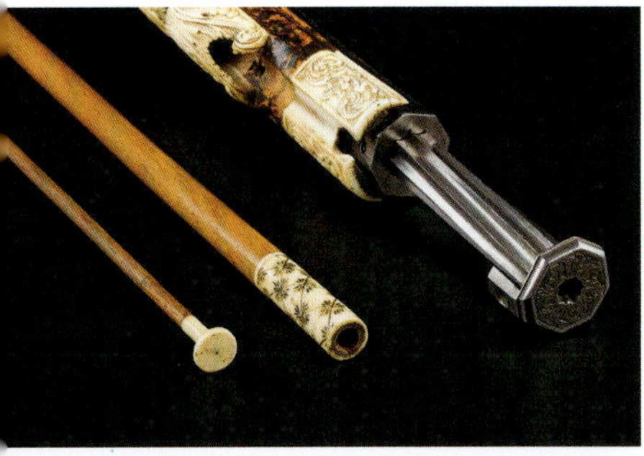

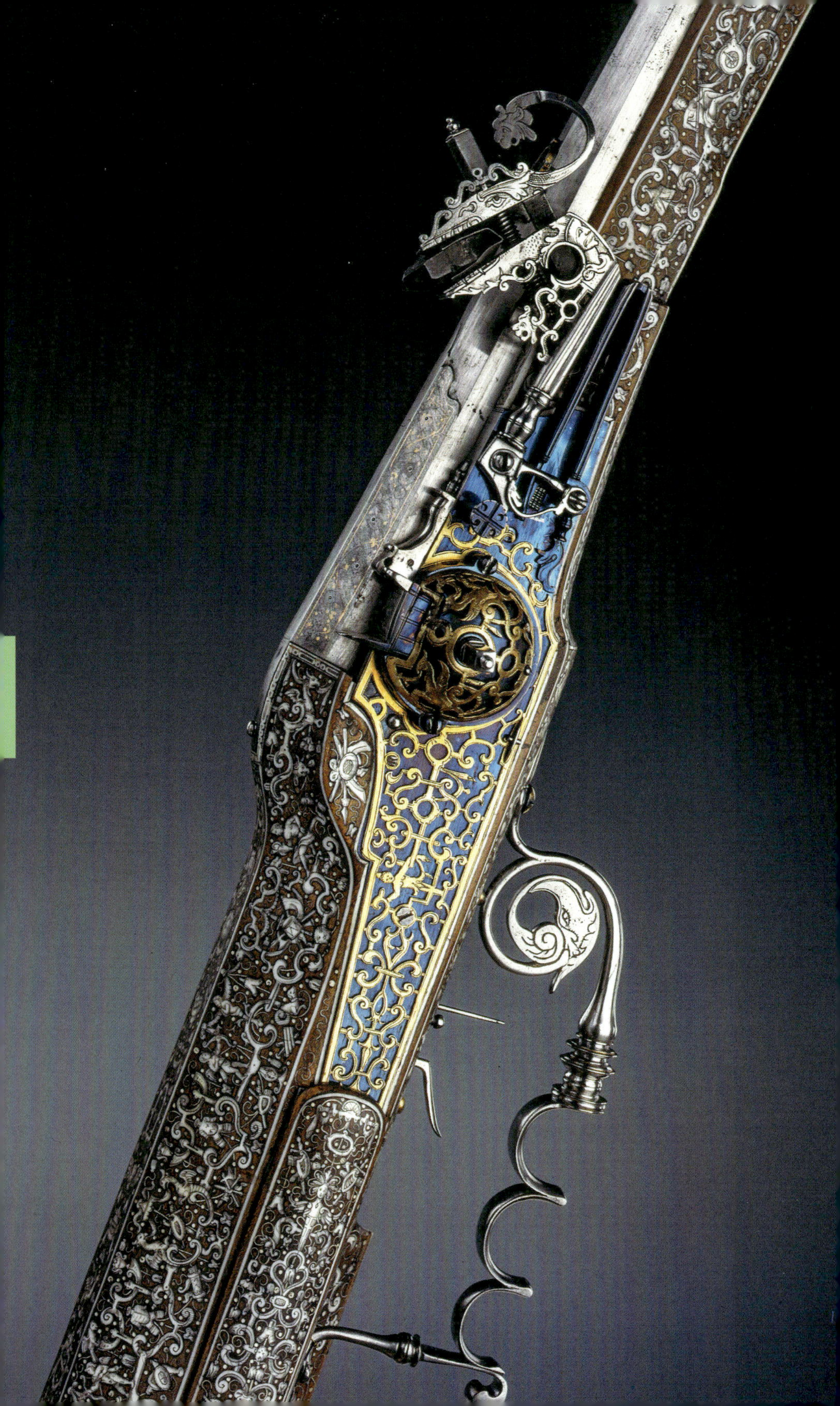

Wheellock rifle

Marx Götersdorfer
Stock: Elias Leckner
Linz, 1601
115.7 cm, Ø 16 mm, 4641 g
Inv. no. G 228

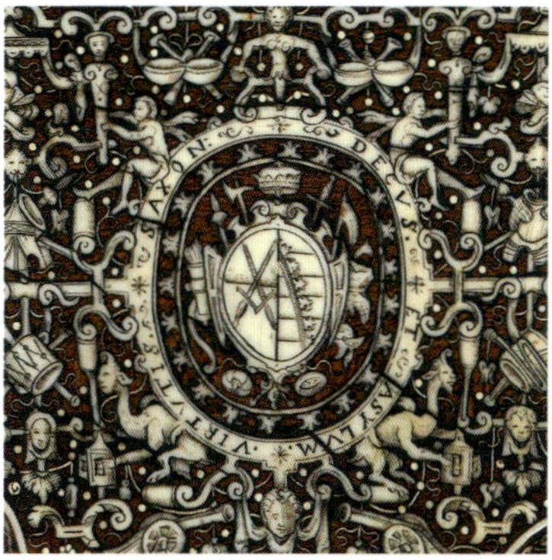

This magnificent wheellock rifle by the Linz gunmaker Marx Götersdorfer is a showpiece of European decorative art from the period around 1600 and is one of the earliest identifiable Austrian guns. The intricately decorated stock made of fruitwood with engraved bone inlays, incorporating the coat of arms of the Electorate of Saxony backed by trophies of arms and surrounded by the motto "SAXON[iae] DECVS ET ASYLVM VIRTVTIS" (Saxony's pride and seat of virtue), was made by Elias Leckner, who signed "EL" below the barrel tang. Götersdorfer himself signed his full name on the barrel chamber.

This luxurious rifle was previously regarded as a gift from Emperor Rudolf II to the young Elector Christian II. However, it was probably a diplomatic gift from Archduke Matthias of Austria, whose residence at that time was in Linz. The motto around the coat of arms can be interpreted as an expression of the future emperor's esteem for Christian II. In 1612, Matthias succeeded his elder brother Rudolf II on the throne of the Holy Roman Empire.

The rifle's elegant overall appearance, the incredibly finely engraved bone inlays and the contrasting colours of the lock plate decoration – gold and blue – represent an early pinnacle of the artistic creativity of Central European gunmakers and decorators. Despite the intricate decoration of the stock and butt, which consists of tiny figures, grotesques, and masks, framed with scrollwork, the rifle has a fully harmonious appearance. Other motifs include trophies of arms, kettledrums and trumpets, modern firearms, a contemporary arquebusier, and a seated figure representing Mars, the god of war (→ cf. fig. p. 80). The multifarious Mannerist ornamentation covers the entire stock and is a demonstrative example of the late Renaissance enthusiasm for ancient Roman decorative art following the rediscovery, in about 1520, of the paintings in the Domus Aurea of the Roman Emperor Nero.

The ornamentation on the rifle may have been directly modelled on prints by the French engraver and decorator of arms Étienne Delaune, who was strongly influenced by the grotesque decorations found in Rome, developed them further, and was active in the circle of the 'School of Fontainebleau'.

Just as delicate as the details on the stock are the subtle gold and silver inlays on the barrel surface and the brass openwork lock plate mount, whose gilded scrollwork decoration mirrors the design of the stock. GK

Wheellock rifle with indirect spanning axle and triple-rotating wheel (so-called *Dreimalumschläger*)

Caspar Zellner, Vienna, c. 1680–1690
144.9 cm, Ø 14 mm, 4984 g
Inv. no. G 277

Caspar Zellner was one of the most famous Viennese gunmakers of the late seventeenth and early eighteenth centuries. This particularly long wheellock rifle is one of Zellner's early masterpieces. In the 1748 inventory, it is described as "a masterpiece", meaning that it was made for the purpose of qualifying as a master craftsman.

The rifle has two special features: firstly, the spanning mechanism of the wheel lock is fascinating – it is a so-called *Dreimalumschläger*, in which the friction wheel is wound up by means of a spur gear, using gearwheels with a multiple transmission ratio (→ cf. pp. 70–71). In addition, the rifle has a barrel designed as a 'hog's back': its upper side is formed by an edge rather than by a flat surface. This edge serves as an additional aiming device alongside the attached sight (→ cf. p. 47).

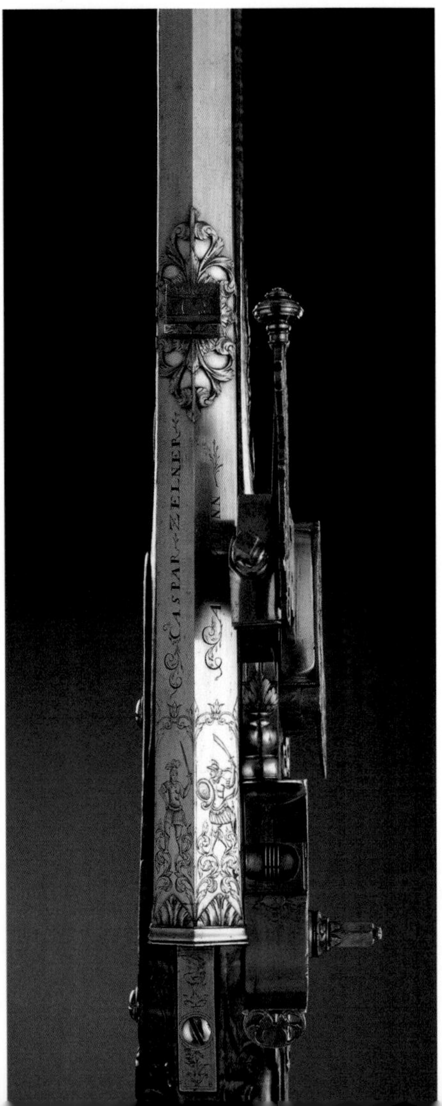

The lock plate is engraved with a view of Vienna, showing palatial Baroque buildings on a fortress, and a Gothic church (→ cf. fig. p. 87). The buildings can perhaps be identified as the Hofburg, with the front facing today's Ballhausplatz, and the Minorite Church. A particularly attractive part of the lock is the dog. The plate covering the dog spring, the back of the dog with the screw, and the jaws of the dog, feature engravings which harmoniously connect with each other and depict, among other things, the Roman goddess of war, Bellona, with trophies, the Old Testament hero Samson in combat with the lion, and a knight in a fantasy chariot. Engraved on the wheel cover is an image of Cupid, who appears to be holding the pan.

The stock is probably made of birch or maple wood and large sections of it are painted with a beer glaze in imitation of flamed burl wood. GK

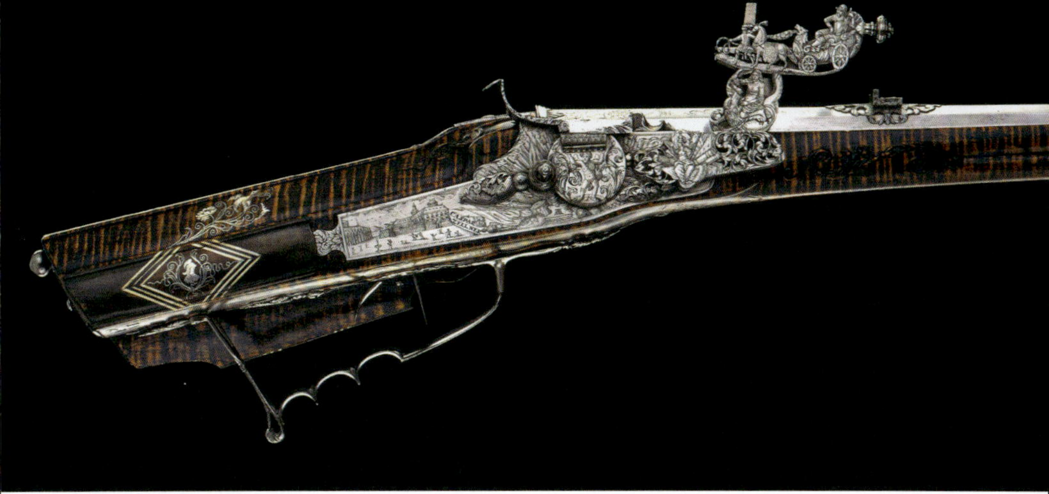

Flintlock shotgun

Georg Keiser, Vienna, c. 1700
154.1 cm, Ø 16 mm, 3574 g
Inv. no. G 1566

This classically elegant flintlock shotgun is impressive, above all, for its stained birch burl stock and butt, the fine silver wire inlays, and the silver mounts, such as the so-called open sight and the thumb plate in the form of a grimacing face (→ cf. fig. p. 81). The weapon was made by Georg Keiser, who came from Cheb (Eger) and qualified as a master craftsman in Vienna in 1674. He was one of the leading Viennese gunmakers for decades. Works by his hand have been preserved in imperial collections as well as in the collections of the Princes of Liechtenstein and Esterházy and in several European museums. From 1702 to 1716, Georg Keiser worked with his son-in-law Felix Meier, who was also a famous gunmaker in Vienna.

This and ten other Viennese shotguns were purchased for Dresden in 1736 from the estate of Duke Friedrich Ludwig von Württemberg-Winnental. GK

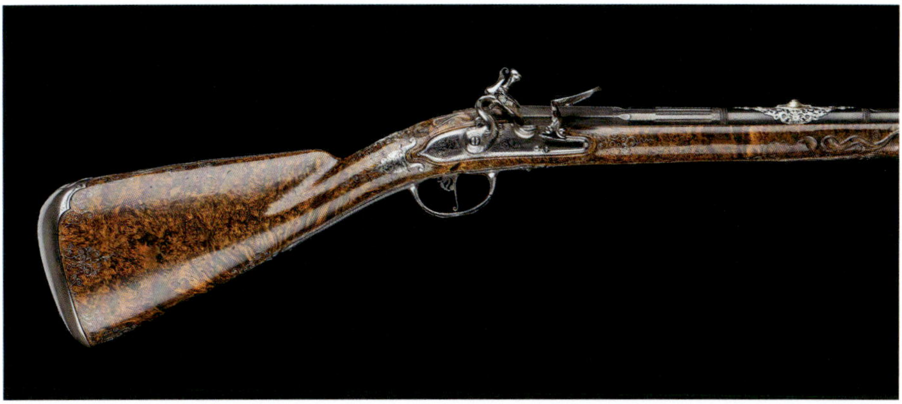

Müllerbüchse-Type Rifles

From 1733 onwards, the first cabinet on the south side of the Long Corridor contained rifles of the type known as *Müllerbüchsen*. These handguns, which are characteristic of the German art of gun making, have precisely rifled barrels with seven or eight grooves, brightly polished wheellocks, and French-style stocks. They appear robust and sturdy and are only sparsely decorated. Hans Lagemann, the son of a miller in Vollmarshausen in the Landgraviate of Hesse-Kassel, is said to have developed them towards the end of the seventeenth century. Hence, they are named after him: *Hessen-Casseler-Müllerbüchsen*. Lagemann's father Jost was probably also involved in the development of these rifles. However, since rifles designated as *Müllerbüchsen*, which are widespread throughout Europe, are rarely signed or marked, it is difficult to determine their geographical origin or chronology. Some bear an "M" on the small, which may possibly be interpreted as a mark of quality – a genuine *Müllerbüchse* produced by Hans Lagemann. The majority of rifles of this type have a wheellock (either with a rounded lock plate polished to a high lustre, or in a flat, planar design). Only a small proportion of the weapons were furnished from the outset with a more modern flintlock.

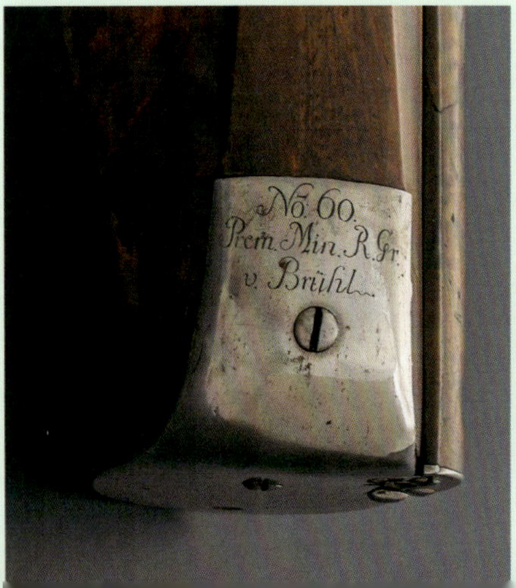

During the reigns of August the Strong and his son August III, the tradition developed at the Dresden court of the king receiving gifts of *Müllerbüchsen* from courtiers or guests, whose names were engraved on the butt cap. The names on the rifles read like a Who's Who of friendly and related royal houses, the Saxon and Polish nobility, the military, and the court household.

The dense two-tier arrangement of the rifles in the showcase is reminiscent of the original presentation of the Müllerbüchsen in the Firearms Gallery. On display are 32 rifles – gifts from various princely houses, diplomats, and guests of the Dresden court, such as the Duke of Saxe-Weissenfels, the Prince of Schwarzburg-Sondershausen, the Prussian envoy ("State Minister Bredow from Berlin"), Count Cosel, the Polish Princes Lubomirski and Poniatowski, the Ministers Count Vitzthum and Count Watzdorf. Count Heinrich von Brühl is represented by two pairs, the first given when he was a cabinet minister and the second dating from his period as prime minister (starting in 1746). These are followed by rifles given by Baron von Seyffertitz, Obermarschall Kettler from Hesse-Kassel, and the military officers Ogilvy and Riedesel. In the mid-nineteenth century, a few rifles were modernised: they were equipped with contemporary percussion lock mechanisms, their barrels were browned, and sighting devices (diopters) were added.

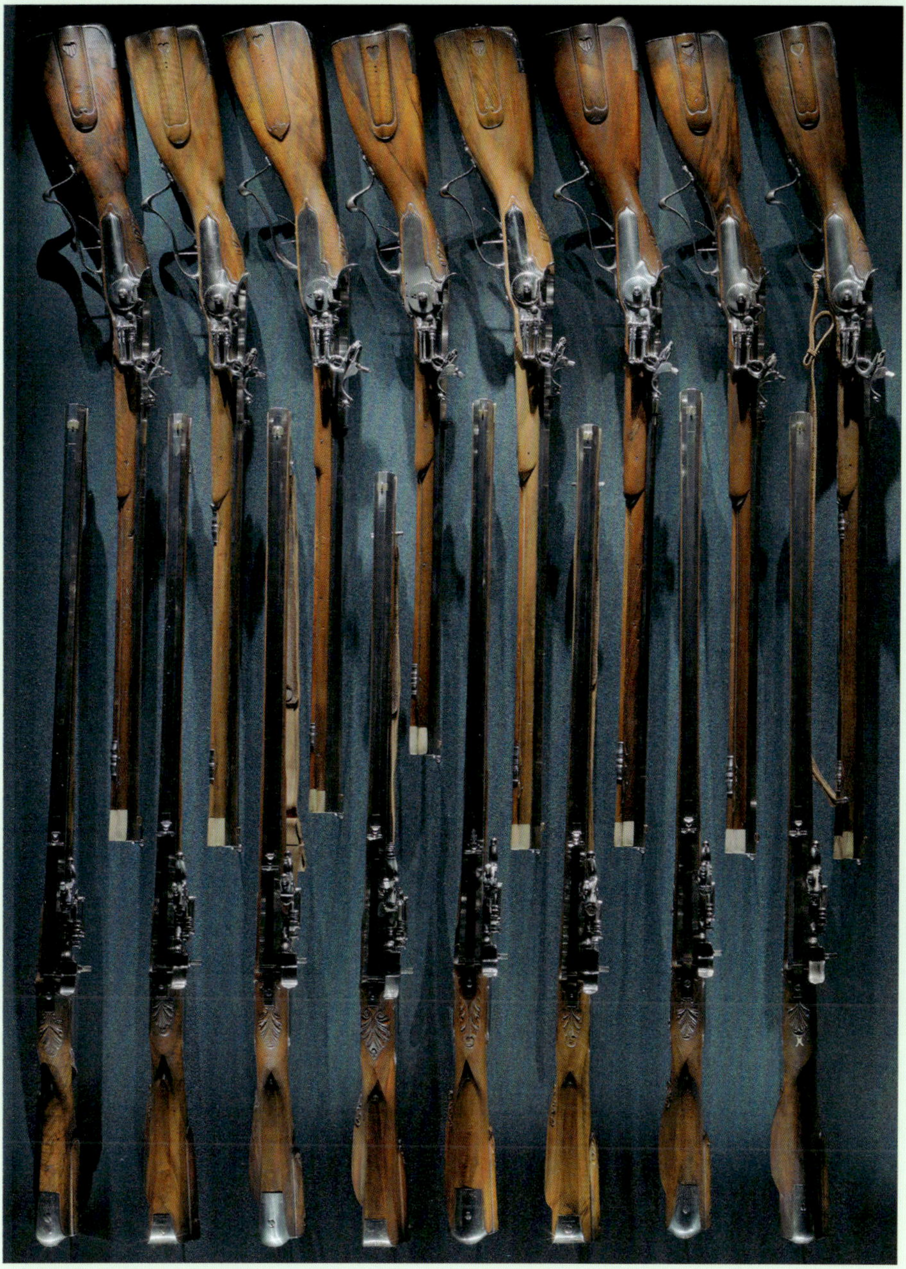

The rifles, which were already over a hundred years old, were then used as stalking rifles in court hunts. One such gun, decorated in neoclassical style with inlays of mother-of-pearl, wood, and bone, bears the monogram of Elector Friedrich August III under an electoral hat and has the Electoral Saxon coat of arms on the butt. The refitting with percussion caps was carried out around 1840–1850 during the reign of King Friedrich August II. GK

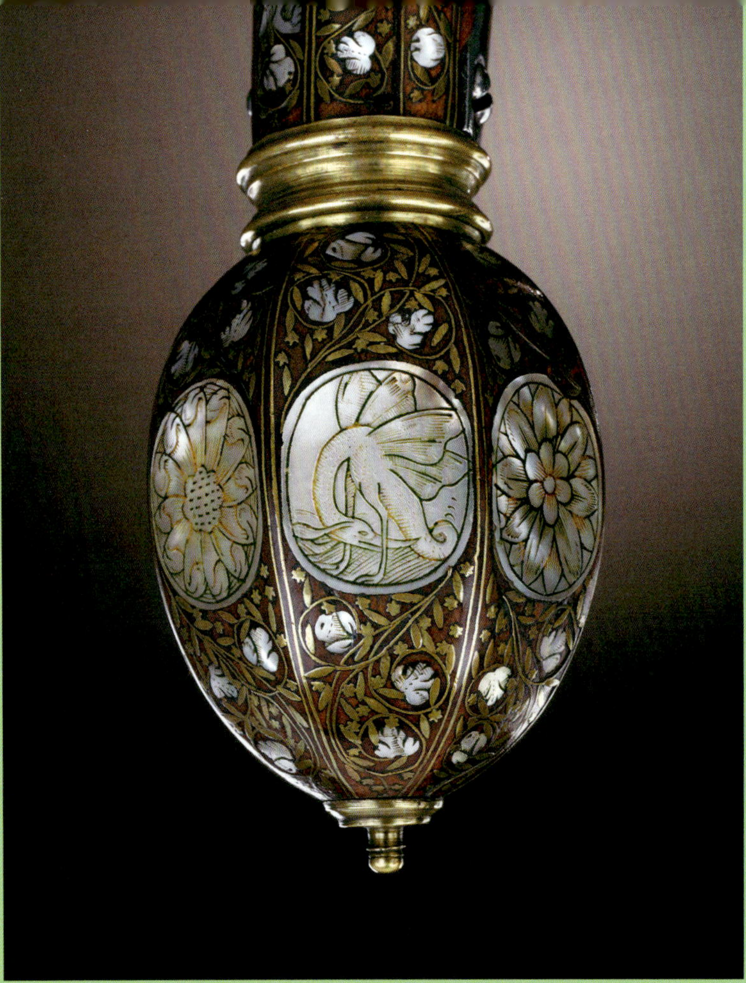

Showcases 2 and 4

France

French wheellock pistols were among the most elegant firearms in Europe in the period around 1600. Their characteristically slender stock and small lockplate are associated with a distinctive mechanical feature. Whereas in Germany the mainspring was accommodated inside the lockplate (which hence had to be quite large), a longer, flexible spring was favoured in France: this was fixed directly onto the wooden stock, which therefore had a more elongated design. The typical ornamentation with inlays of brass wire and engraved mother-of-pearl and bone shows parallels with contemporary French furniture production. Thanks to the collecting zeal of Elector Johann Georg I, luxury weapons of this type are well represented in the Rüstkammer.

In the early years of the seventeenth century, the French court mechanic Marin le Bourgeois developed the flintlock; this ground-breaking invention gradually became established throughout Europe. The flintlock firearms produced by Louis XIV's gunmakers were particularly admired internationally. One court gunmaker at a time was granted the privilege of running a workshop directly in the Grande Galerie of the Louvre; these artists proudly signed their work "A Paris aux Galeries". Their works can also be found in Dresden: Elector Johann Georg II owned a pair of pistols by Guillaume de Vie; later, the famous Bertrand Piraube supplied August the Strong with numerous splendid firearms. The highlights of the collection also include important works by François Laurent, known as Le Languedoc – a court gunmaker who was not based in the Louvre but nevertheless proved to be particularly influential. This was especially due to his close collaboration with engravers, who printed and disseminated his innovative decorative designs. Several pairs of pistols made by Piraube and Languedoc were part of a diplomatic gift from the Sun King in 1715. SR

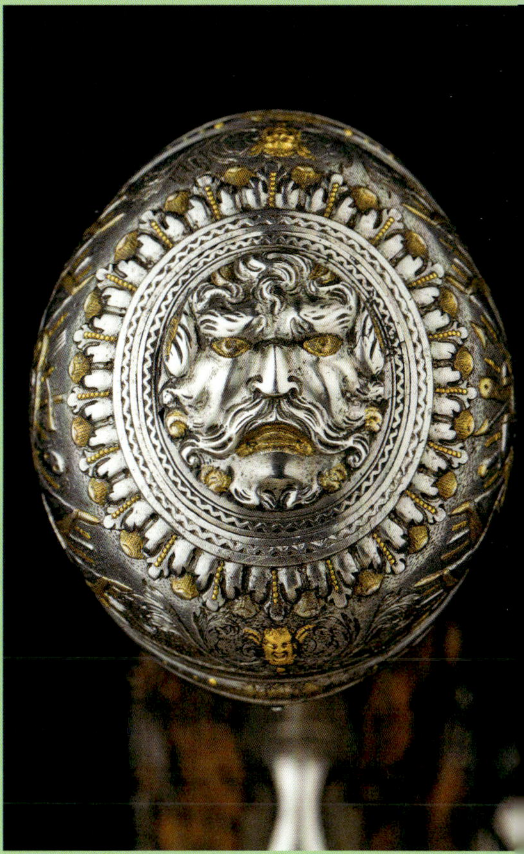

Wheellock pistol

Barrel, lock: Master HP (probably Henry Paris)
Montbéliard, before 1604
78 cm, Ø 8 mm, 1600 g
Inv. no. J 1428

In 1604, Duke Johann Georg (I) married the Duchess of Württemberg Sibylla Elisabeth. This wheellock pistol was given to him by the bride's father, Friedrich I of Württemberg, who had reigned as Duke in Stuttgart since 1593. Friedrich originated from the Württemberg-Montbéliard collateral line and was Count of Montbéliard (Mömpelgard in German), now in France. That is where the pistol was made, as evidenced by the inspection mark on the barrel, which is based on the town's coat of arms.

Although the county of Montbéliard remained politically an exclave of the Holy Roman Empire until 1793, it was culturally part of the Romance linguistic and cultural area. Hence, the form and typology of this small-calibre weapon, with its spherical pommel and crescent-shaped wheel guide, closely resemble those of French firearms from the late sixteenth century. On the other hand, its mechanical characteristics are more similar to the products of German gunmakers, with the mainspring being attached inside a large lockplate. A distinctive feature is the ornamentation on the stock, whose reddish lacquer and slivers of mother-of-pearl simulate marbling. SR

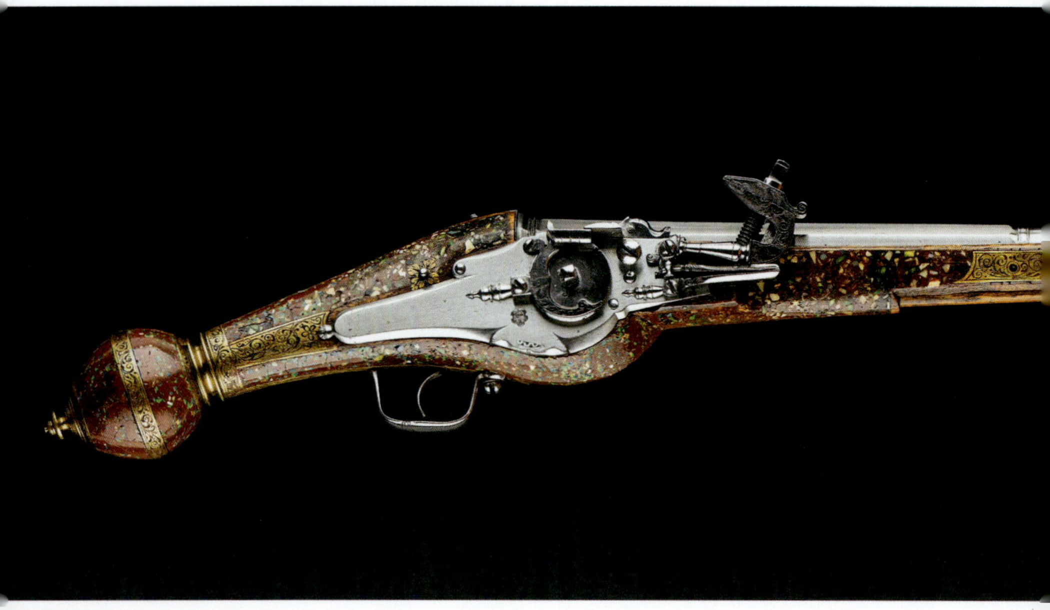

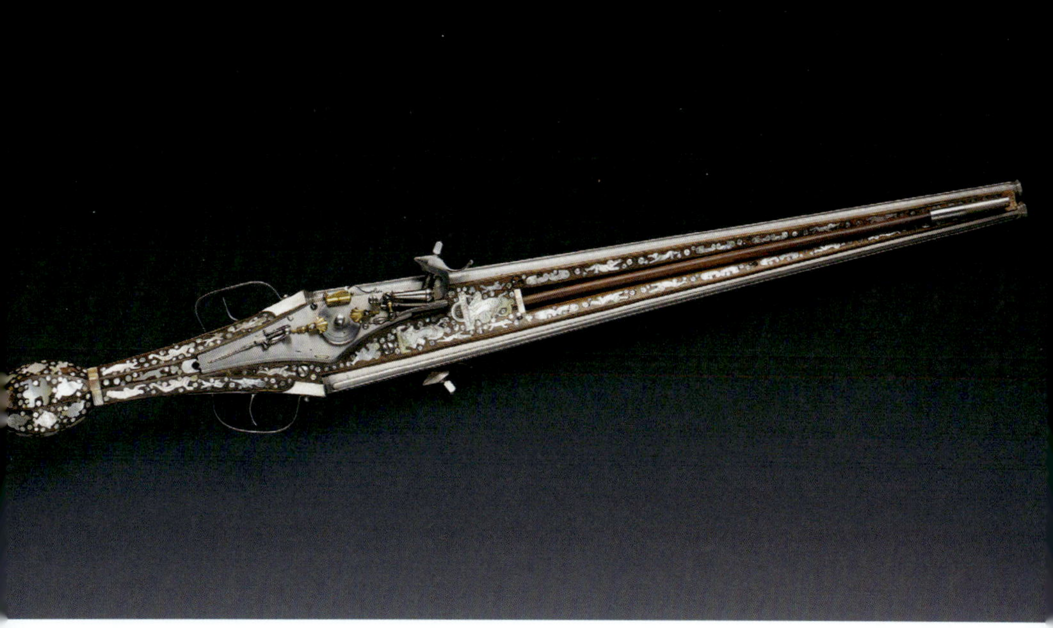

Double-barrelled wheellock pistol

Barrels: Master IF
France, before 1608
72.6 cm, Ø 8/9 mm, 1579 g
Inv. no. J 290

The pistol has two barrels, wheellocks and triggers, which can be operated successively by turning the weapon over. The wooden stock is lavishly decorated with brass wire and engraved mother-of-pearl inlays in the form of angels and mascarons. Two larger mother-of-pearl inlays depict allegories of arithmetic (with books and an hourglass) and astrology (with an armillary sphere and a double child's head symbolising the winds). These images are based on ornamental engravings by the goldsmith and engraver Étienne Delaune. Duke Johann Georg (I) received this precious pistol before 1608 as a gift from the first Saxon court huntsman, Werner von Lützelburg. SR

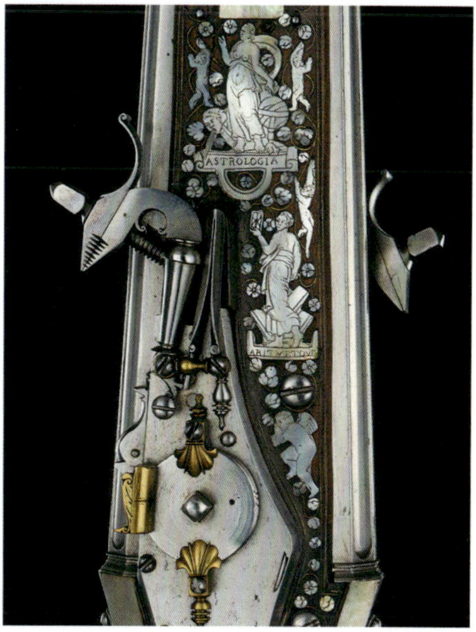

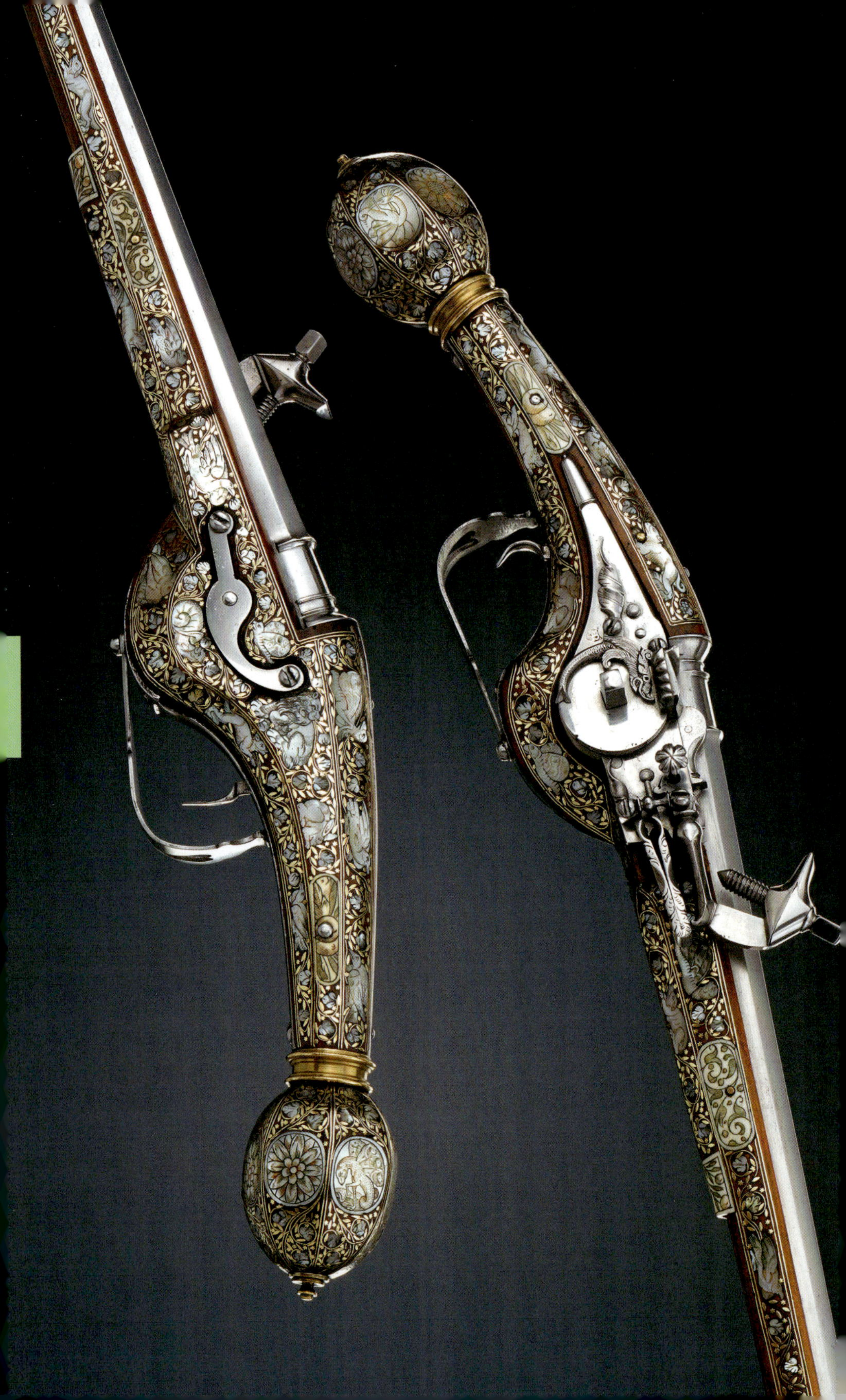

Pair of wheellock pistols

Barrels: Master AM
Locks: Master PP
France, early 17th century
79 cm, Ø 9 mm, 1589/1648 g
Inv. no. J 312, J 320

In terms of both its design and its technical features, this is a prime example of French pistol manufacturing around 1600. The pair has the typical lavish embellishment of the stocks, with scrolling vines in inlaid brass and mother-of-pearl, engraved and coloured bone medallions framing the pins that hold in place the mainspring and the barrel, as well as a multitude of incised mother-of-pearl inlays, hatched in red and green, depicting animals. A comparable design principle can be found in contemporary furniture art, particularly from the Loire Valley; there is also evidence that French gunstockers produced similarly decorated wooden caskets.

This pair of pistols is exceptional in the diversity and high quality of its pictorial decoration. In addition to dogs, birds, and rabbits, we encounter snails and imaginatively rendered insects (several butterflies, a fly, and a grasshopper). There is also a panther and a lion, angel heads, and even a bear in a monk's habit. The highlight of this extravagant bestiary is found on the pommels, which feature large mother-of-pearl medallions adorned with stylised flowers and fantastical hybrid creatures (→ cf. fig. p. 90). SR

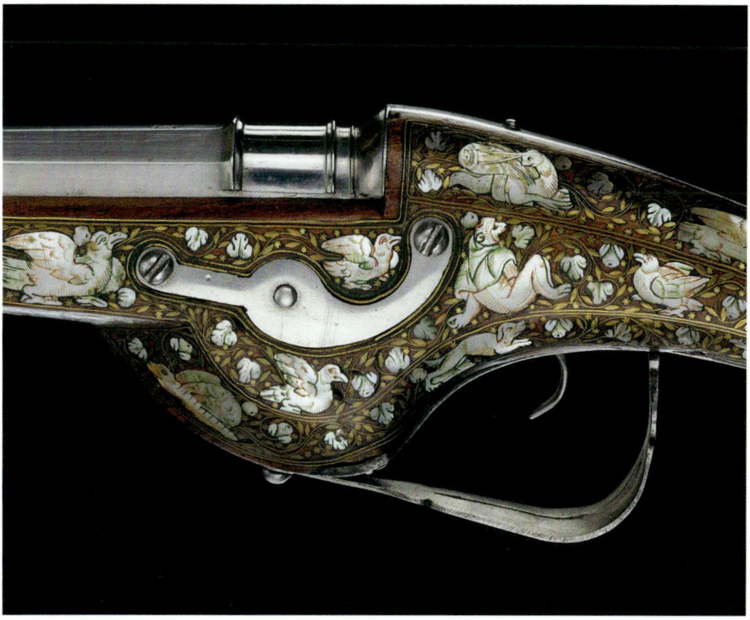

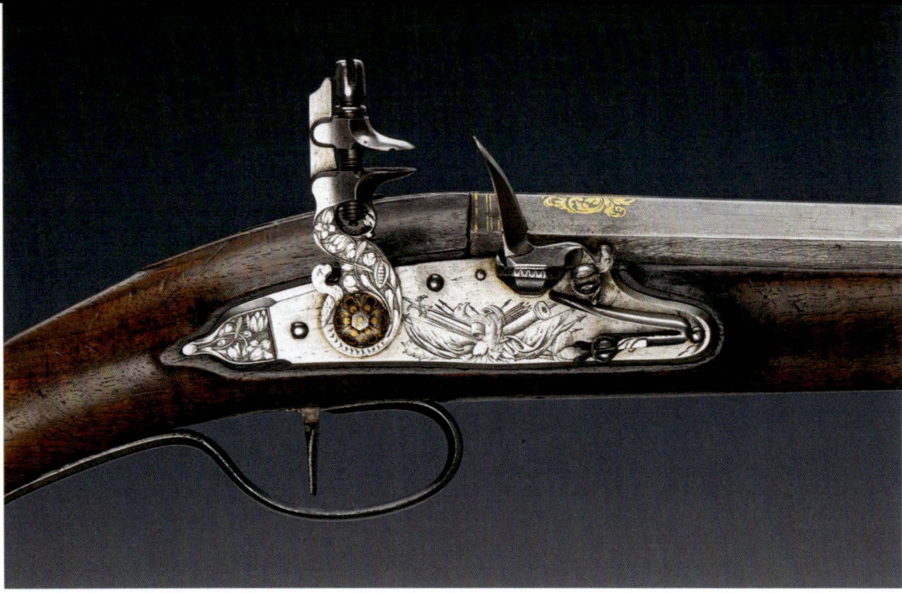

Pair of flintlock pistols

Guillaume de Vie, Paris, before 1667
57.3/57.4 cm, Ø 20 mm, 1045/1073 g
Inv. nos. J 601, J 602

In 1661, the royal gunsmith Guillaume de Vie was granted the right to run a workshop in the Louvre. This privilege, known as a *brevet de logement*, was awarded to him in recognition of his skill in making, engraving, and decorating beautiful weapons. As all the workshops in the Grande Galerie were occupied at the time, de Vie was temporarily provided with an apartment next door.

An inventory entry from 1667 states that these pistols "with Moors' heads" in high-quality ebony carving were frequently carried by Duke Johann Georg II. SR

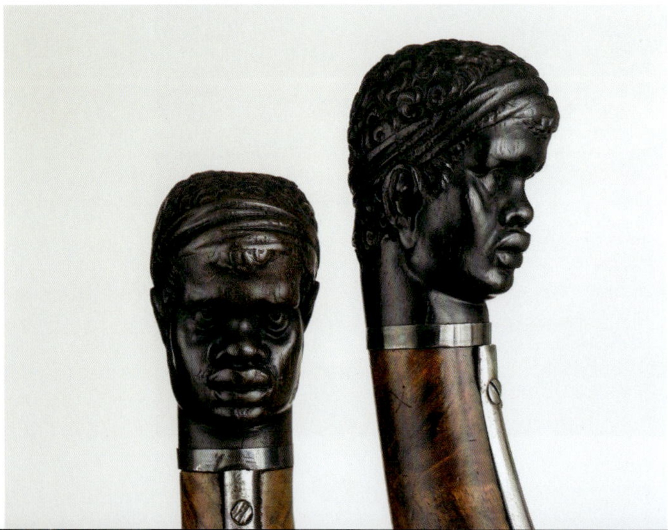

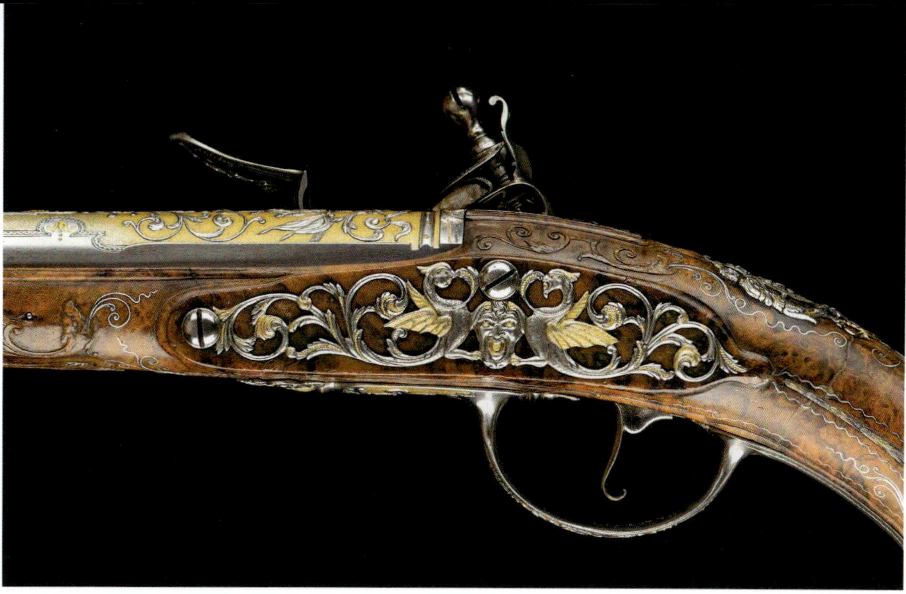

Pair of flintlock pistols

Bertrand Piraube, Paris, c. 1690–1695
50.9/51.3 cm, Ø 15 mm, 1094/1076 g
Inv. nos. J 668, J 669

This pair of pistols (→ cf. fig. p. 91) was part of a state gift from Louis XIV to August the Strong. In 1715, shortly after the ratification of a treaty of friendship between France and Poland, six Spanish stallions from the royal stables in Versailles were brought to Dresden. Each horse was equipped with a full set of tack comprising saddle, caparison, bridle, and other trappings, as well as a pair of pistols. While only two of the magnificent saddles have survived, the complete set of pistols has been preserved. Five pairs bear the signature of the court gunmaker Bertrand Piraube, the sixth that of his colleague Le Languedoc. Although most of the pistols were more than twenty years old when they were presented as gifts, their unique quality was greatly admired. According to a court official involved in preparing the gift, they were even “among the best produced in France”. SR

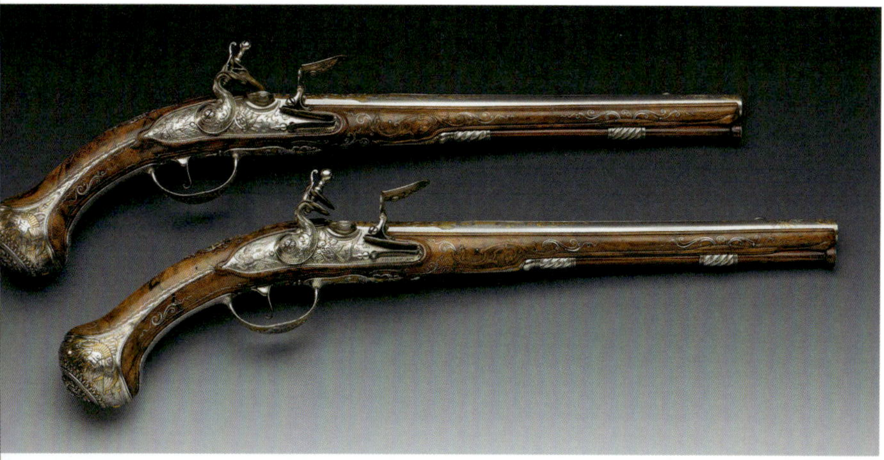

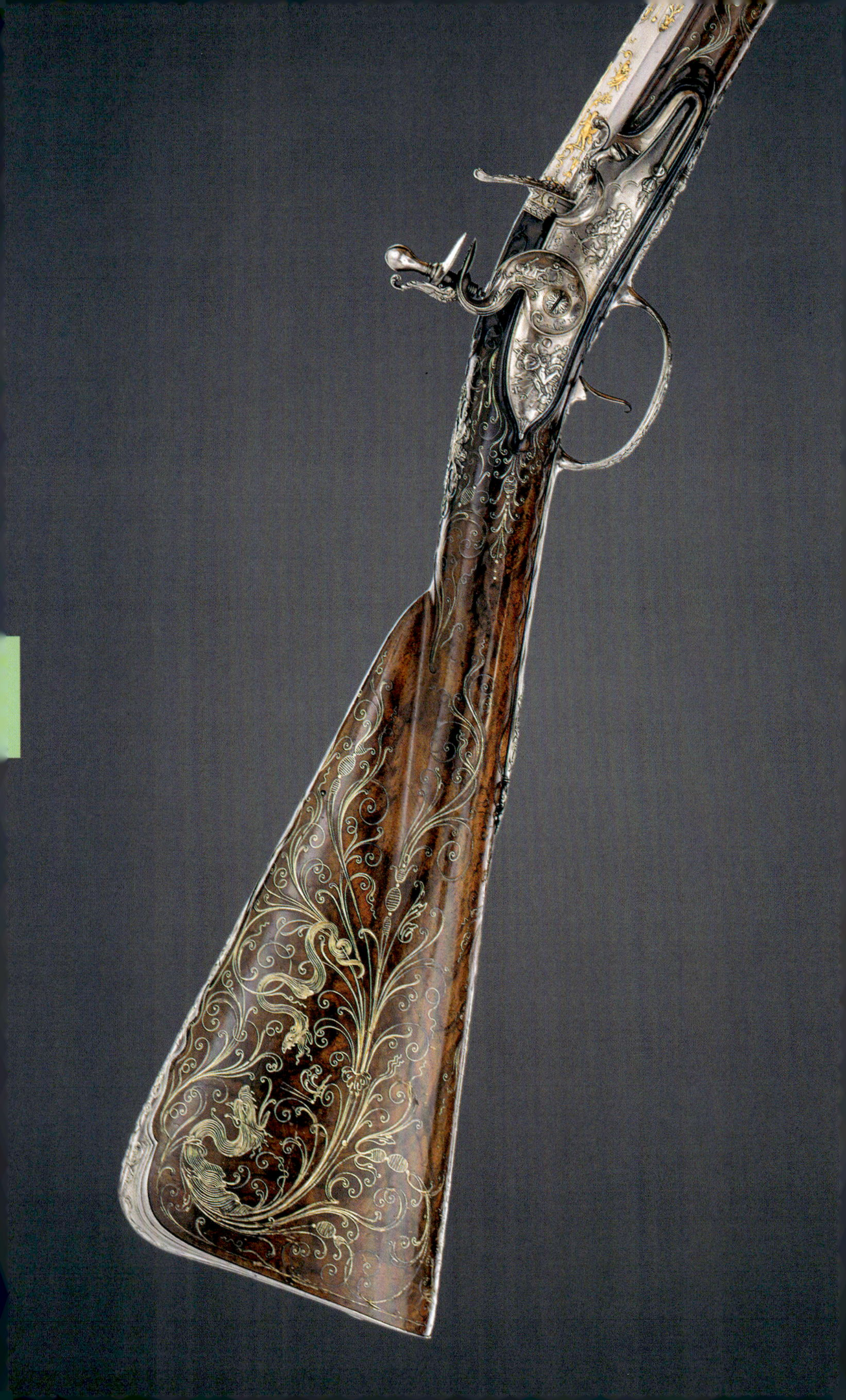

Flintlock shotgun

François Laurent, called Le Languedoc, Paris, c. 1695
158.7 cm, Ø 14 mm, 3079 g
Inv. no. G 735

This shotgun is the finest work of François Laurent, known as Le Languedoc, probably the most important court gunmaker of Louis XIV alongside Bertrand Piraube. The ebullient silver wire decoration on the butt, featuring foliate scrolls and grotesque dragons, is unique. Emblazoned in gold on the barrel chamber is a depiction of Victoria accompanied by putti blowing trumpets of glory.

Le Languedoc's reputation was due in large part to his long-standing collaboration with the engravers Claude Simonin and De Lacollombe, who produced particularly influential collections of patterns for gunmakers based on his designs. Various details of this shotgun (including the butt decoration) correspond to these engravings.

Prince Friedrich August (II) – later King August III of Poland – received the shotgun in 1725 as a gift from the chamberlain Giovan Antonio Castelli Count of Cornegliano, a Piedmontese diplomat in Saxon-Polish service. The following year, Castelli had to leave Saxony in disgrace: his nephew had killed the influential minister Friedrich Vitzthum von Eckstädt in a duel. SR

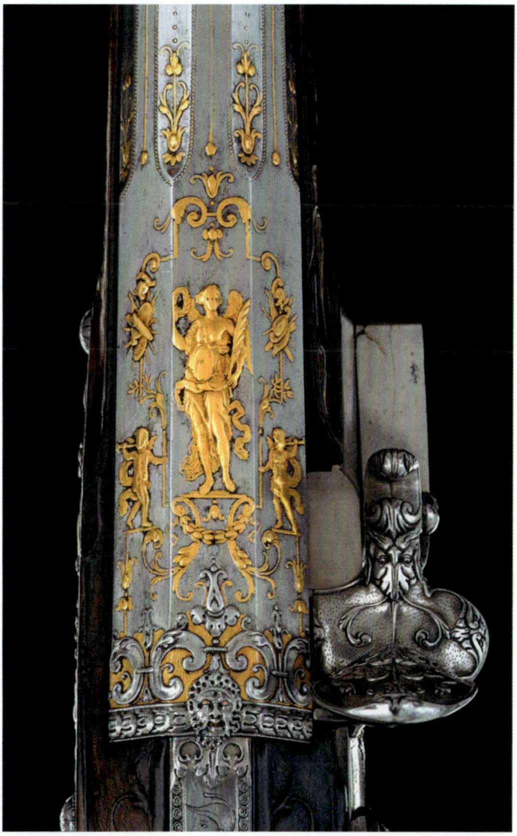

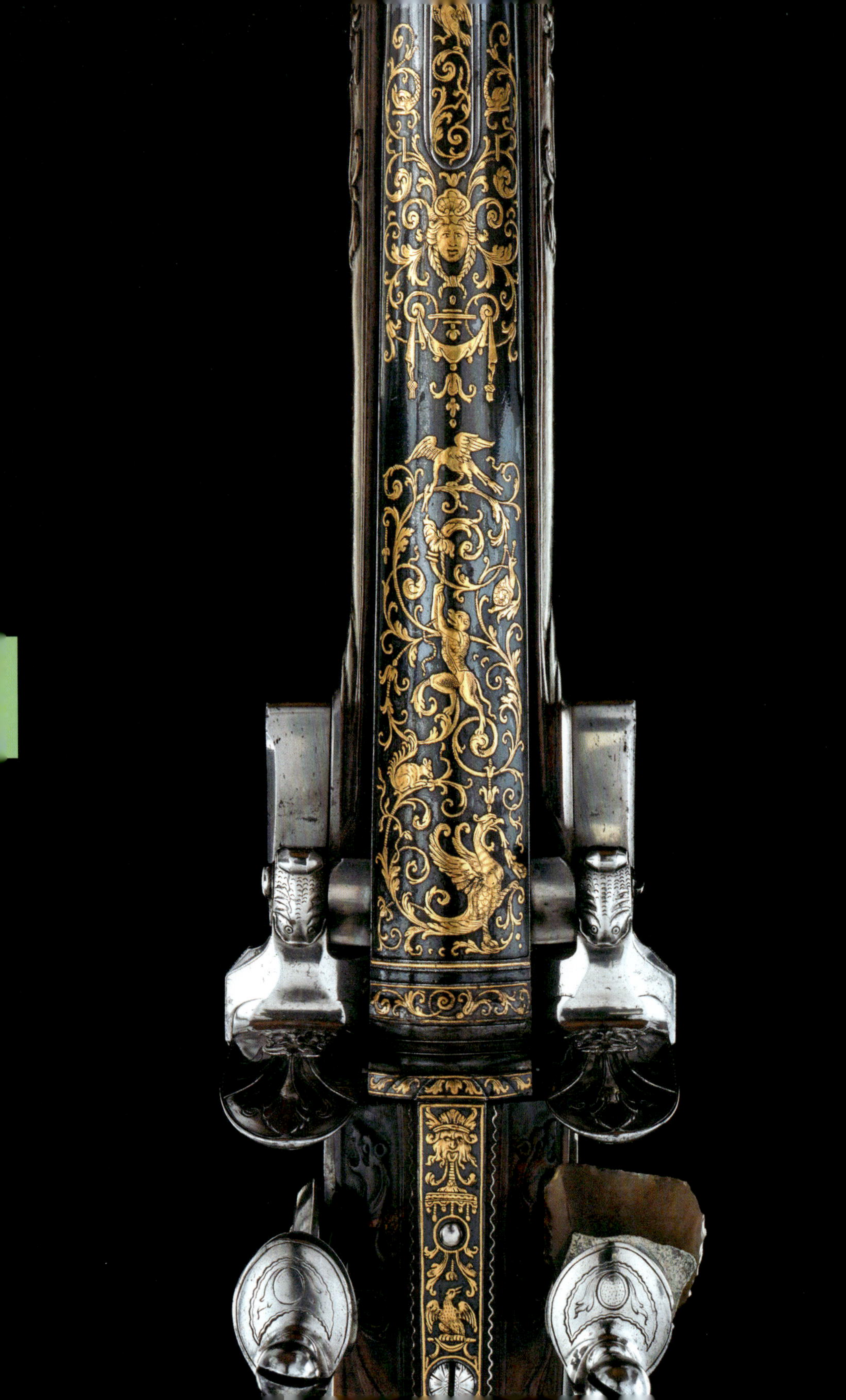

Double-barreled flintlock shotgun (over-and-under)

Bertrand Piraube, Paris, c. 1700
148 cm, Ø 15 mm, 3700 g
Inv. no. G 1388

This gun, first catalogued in 1730, is a so-called over-and-under shotgun, with two barrels one above the other. Bertrand Piraube, *armurier du Roi* at the court of the Sun King, was the most renowned gunmaker of his time. From 1670, he had a workshop in the Grande Galerie of the Louvre. The signature on the two lock plates reads accordingly: "PIRAVBE AVX GALLERIES A PARIS".

The gold-inlaid grotesque decoration on the blued barrels corresponds to the Louis Quatorze style. The foliate scrolling interspersed with snails, squirrels, and herons is reminiscent of designs by the court artist Jean Bérain the Elder. The striking motif of a monkey pulling on a rope is almost identical to an ornament print included in a publication with etchings after his designs. Bérain, who came from a family of gunmakers, was active in the decoration of firearms in his early phase: in 1659, for example, he published a collection of patterns for gunmakers and around 1660 he signed the decoration of a shotgun now held in Stockholm. From 1677 onwards, Bérain also held a *brevet de logement* at the Louvre. It is therefore tempting to speculate that Piraube may have obtained a draft design for the ornamentation on this luxury weapon from his famous neighbour. SR

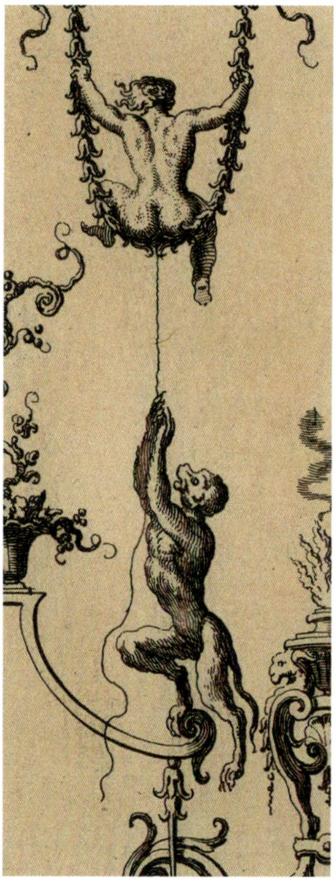

Ornament print after Jean I Bérain, detail, etching, Paris, Bibliothèque de l'Institut national d'histoire de l'art

Double-barrelled flintlock shotgun (turn-over)

Adrien Reynier the Younger, called Le Hollandois, Paris, c. 1730
129.9 cm, Ø 16 mm, 3122 g
Inv. no. G 1387

In a turn-over gun, a single cock operates two superposed barrels, each with its own pan and battery. By activating a locking mechanism concealed in the trigger guard, the barrel section can be rotated 180° around its axis. After the first shot, the gun can be fired a second time without having to reload, simply by cocking the hammer again. The gunmaker, Adrien Reynier, was granted a workshop in the Louvre in 1724.

August III received the rifle in 1739 as a gift from his half-brother, Count Moritz of Saxony, who was a lieutenant-general in the army of Louis XV. He was later appointed Marshal of France and entrusted with supreme command over the French Royal Army. The *Maréchal de Saxe* is regarded as one of the great generals and military theorists of his era. SR

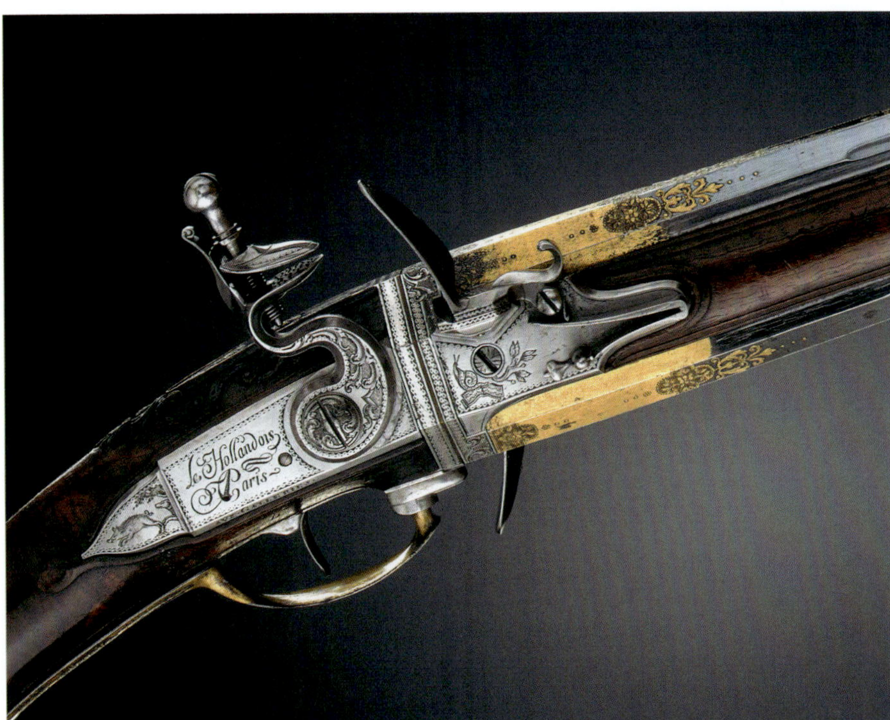

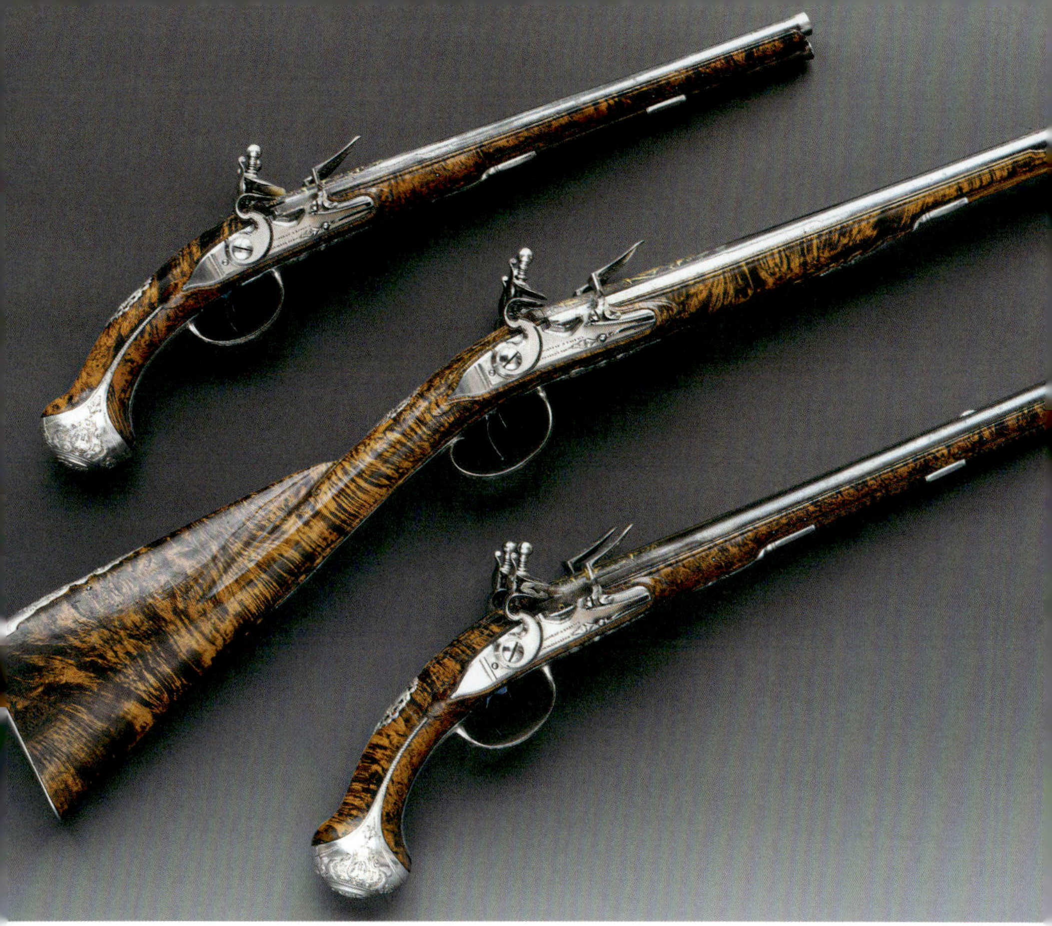

Set of double-barrelled flintlock firearms

Pessonneau the Elder, Lyon, c. 1715
Shotgun: 149.1 cm, Ø 16 mm, 3371 g
Pistols: 55.6/55.8 cm, Ø 14 mm, 1642/1653 g
Inv. nos. G 1361 (shotgun), J 567, J 568 (pistols)

Talented gunsmiths were not only active in Paris: Pessonneau, for example, who was based in Lyon, was particularly appreciated by August III. In 1720, while still a prince, he presented his father, August the Strong, with this set consisting of a double-barrelled shotgun and two double-barrelled pistols – all of which have stocks of fiery grained burl wood. SR

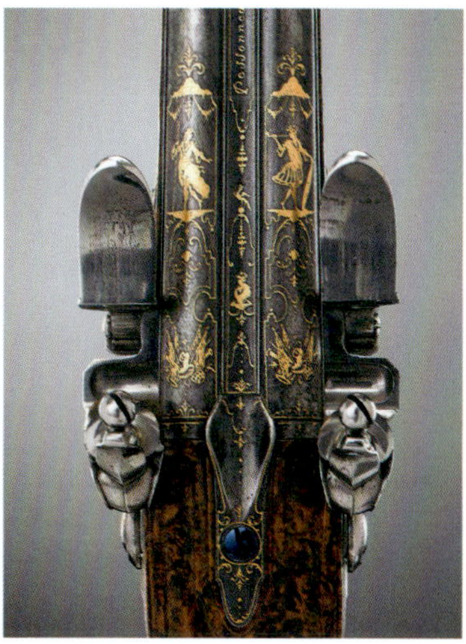

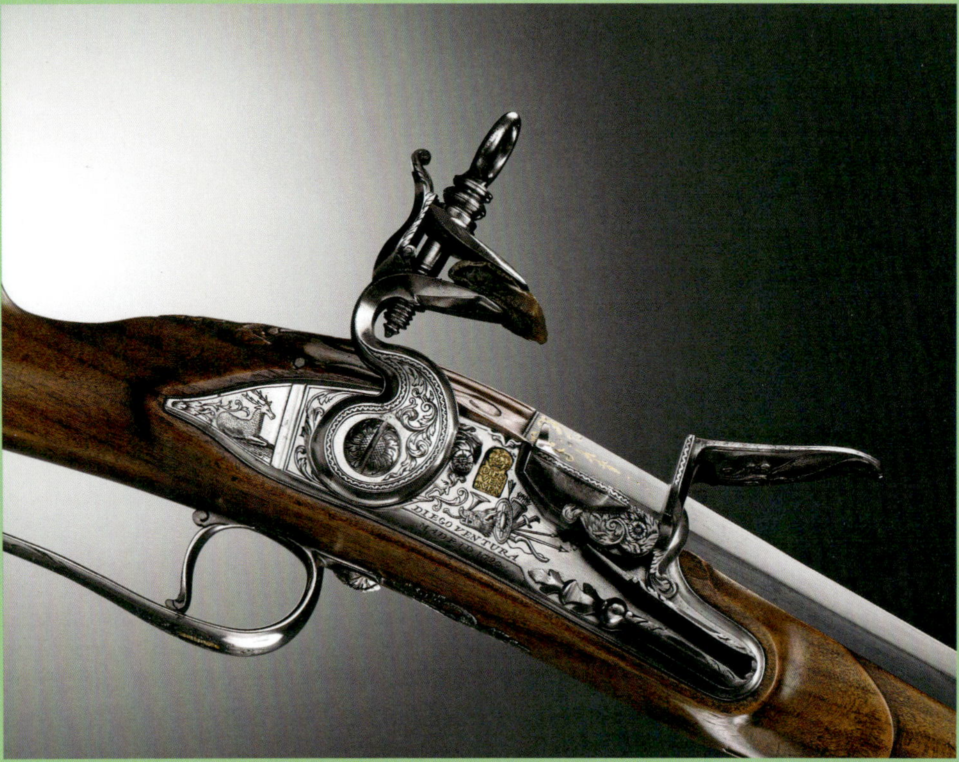
DIEGO VENTURA

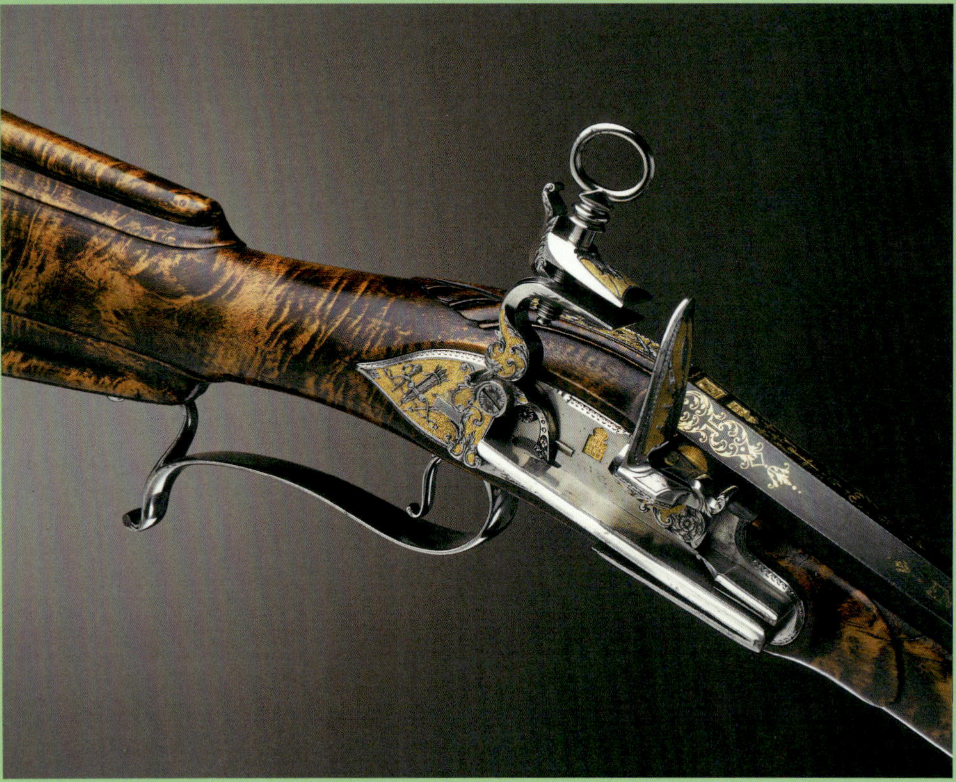

Spain and Portugal

With flourishing production centres such as Madrid and the Catalan town of Ripoll, Spanish firearms manufacturing was much renowned in the eighteenth century. In particular, the shotgun barrels forged from old horseshoes were unrivalled: their magnificent bluing, their gold-plated maker's marks, as well as their gold-inlaid inscriptions, gave them a unique aesthetic appeal. To avoid soldered joints, the barrel was not attached using metal loops on the underside: instead, two silver rings were slid over the barrel and stock.

Until the nineteenth century, Spanish gunmakers remained faithful to traditional features such as the Catalan or Madrid stock and the so-called Miquelet lock (a local snaplock variant). Nevertheless, there was an increase in French influence following the succession (in 1700) of the House of Bourbon to the Spanish throne. The *a la moda* lock was developed, which essentially retained the old snaplock mechanism but resembled a French flintlock in its design. The conspicuous external trigger mechanism of the Miquelet lock was now reduced to two hooks at the base of the cock, usually skilfully disguised as leaf-shaped decorative elements.

The Portuguese art of gunmaking is represented only by a single object in the Firearms Gallery, albeit a very significant one. SR

Snaplock gun

Atienza (?), before 1715
150.6 cm, Ø 16 mm, 3060 g
Inv. no. G 1184

This shotgun with a Miquelet lock and Catalan stock was brought back from Italy in 1715 by the Spanish chamberlain and art agent Juan Alfonso de Baca for August the Strong. The chiselled iron decoration on the lock looks somewhat outmoded; an early inventory even describes the weapon as "a very old-fashioned shotgun". Nevertheless, it was probably new, as a magnificent breech-loading shotgun by the same maker (Paris, Musée de l'Armée) was produced for King Philip V of Spain no earlier than 1714. Both shotguns are signed "ATIENZA". It is unclear whether this refers to the Castilian town of the same name (which, however, is not known as a centre of firearms production) or whether it is the signature of an as yet unidentified gunmaker. SR

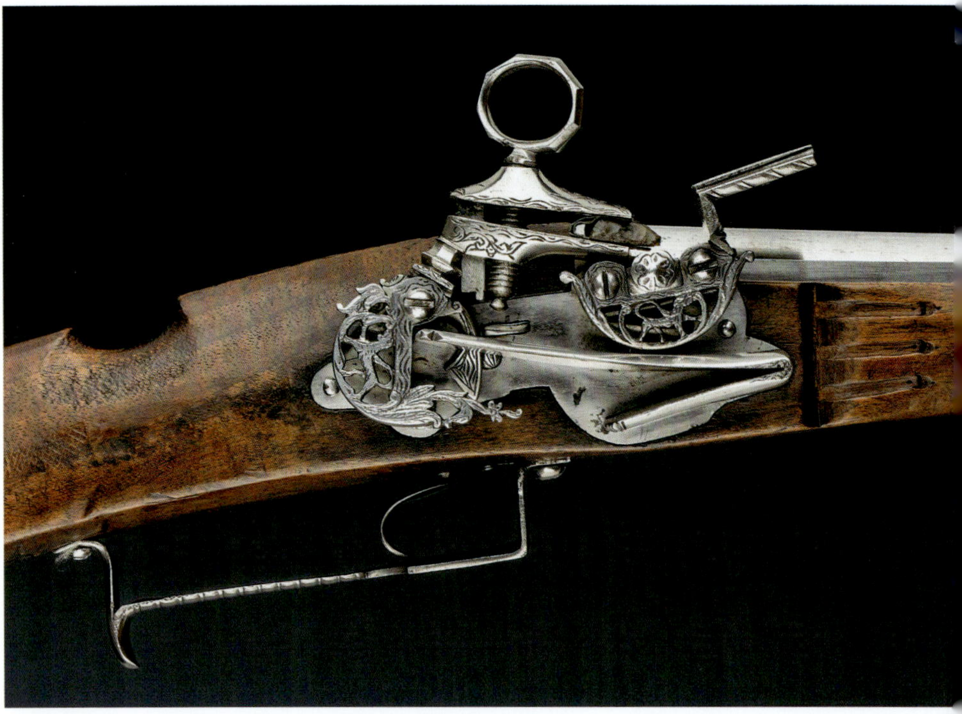

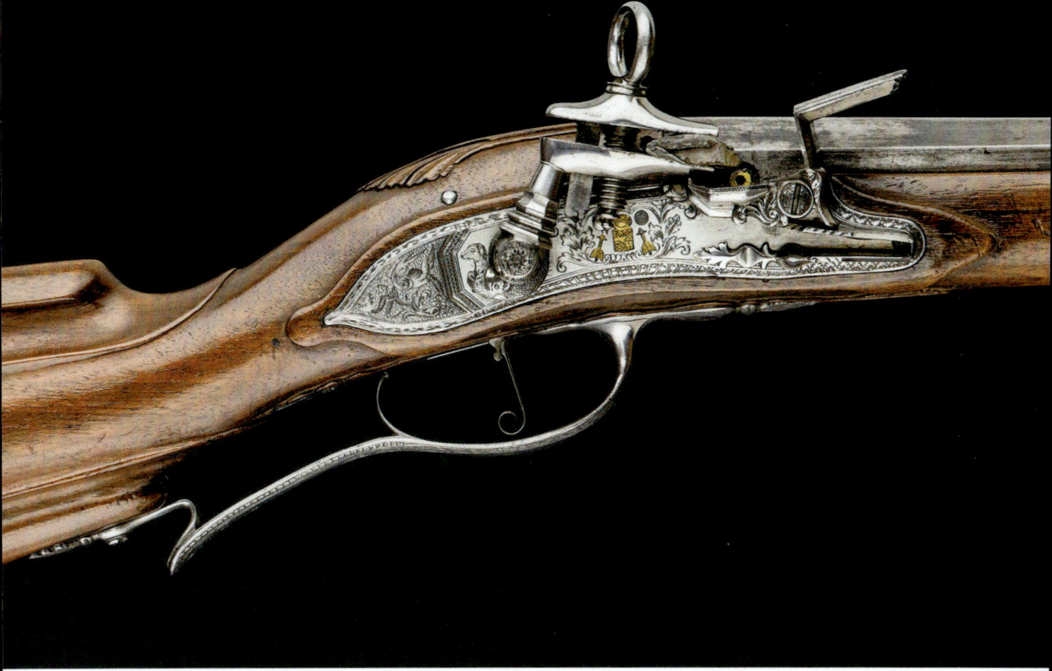

Snaplock shotgun

José Francisco, Lisbon, 1718
148.2 cm, Ø 16 mm, 3279 g
Inv. no. G 1195

In 1718 the Lisbon gunmaker José Francisco, together with his brother, published the treatise *Espingarda perfeyta* (The perfect gun) – a comprehensive treatise on his craft – under the pseudonym Cesar Fiosconi, an anagram of his name. This is an important documentary source on the art of gunmaking in Portugal and far beyond. It includes an engraving showing a snaplock variant developed by the authors, which has an internal mainspring. The mechanical features of this rare shotgun, signed by Francisco and also dated 1718, largely correspond to that illustration. This masterpiece of Portuguese gunmaking was brought to Dresden by the "Cammerier Alphonso" (Juan Alfonso de Baca) in 1719. SR

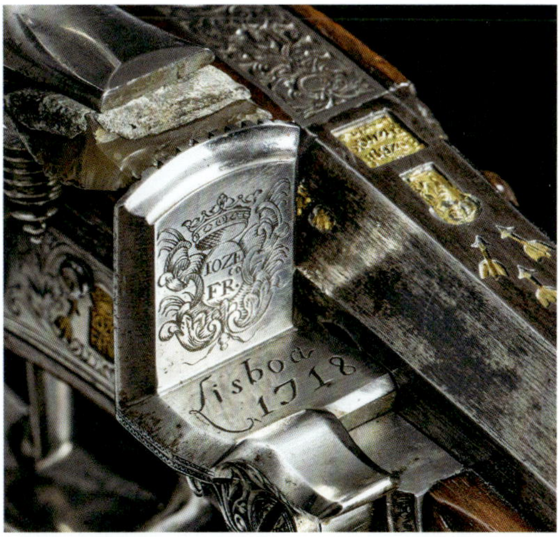

Set of snaplock firearms

Barrels: Joan Peresteva
Locks: Sitjar
Barcelona, before 1721
Shotgun: 146.1 cm, Ø 16 mm, 2879 g
Pistols: 30.5/30.4 cm, Ø 15 mm, 692/689 g
Inv. nos. G 1188, J 736, J 1352

This set consisting of a shotgun and a pair of small pistols is an outstanding example of early eighteenth-century Catalan gunmaking. It is characterised by the sturdy Miquelet locks, the striking design of the shotgun butt (a feature of the so-called Catalan stock), the spherical pistol pommels and the silver openwork inlays. The small pads of red felt on the locks of the pistols are to protect the hand from injury. The set originally included a broad silver-embroidered suede baldric (or *xarpa*) for carrying the pistols, which have belt hooks attached to their side-plates.

The set entered the Rüstkammer in 1721. It was purchased on behalf of August the Strong by General Joseph Antoine Gautier de Seissan, a Frenchman who had served as an officer in the Saxon army until 1719. His eventful biography includes adventurous episodes such as an attempted landing in southern France at the head of an English troop contingent (in 1710), as well as an alleged unsuccessful plot to kidnap the deposed Polish king Stanisław Leszczyński (in 1717). SR

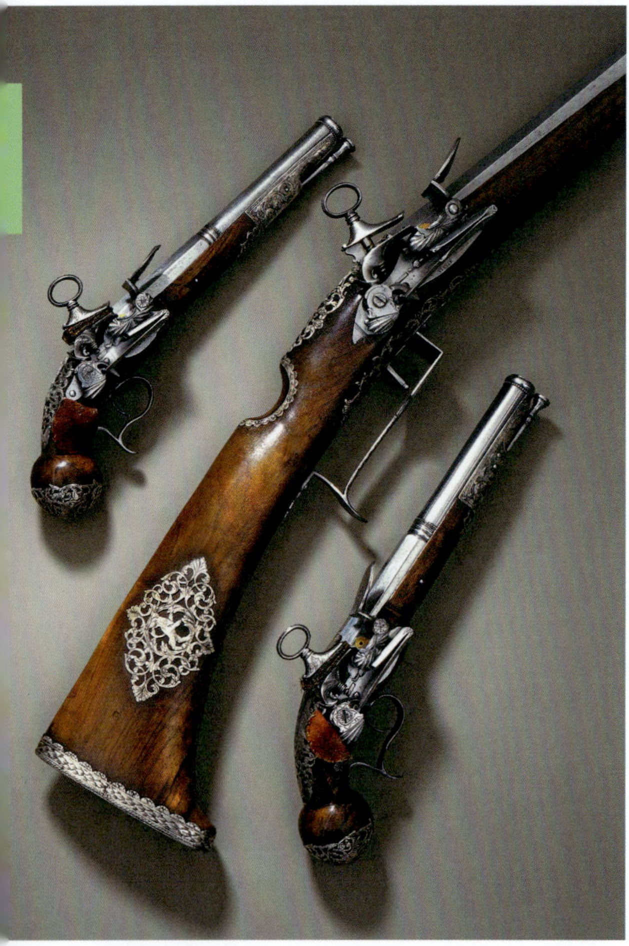

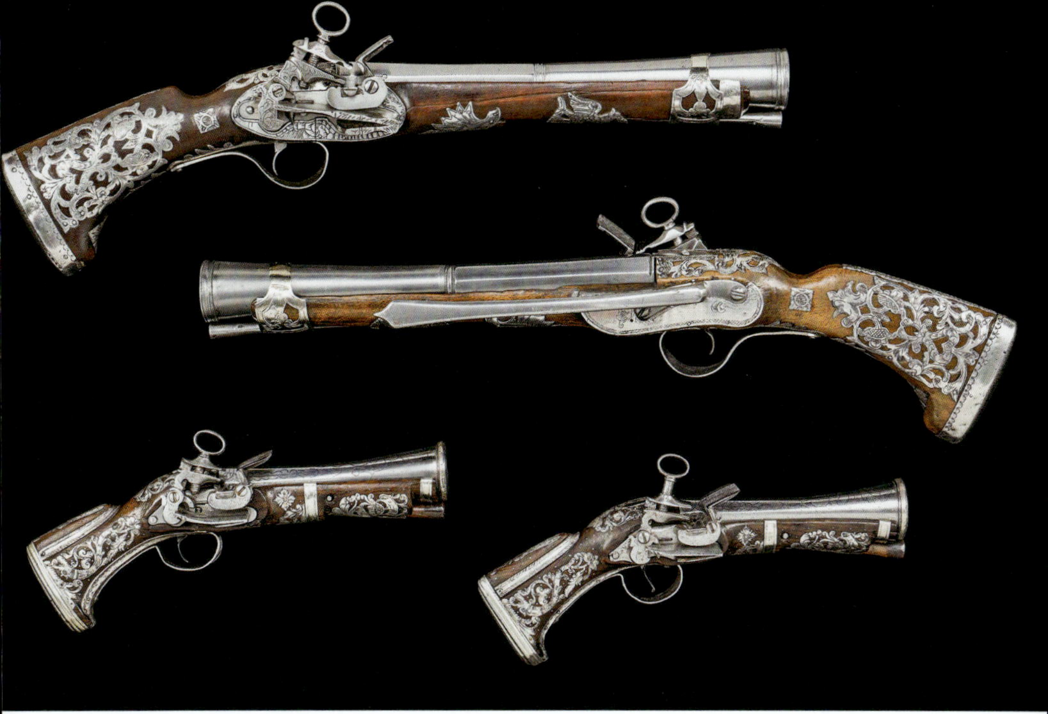

Two pairs of snaplock blunderbuss pistols

Ripoll, probably 18th century
52.9/53.7 cm, Ø max 34 mm, 1842/1730 g
27.9 cm, Ø max. 25/30 mm, 722/744 g
Inv. nos. J 1311, J 1312; J 1313, J 1314

These two pairs of pistols with so-called blunderbuss barrels, carbine butts, belt hooks and somewhat naïve-looking openwork silver inlays are typical of firearms manufactured in Ripoll, the centre of gunmaking in Catalonia. Such weapons, which could fire several bullets at once, were produced in very similar form over a long period of time, well into the nineteenth century. For the most part, these simple utility weapons were intended for export, particularly to the Spanish overseas colonies. The larger pair probably reached South America via this route, where it ended up in the collection of the Saxon diplomat Rudolf Friedrich Le Maistre. He spent almost twenty years in Argentina and Brazil, as ambassador of the North German Confederation and then of the German Empire (up to 1886). After his death in 1903, Le Maistre's heirs donated the pair of pistols – along with other, mostly Mexican objects – to the Dresden collection. SR

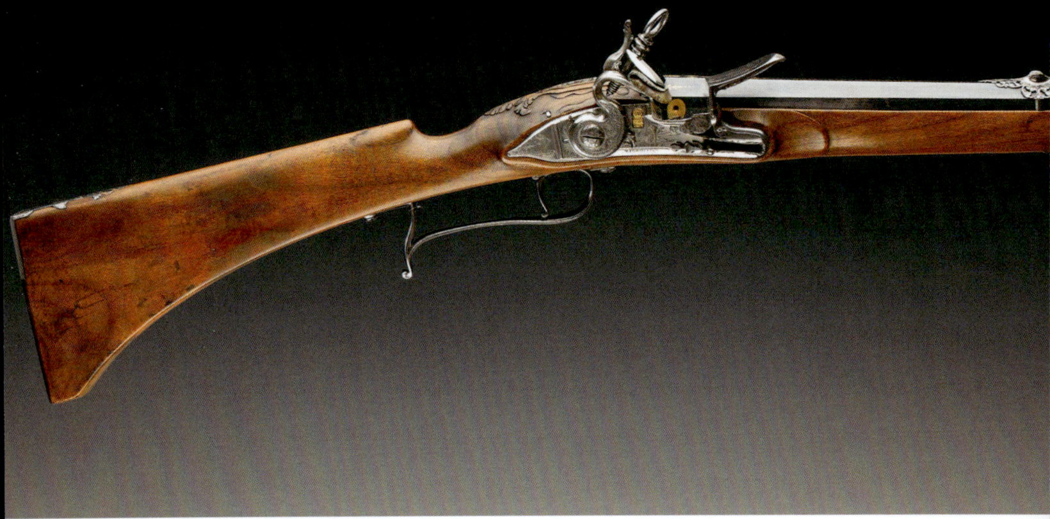

Pair of snaplock shotguns

Diego Ventura, Madrid, 1729
141.5/141.1 cm, Ø 17 mm, 2690/2667 g
Inv. no. G 1210, G 1211

The Spanish aristocrat and court official Juan Manuel López de Zúñiga y Castro, Duke of Béjar, sent August the Strong this pair of shotguns, along with two other guns, at the end of 1732. The gift was delivered in a wooden case with a red leather cover and gilded mounts; the individual weapons each had a case made of green velvet with silver borders. Both shotguns have Catalan-style stocks and elegant *a la moda* locks (→ cf. fig. p. 104 top). The inscription "Son Hermanos", i.e. "they are brothers", is inlaid in gold on the barrels. The phrase is intended to emphasise the bond between the pair of shotguns, but can also be understood as a tactful expression of friendship on the part of the gift-giver. SR

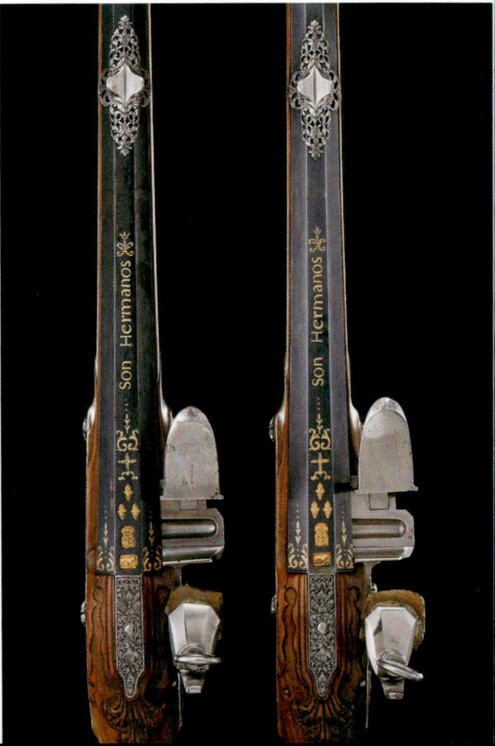

Snaplock shotgun

Joseph Cano, Madrid, 1738
142.1 cm, Ø 17 mm, 2605 g
Inv. no. G 1196

With its lavish gold ornamentation and its 'Madrid' stock made of fiery grained burl wood, this shotgun dated 1738 is probably the most beautiful Spanish firearm in the collection. The lock (→ cf. fig. p. 104 bottom) corresponds to the type known as *a las tres modas*: a variant of the Miquelet lock which, although mechanically in the Spanish tradition, adopts individual elements of the French flintlock (the battery) and the Italian snaplock (the cock design).

The gun, which is signed by Joseph Cano, arrived in Dresden on 8 November 1738 as part of a copious gift from the Madrid court. This included another pair of pistols by Cano, as well as five shotguns by other gunmakers, each in cases made of gold-trimmed red velvet. The state gift also encompassed Spanish horses and American tobacco from the royal tobacco factory in Seville. The occasion for the gift must have been the marriage of the Saxon princess Maria Amalia to King Charles VII of Naples: the latter's mother, the Spanish Queen Elisabetta Farnese, had conducted the wedding negotiations. In the same year, August III sent her several valuable porcelain services as a gift.

This magnificent shotgun played an important role in the career of gunmaker Joseph Cano, as it was his first commissioned work for the Spanish court. He proudly referred to it when he successfully applied for the position of court gunmaker the following year. SR

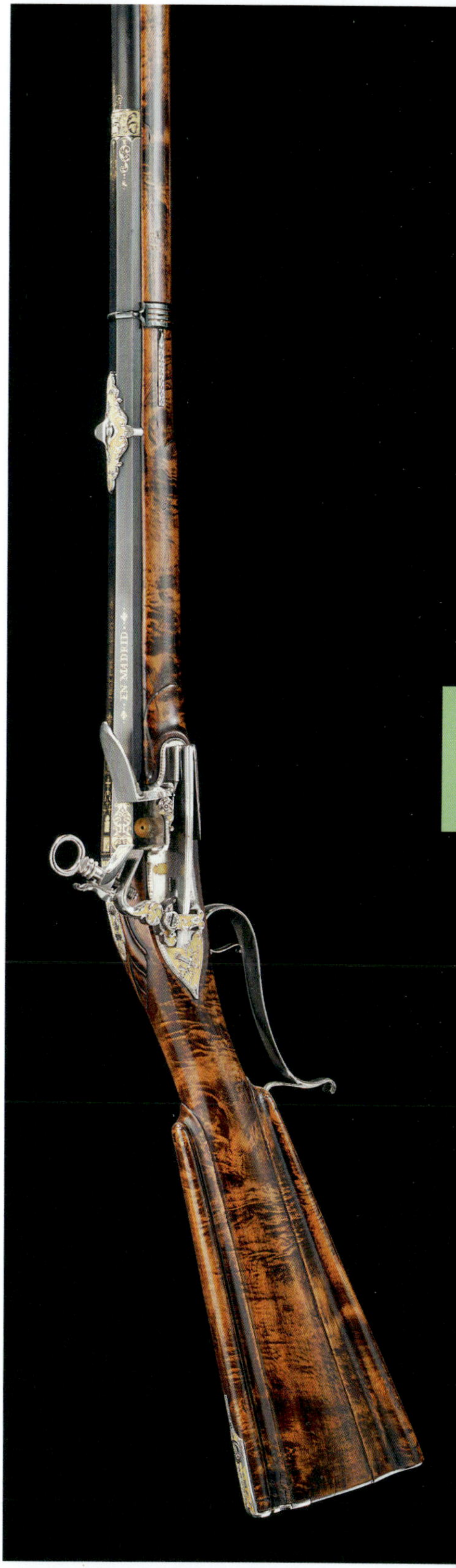

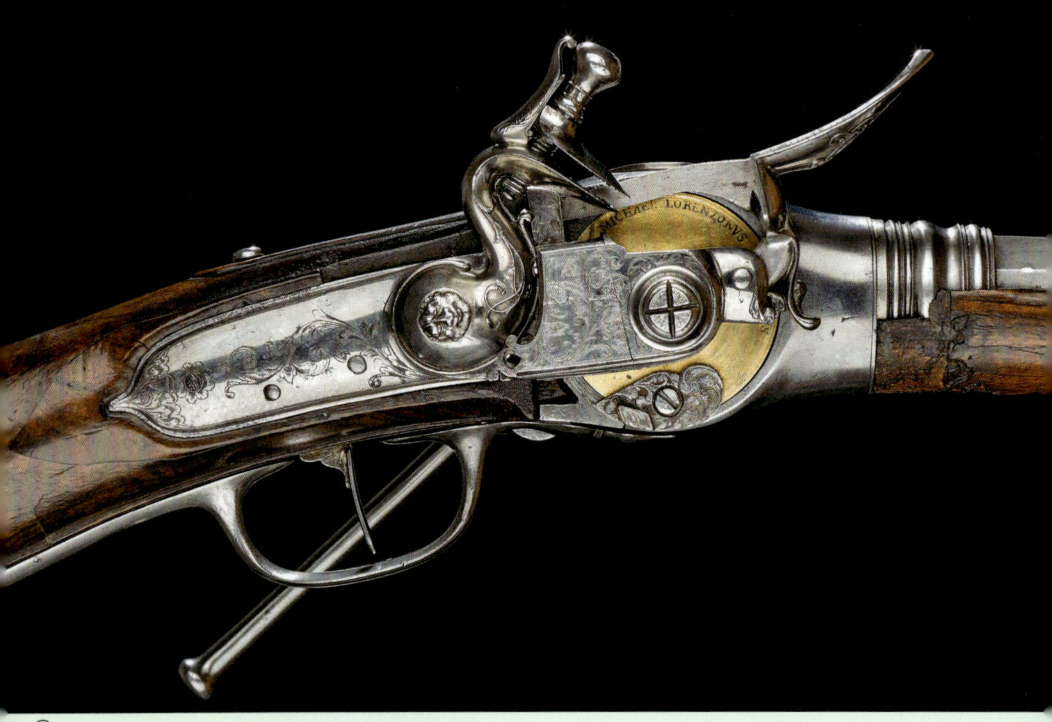

①

⊕ Shoot faster!

One of the great challenges for gunmakers was to manufacture firearms that could fire multiple shots. As early as the mid-sixteenth century, they developed wheellock pistols with multiple barrels and locks (→ cf. p. 93). And around 1600, revolver systems for wheellock, and later flintlock, guns started to become widespread. A more sophisticated technical solution were so-called repeaters – mechanisms whereby several balls and powder charges were stored in a magazine and only a few simple movements were required to prepare for the next shot.

Towards the end of the seventeenth century, the Florentine court gunmaker Michele Lorenzoni produced repeating guns that could fire thirty shots in succession (fig. 1). Two separate tubular magazines for the balls and powder charges were concealed in the butt. To prepare for firing, the shooter had to hold the rifle with the barrel pointing downwards and turn a lever at the back forwards and back again. This lever is connected to a revolving cylindrical brass breech block with two cavities: a shallower one, which places a ball in the barrel, and a deeper one, which positions the

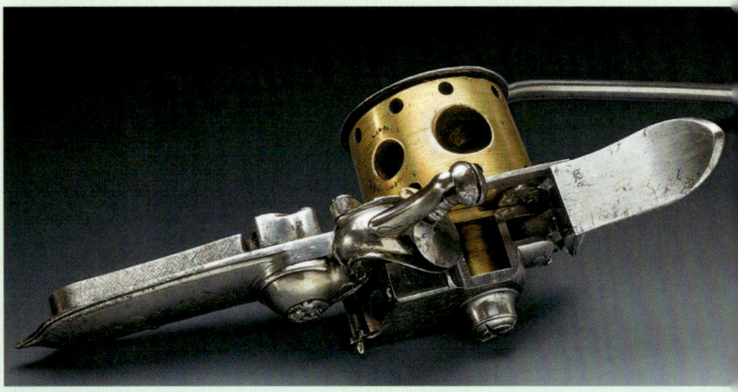

②

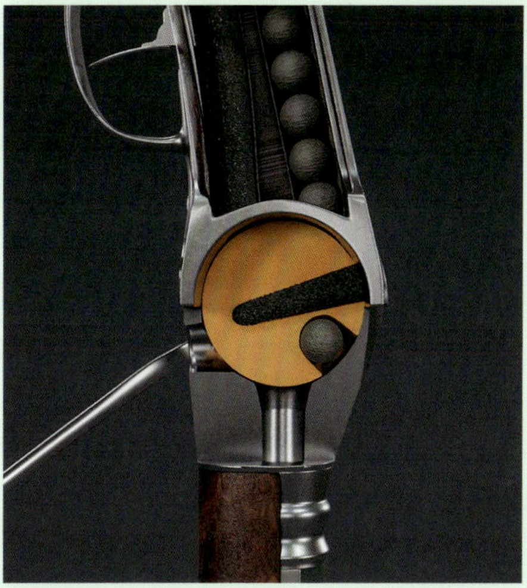

③

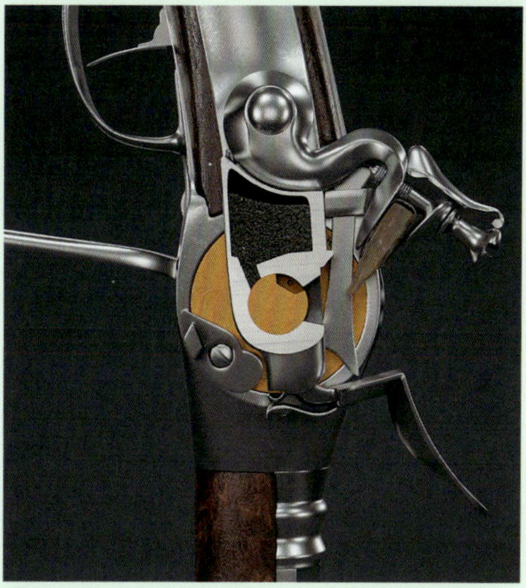

④

powder charge behind the ball (figs. 2, 3). The latter cavity is connected to the touch hole and also serves as the chamber during firing. At the same time, the priming pan was filled from a smaller powder magazine (fig. 4). The lock was also automatically cocked and the pan covered. To demonstrate the working of this repeating system and a number of other objects from the Firearms Gallery, a series of digital videos (figs. 3, 4) have been produced as part of a cooperation project between the Rüstkammer and HTW Dresden (University of Applied Sciences) between 2021 and 2025 (cf. https://ruestkammer.skd.museum/ausstellungen/gewehrgalerie-im-langen-gang/).

Whether the Florentine court gunmaker actually conceived the design described here is a matter of dispute among scholars, but the so-called Lorenzoni system is named after him today. The serious disadvantage of this design was the high risk of explosion: the positioning of both magazines in the butt (*a tutto dietro*, i.e. 'all at the rear') could lead to serious facial injuries. To reduce this risk, Lorenzoni developed other models in which initially only the powder magazine, and then both the powder and the ball magazines, were positioned at the front, under the barrel (the so-called Lorenzoni *misto* and *a tutto avanti* variants, i.e. 'mixed' and 'all at the front'). These fragile and malfunction-prone weapons were unsuitable for military purposes: it was not until the nineteenth century that repeating firearms were to play a significant role in warfare.

Since 1730, the depicted hunting gun (inv. no. G 60) has been linked to Elector Johann Georg III's stay in Florence in 1684; according to the earliest inventory entries, however, it was purchased by Electoral Prince Johann Georg (IV) in Italy during his Grand Tour in 1690. It is one of Lorenzoni's early works and was possibly made before his employment in Florence, as the signature "MICHAEL LORENZONVS SENIS" (i.e. Michele Lorenzoni in Siena) may suggest. SR

Italy

The city of Brescia and its hinterland, part of the Republic of Venice since 1426, developed in the sixteenth century into one of the first major European centres of firearms production – originally primarily for military use. By the start of the seventeenth century, however, Brescia was internationally famed for civilian luxury firearms: wheellock carbines and pistols manufactured there were coveted collector's items and were indispensable for a *cabinet d'armes* such as that of King Louis XIII of France. Thanks to the connections of the local nobility and the active support of the Venetian authorities, the firearms manufacturers from Brescia and the surrounding area enjoyed direct access to an exclusive international clientele.

The consistent use of wood embellished with chiselled and incised iron, without gilding or inlays of other materials, determines the unique aesthetic appeal of these elegant weapons. Particularly impressive are the decorative iron inlays and mounts, whose intricate openwork patterns almost resemble lace – another art form with a long-standing tradition in northern Italy. Unlike other manufacturing locations, Brescia adhered to a system of specialisation in firearms production: barrels, locks, and mounts were made by different masters and were often individually signed or marked. It was up to the customer to approach the various craftsmen and have the different parts assembled, with the result that every Brescian firearm was a unique, one-off item. Among the most famous masters were the Cominazzo barrel-making family from Gardone Val Trompia and the Beretta dynasty, which is documented from the early sixteenth century onwards. SR

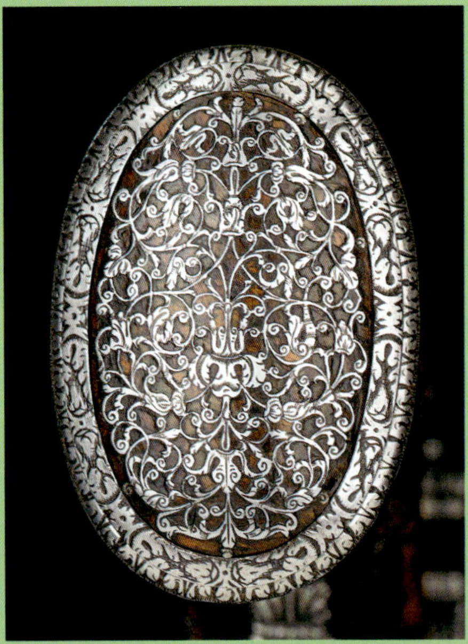

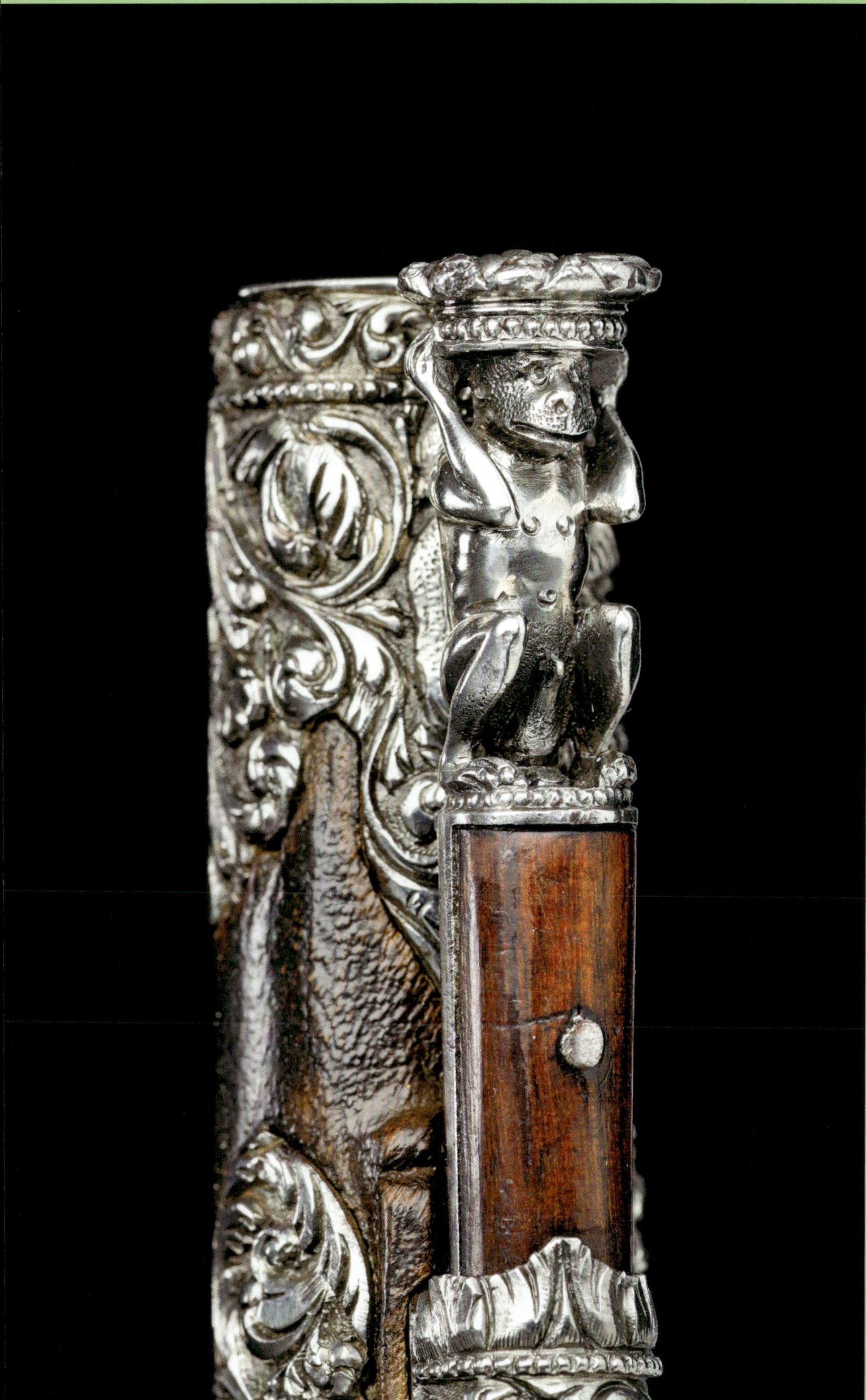

Wheellock gun

Lock: Italy or Germany, 1585
Stock: Germany
Barrel: probably 19th century
119.7 cm, Ø 16 mm, 4645 g
Inv. no. G 982

Early Italian wheellock firearms often bear a close resemblance to guns produced in southern Germany during the same period. The reason for this was the large-scale export of un-stocked Brescian firearms across the Alps, as well as the activity of many German gunmakers in northern Italy. It is precisely this close cultural interdependence that makes it difficult to determine the origin of this magnificent sixteenth-century gun. It came into the Dresden collection in 1938 from the possession of Prince Johann Georg von Sachsen, the brother of the last King of Saxony, Friedrich August III. It is presumed that it had previously belonged to the Roman bibliophile Giovan Francesco De Rossi.

The stock was certainly made north of the Alps, and is probably of German origin, but the lavish gold and silver-inlaid lock may well be of Italian production. The date 1585 and the inscription "MARIO A.G.LARA" are found on the pan and the dog, and this was long considered by experts to be the earliest example of an Italian gunmaker's signature. In fact, however, the inscription does not refer to the maker, but rather to the person who commissioned the gun: the Italian professional soldier, Captain Mario dell'Anguillara. This scion of the ancient Roman noble family of the Counts of Anguillara fought in the service of Venice, France (against the Huguenots and the Ottomans) and Spain (against England), among others. His coat of arms, consisting of two crossed eels (Italian: *anguille*), is emblazoned on the lock plate and in several places on the stock. SR

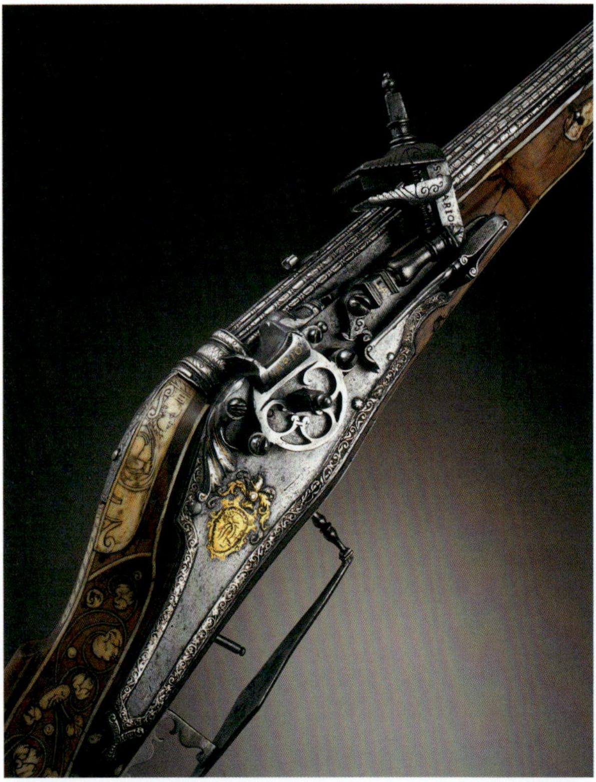

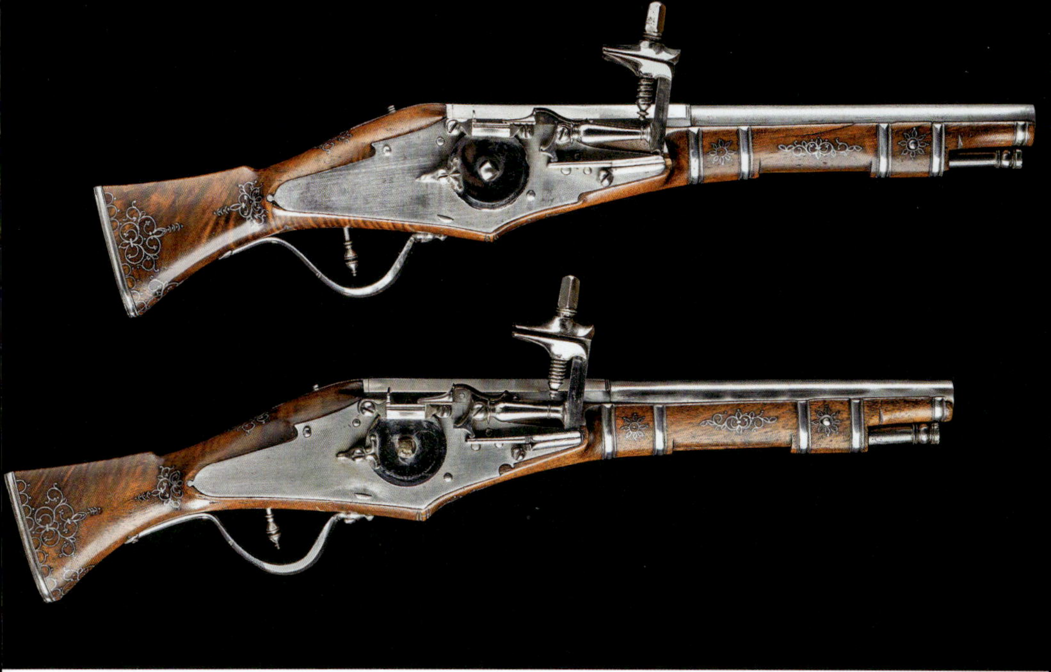

Pair of wheellock pistols

Locks: Master PG
Probably Venice, early 17th century
43.7/44.3 cm, Ø 11 mm, 1145/1149 g
Inv. nos. J 552, J 553

This pair of pistols, dating from around 1600, are among the oldest Italian firearms in the collection. Elector Johann Georg I received the pistols between 1618 and 1632 as a gift from Lieutenant-Colonel Andreas Matthias von Kehraus. This military commander fought on the imperial side in the Thirty Years' War, but had begun his career in the service of the Electorate of Saxony.

The pistols, which are fitted with belt hooks, have a small hole on the lower side of the stock, through which the mainspring could be inspected. This feature and the relatively plain iron wire inlays are unusual for Brescia. A very similar shotgun in Vienna, which bears the same maker's mark, was presumed to have been made in Milan. According to the Rüstkammer inventory, however, the pistols "are said to have been made in Venice". SR

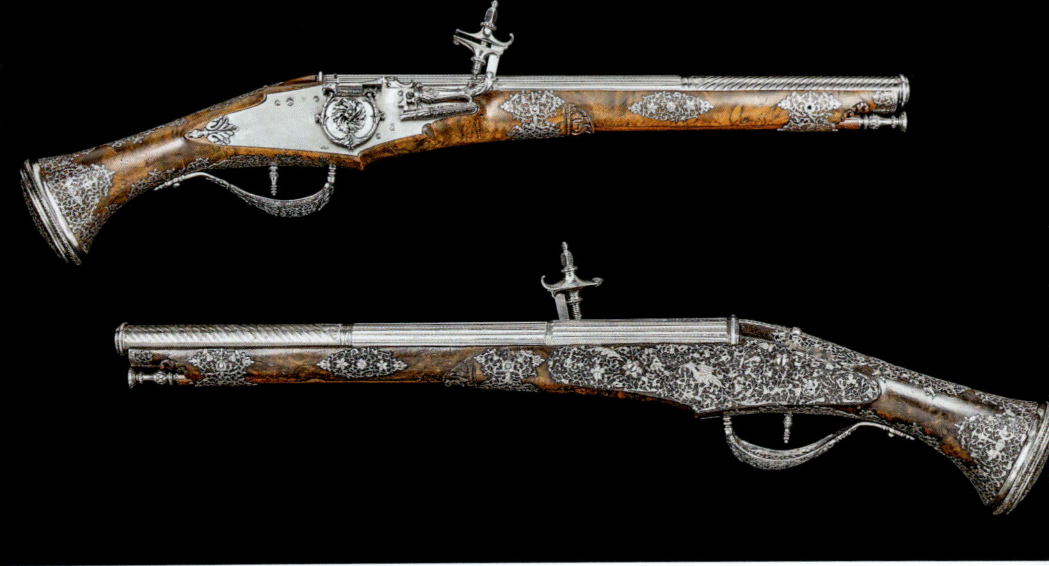

Pair of wheellock pistols

Barrels: Lazarino Cominazzo, Gardone Val Trompia
Locks: Master VP, Brescia
c. 1640
53.4/53.5 cm, Ø 15 mm, 1106/1145 g
Inv. nos. J 515, J 516

This pair of pistols was owned by the future Elector Johann Georg (III) before 1680. It is possible that the pistols were part of a larger group of "Präßanisch Gewehr" (i.e. Brescian firearms) which had been "purchased from an Italian" for his father Johann Georg II in 1665. The pair is an outstanding example of Brescia's luxury production in the second quarter of the seventeenth century. The barrels, filed to create a decorative grooved pattern, are signed by the famous Lazarino Cominazzo, the most important representative of the dynasty of barrelsmiths of the same name. The locks, marked "VP" on the inside by an unknown maker, feature particularly finely chiselled leaf ornamentation on the wheel covers and dogs. Even more impressive are the virtuoso openwork mounts and iron plates that almost completely cover the warm walnut of the stock (→ cf. fig. p. 114): hidden among the intricate tendrils are birds and half-length figures. This "skilfully pierced, well-made work" already came in for particular praise in the handover report drawn up in 1665. SR

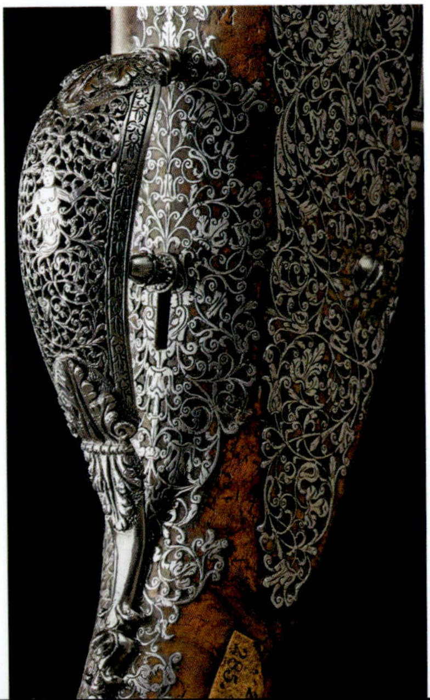

Set of wheellock firearms

Barrels: Lazarino Cominazzo, Brescia / Gardone Val Trompia
Locks: Master IC (probably Jacopo or Gerolamo Colombo), Brescia
Stocks: Marco Spinone, Brescia
c. 1660
Carbine: 98.7 cm, Ø 14 mm, 1822 g
Pistols: 57.5 / 57 cm, Ø 13 mm, 994 / 999 g
Inv. nos. G 1441, J 428, J 533

The barrels of this set of wheellock firearms, consisting of two pistols and a delicate carbine, are cut in an elegant fluted and chevron banded pattern and bear the signature "LAZARINO COMINAZZO". It is a typical product of the Cominazzo dynasty of barrelsmiths based in Gardone val Trompia, which had many active members from the sixteenth to the eighteenth century. Lazarino Cominazzo enjoyed international fame and was commissioned by the Venetian government to produce several barrels for a set of weapons to be given as a gift to the King of France in 1638. However, as other family members also bore the name Lazarino – or adopted it as a nickname, probably for commercial reasons – the attribution of individual signed barrels to specific makers often remains problematic. As early as the seventeenth century, the term *canne lazzarine* (i.e. Lazarino barrels) became widespread in Italian sources as a generic term for all Cominazzo barrels, since the name was regarded as a recognised mark of quality.

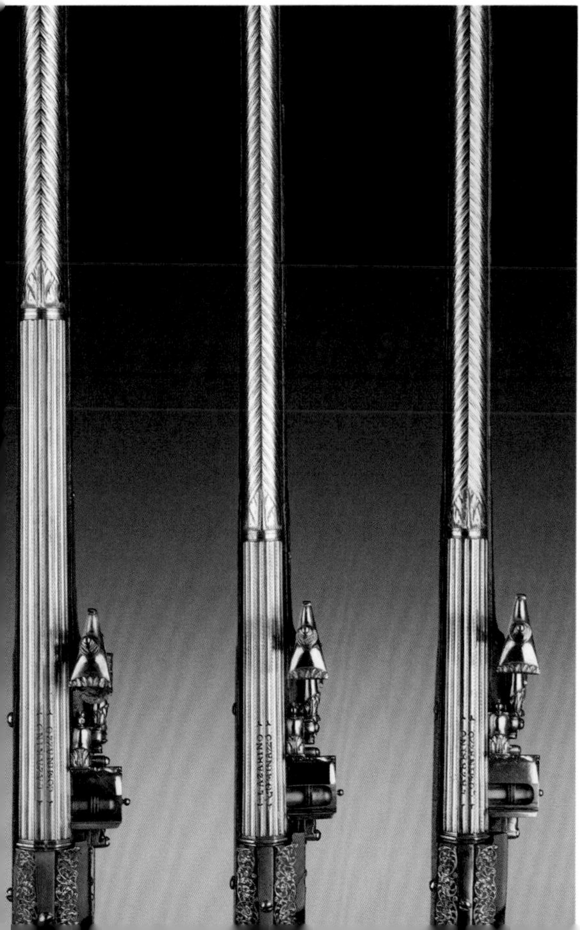

Biographical information about the Cominazzos reveals an unusually high number of violent incidents. The famous Lazarino, for example, had to move to Florence for several years because of a criminal offence; after his return to Gardone, he was reportedly shot by a fellow gun manufacturer – in retaliation for the murder of the latter's mother. This situation was due in part to the specific legal environment in Brescia and Gardone. Whereas strict gun laws were in force in Milan, for example, there were no restrictions on the carrying of firearms in the Venetian gunmaking centres. SR

Pair of flintlock pistols

Barrels: Lazarino Cominazzo, Brescia/Gardone Val Trompia
Locks: Giovanni Beretta, Brescia
Stocks: Marco Spinone, Brescia
c. 1660
56.2/56.1 cm, Ø 14 mm, 803/822 g
Inv. nos. J 578, J 579

The Beretta family is one of the most prominent dynasties of Brescian firearms manufacturers, whose members can be traced back to Gardone and Brescia without interruption since the early sixteenth century. Unlike the Cominazzos, this family included both barrelsmiths and gun-lock makers: Giovanni, who was active around 1660, is one of the earliest Brescian makers of flintlocks. The Fabbrica d'armi Pietro Beretta, founded in Gardone in 1832, is still run by members of this family today. SR

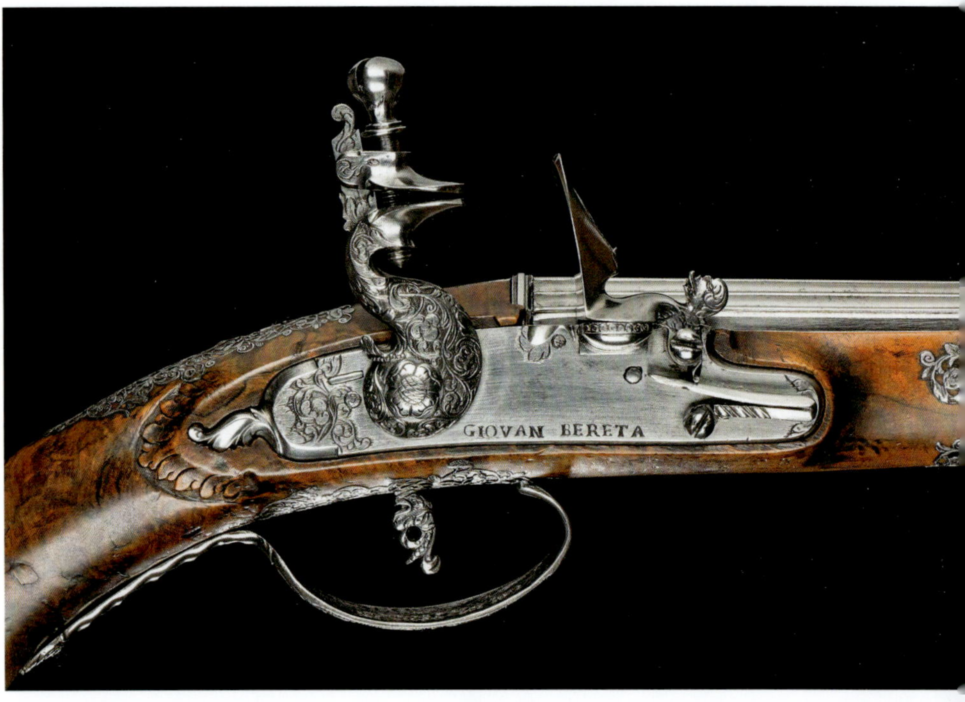

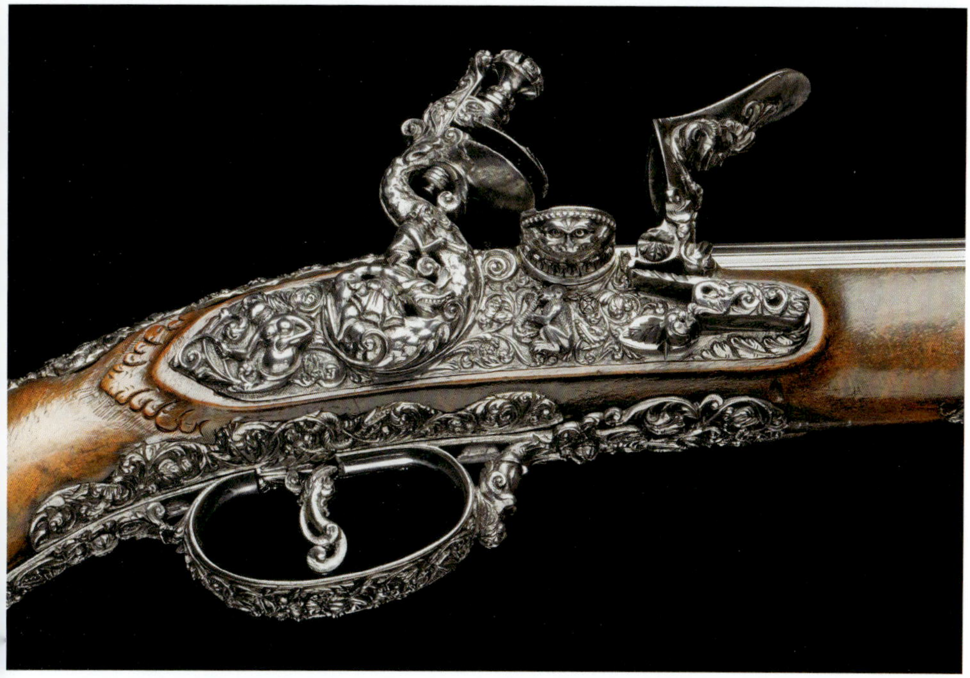

Pair of flintlock pistols

Barrels: Lazarino Cominazzo, Brescia / Gardone Val Trompia
c. 1670
56.2/56.6 cm, Ø 12 mm, 1085/1067 g
Inv. nos. J 1415, J 1416

This pair of pistols, which can be dated to the third quarter of the seventeenth century, entered the Firearms Gallery in 1746 as part of the so-called "Weissenfels Hereditaments". The locks, mounts and fittings are extensively decorated with chiselled iron ornaments: half-length figures, mascarons and a multitude of playful monkeys are hidden among the scrolling vines. A particularly whimsical feature are the ramrod tips in the shape of monkeys (→ cf. fig. p. 115). These are positioned underneath the muzzle of each barrel; to load the gun, the ramrod is taken out and turned round, so that the tip disappears into the barrel. The flower-shaped disc held up by the monkey pushes the bullet down into the barrel chamber. SR

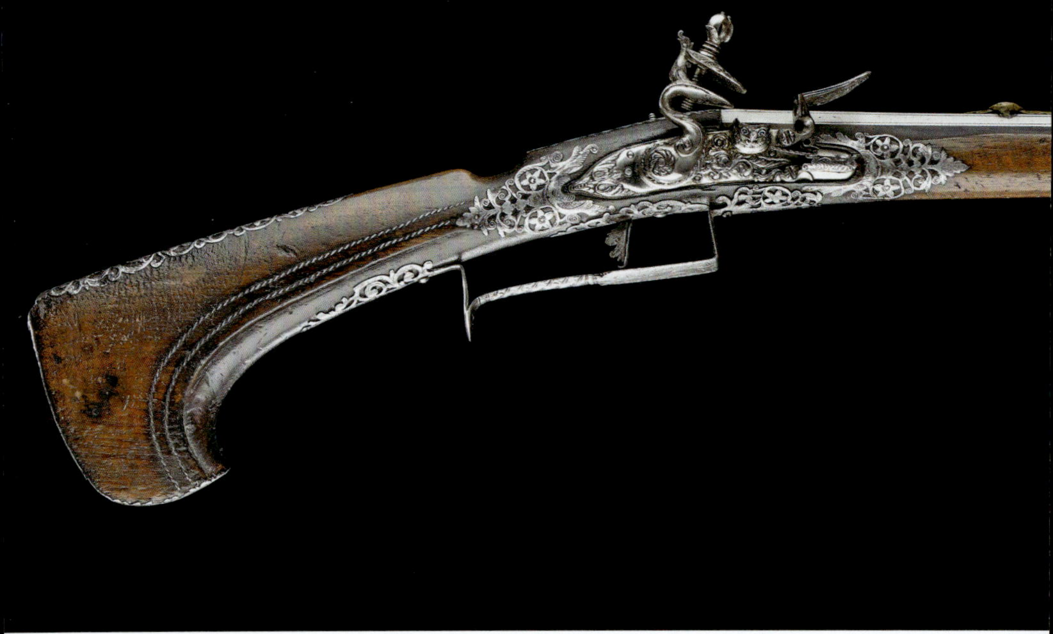

Flintlock shotgun

Probably Corsica, before 1732
156 cm, Ø 15 mm, 2940 g
Inv. no. G 1416

In 1729, the first of several revolts broke out in Corsica against the Republic of Genoa, which had ruled the island since the Middle Ages. At the request of the Republic, Emperor Charles VI sent a contingent of troops to pacify the island. However, the expedition was unsuccessful against the Corsican guerrillas, so that Genoa had to provisionally agree to the rebels' demands in 1732. Baron Ulrich Friedrich Woldemar von Löwendahl, an up-and-coming general in Saxon service, also took part in the campaign. In 1733, he gave this shotgun "which he had brought with him from Corsica" to the new Elector, Friedrich August II.

It can be assumed that this distinctively designed weapon is a rare specimen of local gun manufacturing. The stock, with its openwork iron inlays, clearly resembles the design of Catalan shotguns (→ cf. p. 108), which also influenced contemporary Sardinian firearms production. Whereas there the snaplock was common, this shotgun is fitted with a modern flintlock. The curvature of the butt section is also unusual. SR

Flintlock blunderbuss with folding butt

Barrel: Lazaro Cominazzo, called Lazarino, Brescia / Gardone Val Trompia
Lock: Giovanni Poeta, Brescia
Before 1723
95.1 cm; Ø max. 30 x 48 mm; 2632 g
Inv. no. G 1464

The Neapolitan prince Alfonso Filomarino, a lieutenant-colonel in August the Strong's Garde du Corps from 1726 onwards, presented this gun to Duke Johann Adolf II of Saxe-Weissenfels in 1729. After the duke's death in 1746, it was transferred to the Firearms Gallery as part of his "hereditaments". It is a particularly dangerous weapon in two respects. The blunderbuss barrel with its flaring oval muzzle is suitable for firing several bullets indiscriminately. In addition, a hinge permits the butt to be folded down by activating a catch. This, along with the belt hook on the rear side, enables the weapon to be concealed under clothing. SR

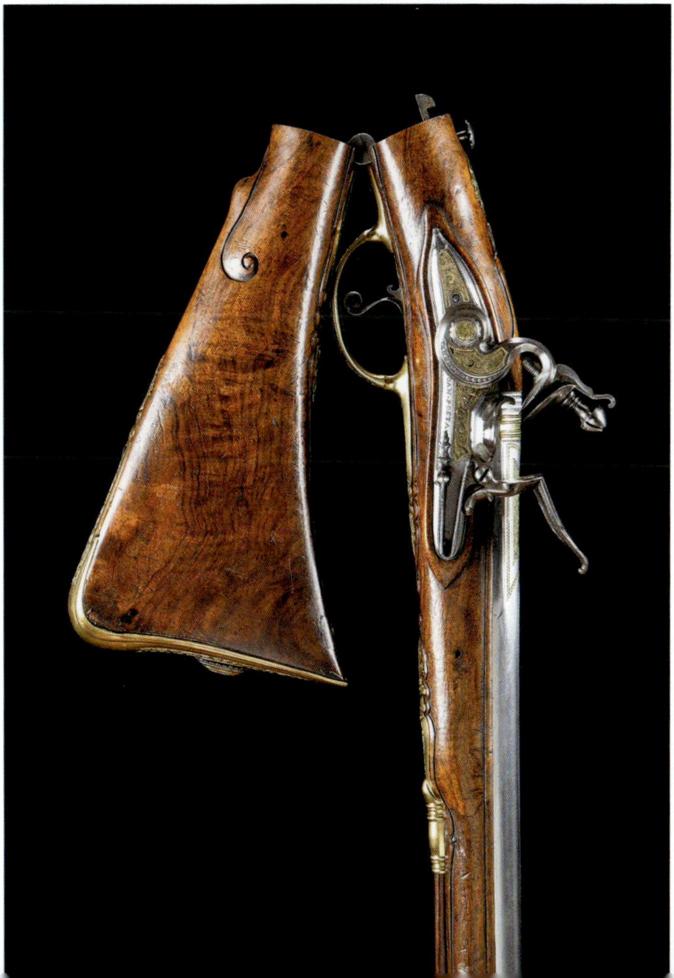

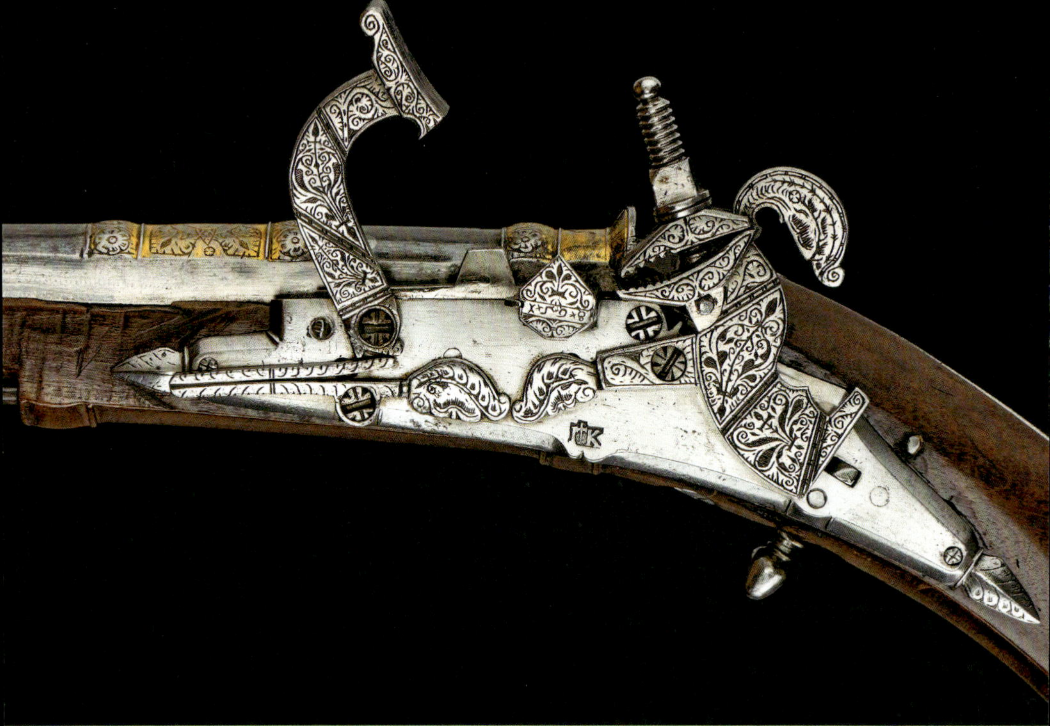

Showcase 10

Scotland, England, Liège

In 1603, the Scottish and English crowns were united in personal union under King James VI/I (son of Mary, Queen of Scots). Nevertheless, Scottish firearms retained their own distinctive style. In the late sixteenth century, a snaphaunce lock variant with original technical and design features had emerged there. The production of these characteristic weapons (mainly pistols) continued virtually unchanged for almost a century. Their somewhat exotic appearance made them sought-after collector's items – including in Dresden, where Elector Johann Georg I owned three pairs of such pistols.

Around 1600, English gunmakers followed Scottish, and later Dutch, models. It was only with the consolidation of English naval power towards the end of the seventeenth century that gunmaking in London came into its own. The focus was primarily on functionality and technical innovation. This development was spurred by the immigration of Huguenot gunmakers from France, such as the famous inventor Isaac de la Chaumette in 1721. At the beginning of the eighteenth century, so-called Queen Anne pistols were popular – small breech-loading pistols with turn-off barrels (meaning they could be unscrewed), although this barrel design had already been developed in 1640–1645 by a Dutch gunmaker in London (→ cf. p. 135). From the middle of the eighteenth century, Queen Anne pistols were often combined with a particularly compact flintlock mechanism, known as the boxlock (→ cf. p. 128).

The Principality of Liège was an independent prince-bishopric within the Holy Roman Empire and had been a leading centre for the manufacture of military armaments since the Renaissance. From the late seventeenth century, luxury firearms were also produced there, with French influence initially predominating. Later, English models became so important that even forgeries with deceptive 'London' signatures were produced. SR

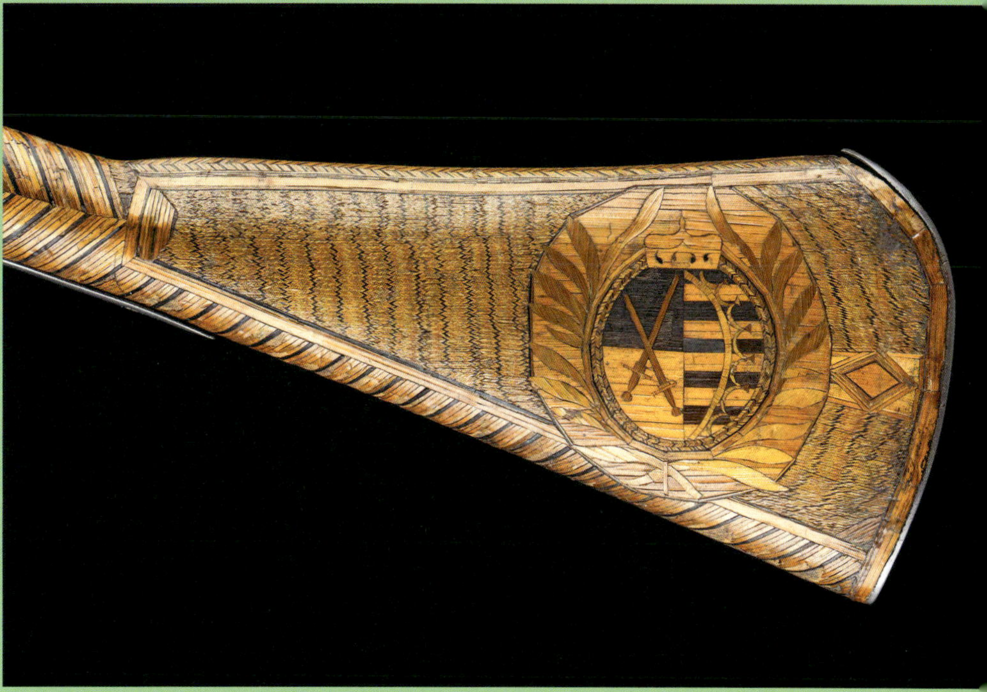

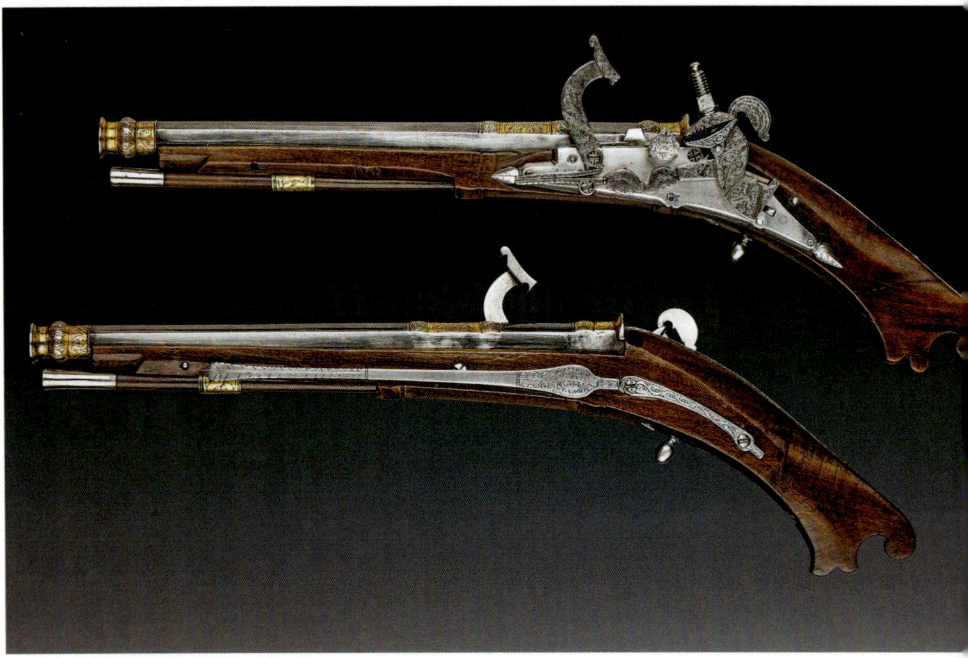

Pair of snaphaunce pistols

Master IK (probably John Kennedy, Edinburgh), 1598
39.7/40 cm, Ø 11 mm, 721/717 g
Inv. nos. J 1431, J 1432

These “two short Scottish hand guns” from among the ducal property of Johann Georg (I) bear the date 1598 on the barrels and flash pans. They are the oldest reliably dated firearms of Scottish manufacture, making them key works for the reconstruction of this fascinating school of gunmaking. The mark “I†K” probably refers to John Kennedy, who is documented as a *dagmaker* (pistol maker) in the *Incorporation of Hammermen* (the guild of all metalworkers) in Edinburgh during the period 1596–1611.

In the Highlands, pistols were not carried on the saddle but on the belt, since most travelling in the mountains was done on foot. Hence, Scottish pistols have belt hooks on the back. Usually, the lock of one pistol of a pair is on the left and of the other on the right, so that they can be inserted on both sides of the body. Other peculiarities of Scottish production are also fully developed in this early pair. These include the characteristic cock design (with a large comb attached to the lower jaw), the absence of trigger guards, the use of brazilwood for the stocks, and the fishtail-shaped butt. Also typical are the engravings on the lock, featuring elegant scrolling ornamentation, which is divided into precise geometric fields (→ cf. fig. p. 124). SR

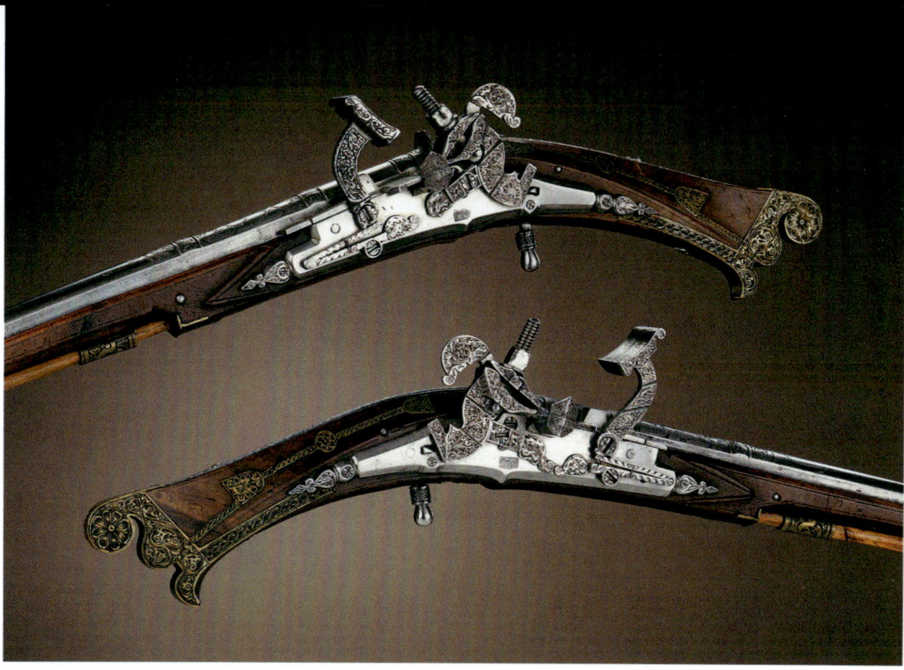

Pair of snaphaunce pistols

Master AM (probably Alexander Muir, Edinburgh), 1611
42.9/42.6 cm, Ø 11 mm, 646/638 g
Inv. nos. J 836, J 837

This pair of Scottish snaphaunce pistols bears the date 1611 and the mark AM on the barrels and locks. The latter can possibly be attributed to the gunmaker Alexander Muir, who is listed in the 1598 roll of Edinburgh burgesses. The technical features and decoration are broadly similar to those of the pair dated 1598 (→ cf. p. 126), with the difference that in this case the fragile contours of the fishtail butts are reinforced with engraved brass inlays. This creates a harmonious colour combination with the iron locks, which are also engraved, and the wooden stocks. The steel on one of the two locks is of inferior quality and probably derives from an early repair. The barrels are decorated with an abstract knot motif in the Celtic tradition.

Early modern portraits of Scottish nobles show that these characteristic firearms were an integral part of traditional Highland dress. Worn on the belt, the pistols were part of a uniform ensemble, along with the dirk (a long dagger), the basket sword, and the tartan kilt or plaid. SR

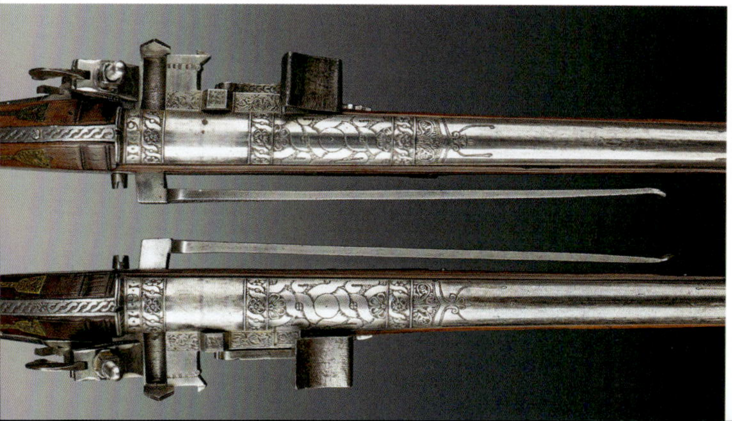

Breech-loading flintlock shotgun

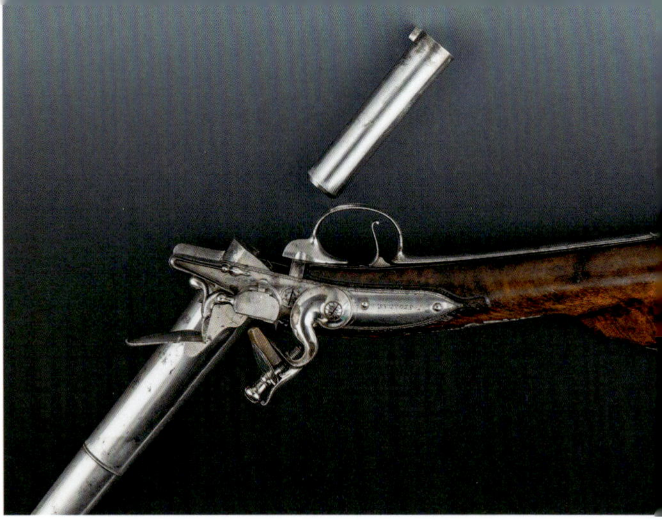

Israel Segalas the Elder,
London, before 1732
116 cm, Ø 18 mm, 2673 g
Inv. no. G 63

This flintlock shotgun by the London gunmaker Israel Segalas the Elder (a Huguenot immigrant from France) features an unusual break-action breech-loading design. A metal cartridge filled in advance with powder and a ball can be placed in the chamber from the rear, which speeds up the loading process considerably. Only one of the original six cartridges (with their own leather pouch) has survived. Unlike most comparable systems (→ cf. p. 75), the barrel tilts upwards instead of downwards, so that the shooter has to turn the rifle over before loading. Through the tilting action, the pan is also automatically filled with a charge from the primer magazine located below it.

August the Strong purchased this shotgun in Warsaw in 1732 "from the gun trader Friederici". The arms dealer Johann Gabriel Friederici was commissioned, among other things, to supply weapons for the Saxon army. SR

Pair of breech-loading flintlock pistols with folding bayonets

Probably Liège, late 18th century
Imitation after Israel Segalas the Younger, London
31.8/31.9 cm, with bayonets folded out 43.3/43 cm, Ø 14 mm, 735/752 g
Inv. nos. J 834, J 835

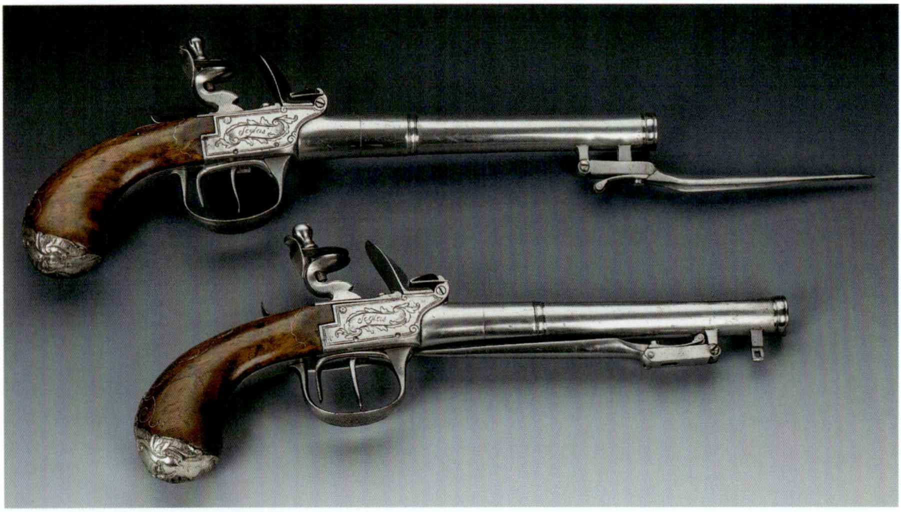

This pair of pistols features the so-called boxlock construction, a flintlock variant typical of England in the second half of the eighteenth century. The lock is not screwed to the side of the stock, but is forged together with the barrel breech; the cock and flash pan are positioned in the central axis of the weapon. The rifled barrels can be unscrewed, which allows the gun to be used as a breechloader. A folding bayonet is fitted underneath each barrel in place of the now superfluous ramrod; when an additional trigger is pulled, a spring is activated causing the blade to spring out.

The pistols are signed "Seglas London", indicating the gunmaker Israel Segalas the Younger. However, several clues (such as the different spelling and the absence of the London proof mark) reveal this to be a forgery. The pair was probably made in Liège, where such 'English' weapons are known to have been produced on a large scale. The pistols were purchased for the Firearms Gallery in 1915. SR

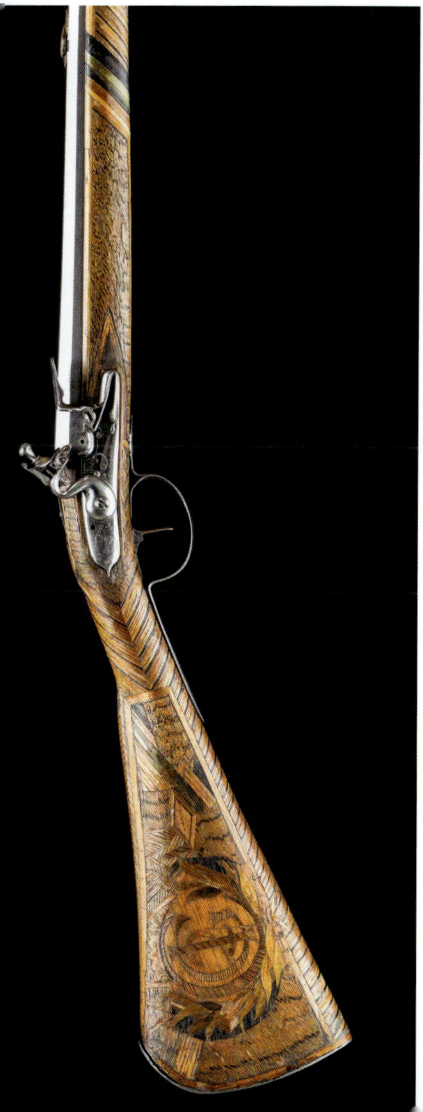

Flintlock shotgun

Guillaume Doyen, Liège, before 1675
Straw marquetry: probably Saxony, 1675
145.9 cm, Ø 13 mm, 2187 g
Inv. no. G 1255

This simple flintlock shotgun by the Liège gunmaker and arms dealer Guillaume Doyen was spectacularly refurbished in Saxony in 1675: the stock was completely covered with delicate straw marquetry. On the butt, this coloured straw inlay forms the coat of arms of the Electorate of Saxony (→ cf. fig. p. 125) as well as the inscription "VIVAT CIG2 1675", with the initials interlaced to form a monogram referring to Elector Johann Georg II.

It is conceivable that this unusual decoration was created in connection with a court festivity. On 25 March 1675, for example, the Dresden court celebrated Carnival with a so-called *Nationenwirtschaft* (tavern of the nations) – a form of entertainment in which the costumed participants took on roles representing different (exotic) peoples. However, the inventories do not provide any evidence to prove such a connection: the shotgun is first described in a late inventory of the Jägerhof (1799); it was integrated into the Firearms Gallery in 1832. SR

⊕ Shooting with air

Blowpipes were already a popular feature of courtly games and garden entertainments in Europe in the fifteenth century. This simplest type of pneumatic weapon could be used with clay balls for hunting small birds and with darts for target shooting. In 1717, August the Strong had a series of 12 iron blowpipes (fig. 3) produced in the Saxon gunmaking centre of Olbernhau. They were each accompanied by a tool resembling pliers, which had rounded ends for moulding clay balls, as well as leather pouches for carrying balls and darts.

In response to scientific and technical developments, gunmakers began experimenting with mechanical compressed air systems for firearms in the seventeenth century. The main component was a compressed air reservoir, which was filled using an air pump. In the eighteenth century, these airguns were highly regarded as hunting weapons and as exciting technical innovations – not least because they made very little noise and could relatively easily be used for firing multiple shots. The air reservoir could be located in different places on the gun. One popular form was a spherical valved air reservoir made of brass or copper, which could be screwed onto the outside of the gun, as illustrated by an unsigned airgun (fig. 5), perhaps made in Poland, which August the Strong received from a Prince Lubomirski (inv. no. G 86). These globe reservoirs (there were usually two) could be screwed onto an accompanying air pump (fig. 4) for charging (shown here is an example from the collection of Elector Friedrich Christian, inv. no. G 87). The airgun manufactured by the Berlin gunmaker C. A. Rode (inv. no. G 90, before 1730) demonstrates an alternative design: in this case, the air reservoir is concealed within the conspicuously thick but small-calibre brass barrel; the pump is incorporated into the butt (fig. 1, 2). A third possibility was a so-called butt reservoir, which was built into the stock; a valve in the butt plate allowed an external pump to be connected in order to fill the reservoir with compressed air.

Interest in pneumatic weapons in the eighteenth century was part of a general enthusiasm for experimental science. This is illustrated by the small brass air reservoir with screw-on stand (fig. 6). It originally belonged to an airgun produced by the instrument maker Johann Gottfried Zimmer at Reinharz Castle (today in Saxony-Anhalt). The imperial count Hans Löser (1704–1763), who resided there, established a renowned workshop for producing scientific instruments. Several objects from Reinharz Castle (such as a vacuum pump) are on display in the Dresden Mathematisch-Physikalischer Salon. SR

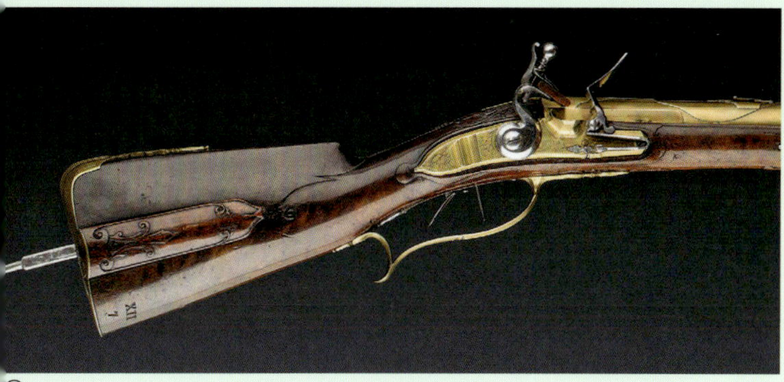

①

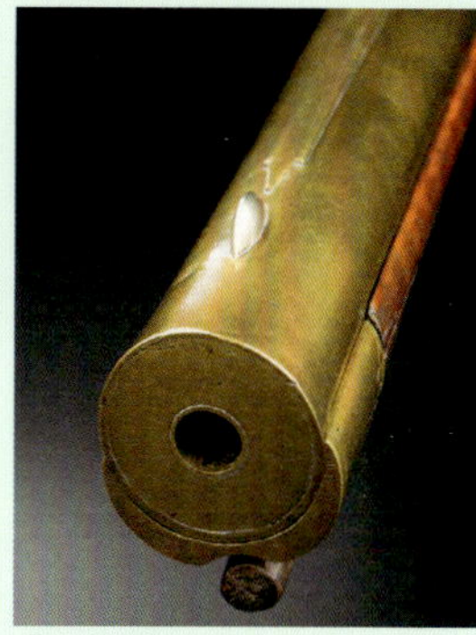

②

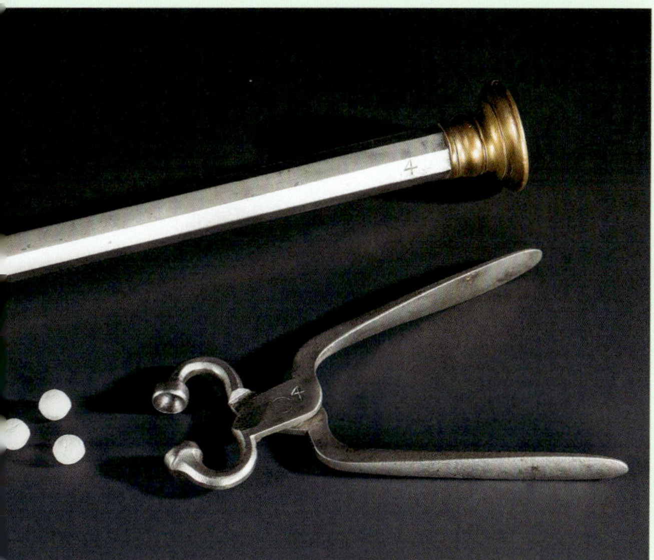

③

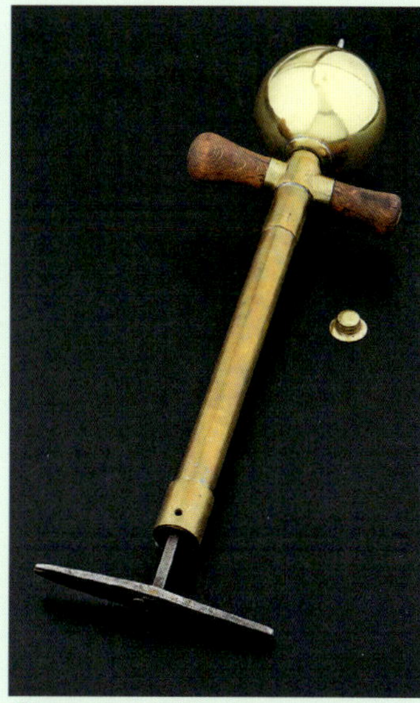

④

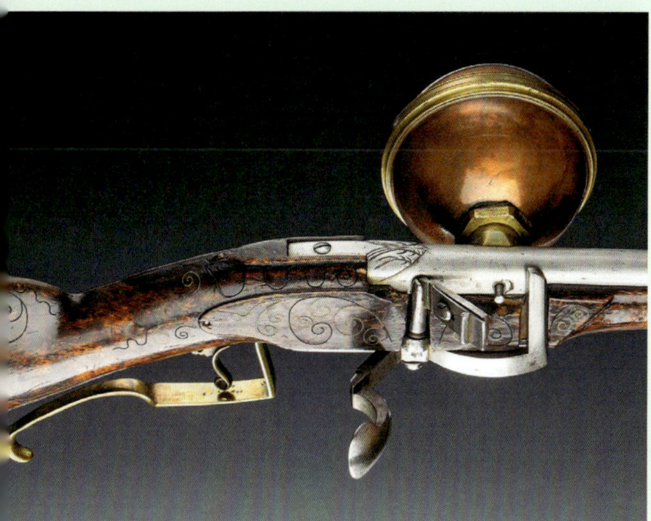

⑤

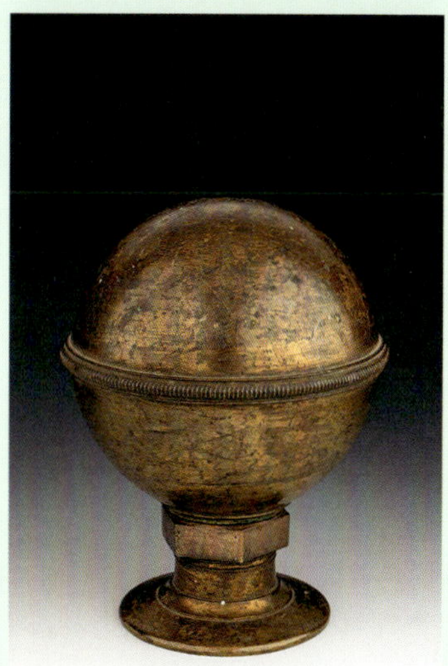

⑥

The Netherlands and its colonies

In the course of the eighty-year Dutch revolt against Spanish rule (1568–1648), the Republic of the Seven United Provinces grew to become a significant factor in European geopolitics. Of decisive importance in this were its successes as a major global trading power. As a result of the conquests made by the Dutch West India Company (GWC) in America and Africa and, above all, by the Dutch East India Company (VOC) in East Asia, this small trading nation acquired an extensive colonial empire.

As part of the flourishing of art and culture in the so-called *Gouden Eeuw* (Golden Age), there was also a surge in the production of valuable luxury firearms. Amsterdam, Utrecht, the Frisian town of Leeuwarden, and Maastricht in the south were among the most important manufacturing centres. The technical aspects of these weapons were predominantly influenced by the French gunmaking tradition. In terms of materials and design, however, the Dutch taste for exotic luxury came to the fore. Precious materials from overseas, such as ebony and ivory, were used for the stocks, and the decorative motifs employed strongly idealised notions of the 'Orient'. On the other hand, indigenous manufacturers in the colonies were commissioned to decorate Dutch weapons using the stylistic forms and techniques of the local artistic tradition. The resulting hybrid luxury objects were particularly prized by the Dutch trading patriciate. Hence, the exhibits described below serve as examples of how the elusive dream of an imaginary 'elsewhere' was juxtaposed with the complex reality of Dutch colonialism. SR

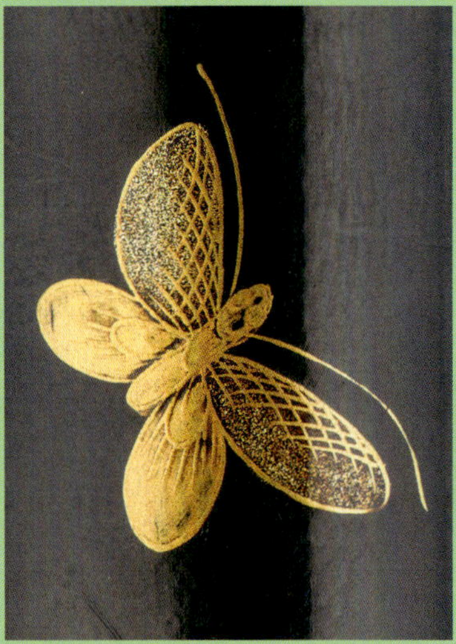

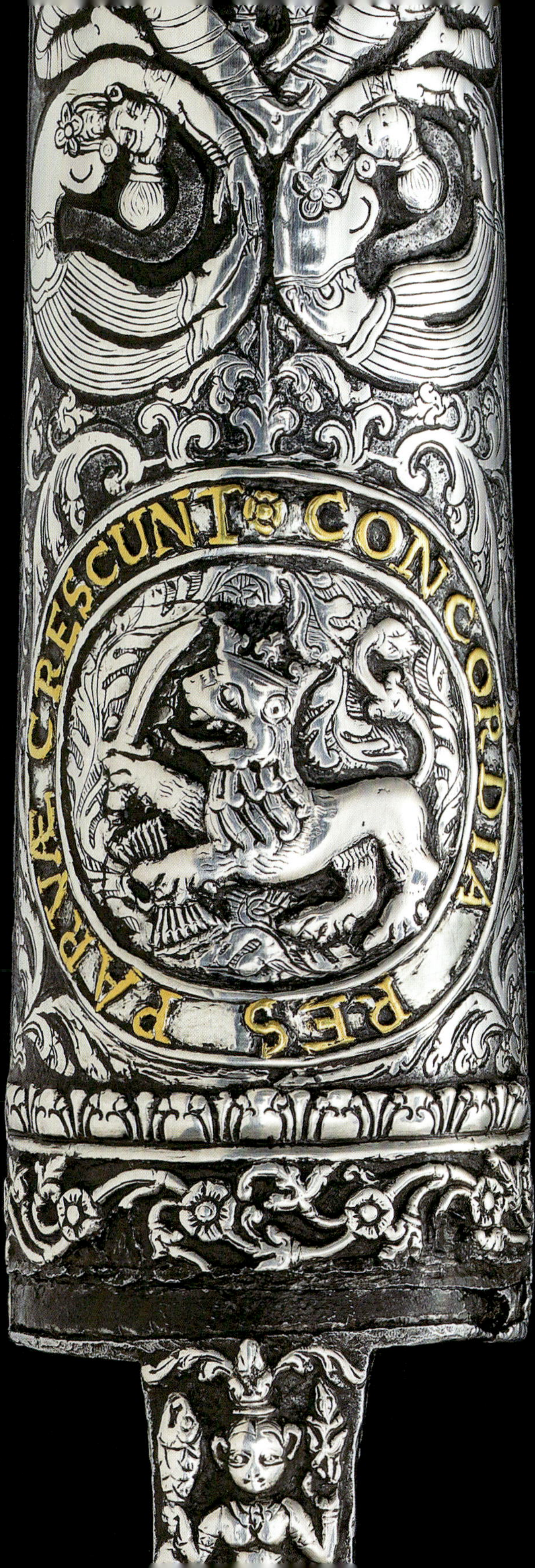
PARVÆ CRESCUNT CONCORDIA RES

Pair of flintlock pistols

Jacob Kosters, Maastricht, c. 1660
49.2/49.5 cm, Ø 12 mm, 980/936 g
Inv. nos. J 410, J 1386

A number of particularly splendid pairs of pistols with solid ivory stocks and pommels in the shape of character heads were made in Maastricht during the period 1650–1680. Whereas the locks were each made by different local gunmakers, the high-quality carvings can be traced back to a single, as yet unidentified, artist's workshop. They mostly depict heads of warriors from classical antiquity, but occasionally they feature figures in oriental costume, as here.

What is remarkable in this case is the unusual design of the turbans: they are covered with a crisscross textile pattern and have a plume of feathers at the side; the apex is formed by a flower. This design has no equivalent in the historical national costumes of the Mediterranean region and can be attributed entirely to the artist's imagination. It is conceivable that he took his inspiration from the ladies' fashions of the Italian Renaissance. In contemporary Dutch painting, exotic costumes were used with similar creative freedom. Artists such as Rembrandt and Vermeer, for example, intensively explored the genre of 'Oriental' character heads (*tronies*).

Elector Friedrich August (II) received this pair of pistols shortly before his thirteenth birthday in 1709. They were given to him by Georg Heinrich von Nischwitz, a courtier in the service of his mother, Queen Christiane Eberhardine. SR

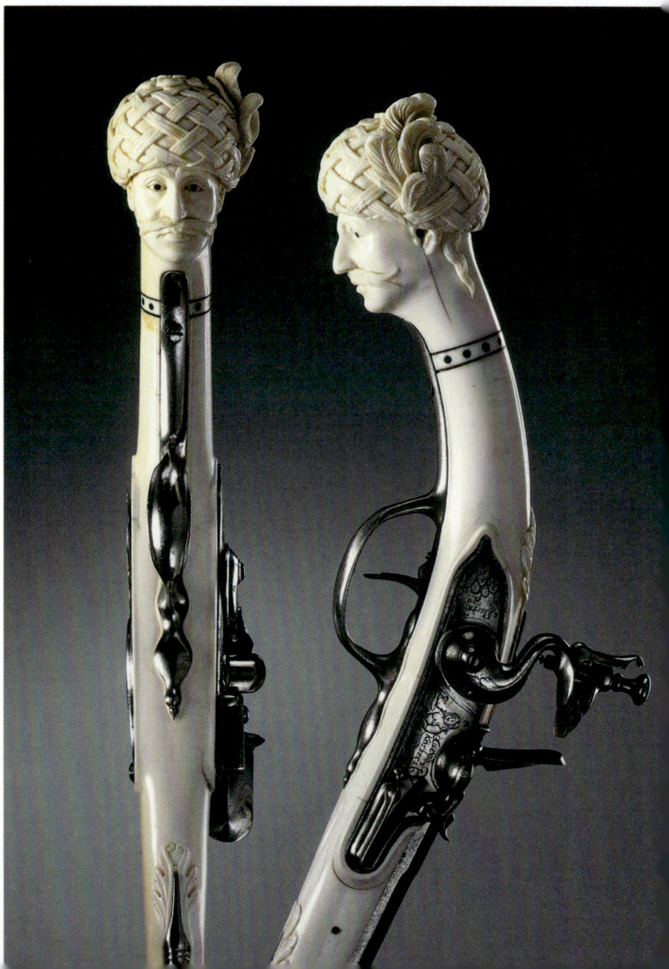

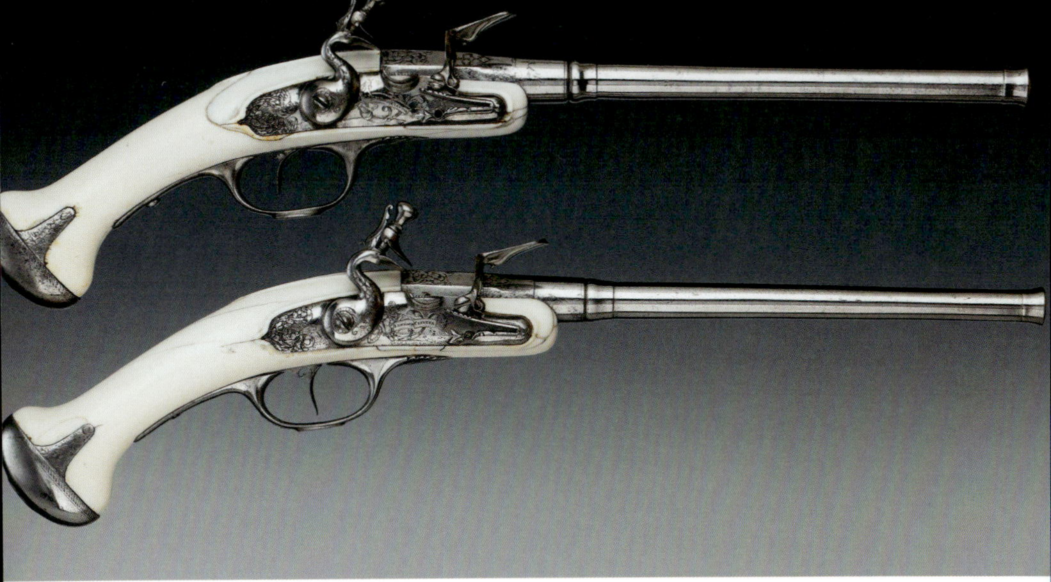

Pair of flintlock turn-off pistols

Leonard Cleuter, Liège, before 1663
45.2/45.3 cm, Ø 11 mm, 929/957 g
Inv. nos. J 673, J 674

Starting in 1650, Leonard Cleuter, a native of Maastricht, earned his living as a gunmaker in the nearby principality of Liège. When he went bankrupt in 1664, he changed his profession: he recruited a regiment of mercenaries and began a career as an officer, which would take him to Italy in the service of the Pope.

The ivory stocks of this pair of pistols are typical of Cleuter's native city of Maastricht. The rifled barrels can be unscrewed, enabling the bullet to be inserted from the breech end, thus eliminating the need for a ramrod. Compared to a muzzleloader, a slightly larger calibre could be used, which made the shot more powerful and precise. The explosion would squeeze the bullet into the rifling, thus significantly reducing the loss of chamber pressure. A very similar rifle (which may perhaps originally have belonged with these) is to be found in the Imperial Armoury in Vienna. Elector Johann Georg II received this exclusive pair of pistols on St John's Day 1663 from "Reinhard the Goldworker" – possibly the court goldsmith Christian II. Reinhardt. SR

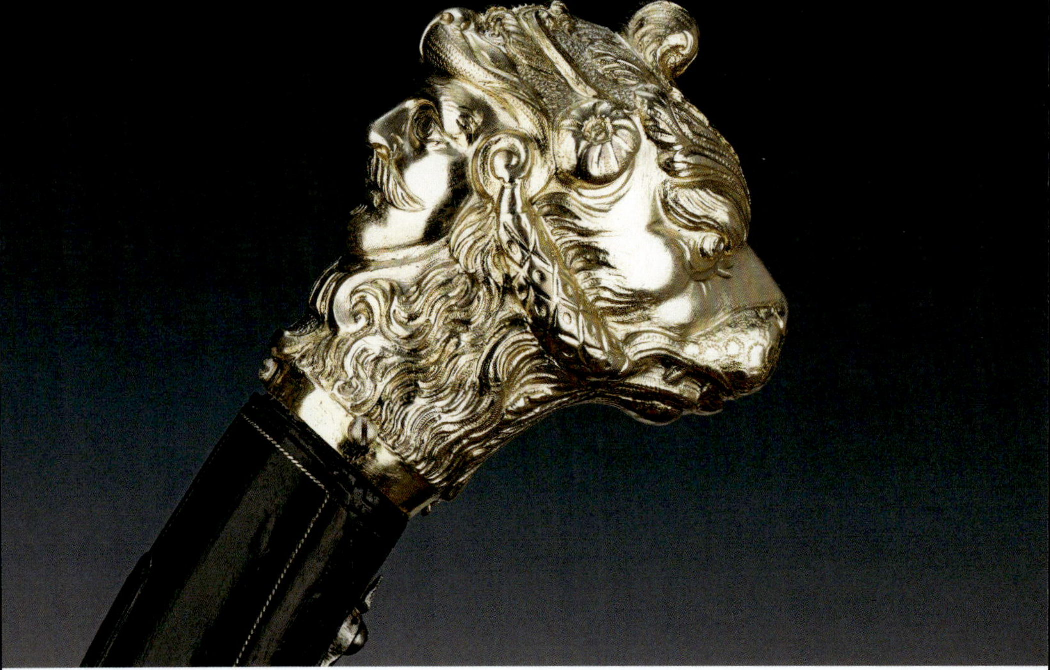

Pair of flintlock pistols

Master FC (probably Frans Claessen), probably ’s-Hertogenbosch,
c. 1640–1650
64.9 cm, Ø 14 mm, 1037/1045 g
Inv. nos. J 752, J 753

Despite similarities with early French flintlock firearms, this pair of pistols is thought to have been made in the Netherlands. Of particular interest are the silver embossed pommels, which combine the face of a man with a lion’s head (probably a reference to Hercules with the hide of the Nemean lion). If the weapon is carried in a saddle holster, the owner sees the calm face of the hero; passers-by on foot, on the other hand, are confronted with the fierce gaze of the wild beast. SR

Flintlock shotgun

Master IS (presumably Jan van Solingen), Amsterdam
Lacquer work: Japan
Late 17th/early 18th century
168 cm, Ø 16 mm, 3666 g
Inv. no. G 2056

From 1639, the Dutch East India Company (VOC) was the only trading organisation from the West permitted to operate in Japan. From its trading post near Nagasaki, it supplied the whole of Europe with precious items such as the popular Japanese lacquerware. Against this background, weapons started to be produced for the European luxury market, in which Dutch types and technology were combined with Japanese decorative art: for example, Western-style smallswords were produced with precious shakudō hilts. Such collaboration in the decoration of firearms was less common, but evidence suggests that it took place. This shotgun produced in Amsterdam around 1700, for example, is embellished with depictions of flowers, animals, and landscapes in Japanese lacquer work (→ cf. fig. p. 132). The technical features of the painting (such as the use of gold powder and small metal inlays) suggest that it is indeed the work of a Japanese artist and is not a European imitation. The object was purchased for the Firearms Gallery on the antiques market in 1903. SR

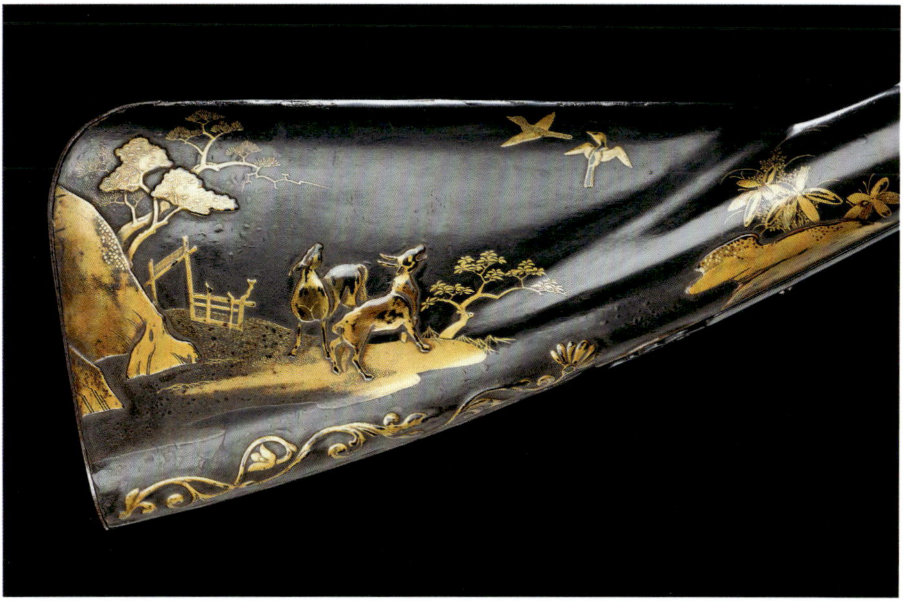

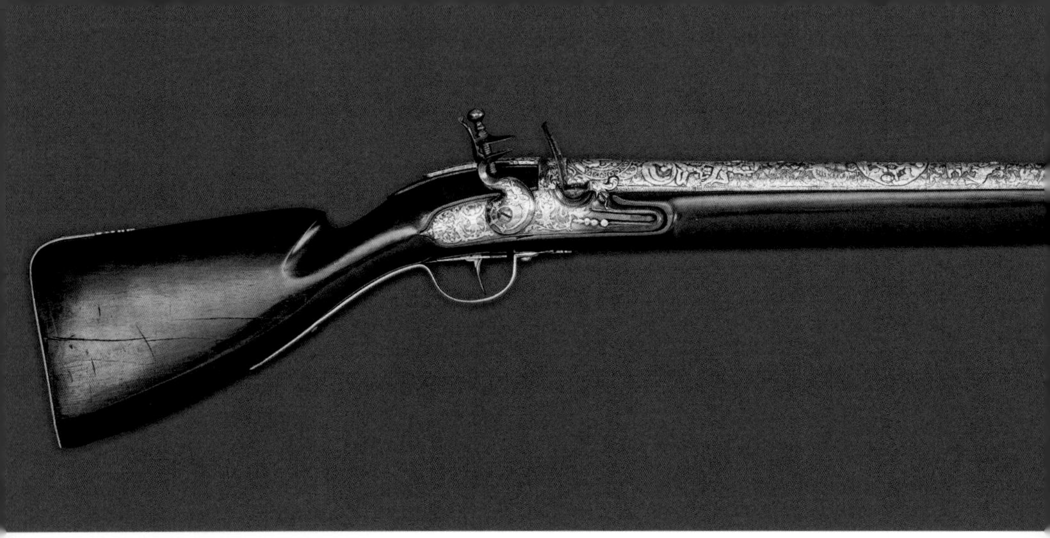

Long flintlock shotgun

Barrel: Widiewarddene the Elder Achari, Sri Lanka
Lock: Master MiW, probably Sri Lanka
c. 1670
2715 cm, Ø 18 mm, 12478 g
Inv. no. G 1548

The island of Ceylon (now Sri Lanka) played a key role in the global spice trade. Between 1640 and 1658, the VOC succeeded in expelling the Portuguese from the island and establishing their own colonial administration, based in Colombo, which controlled the entire coast. This secured the Netherlands a monopoly on the cinnamon trade. In the interior of the island, the Kingdom of Kandy was only able to maintain its independence through stubborn armed resistance and shrewd alliances.

This rifle, with a length of more than 2.70 metres, is a masterful example of Sri Lankan metalwork and a fascinating testimony to intercultural dialogue. The barrel is decorated all over with silver-inlaid foliate scrolling. Among the tendrils are Hindu deities, acrobats, lions, elephants, dragons, and mascarons. At the muzzle of the barrel is a scene depicting the reception of a dignitary, with bodyguards, dancers, and musicians. Shotguns of similar length (so-called punt guns) were used for waterfowl hunting in the Netherlands; in this case, however, the weapon was clearly intended for ceremonial or display purposes. It is known that the noble guard of the King of Kandy was equipped with comparable silver-inlaid shotguns (one of which is on display in the Firearms Gallery, inv. no. G 1182). This specimen, however, was evidently commissioned by the VOC: the chamber is emblazoned with the lion of the Dutch Republic with its gold-inlaid motto (→ cf. fig. p. 133). This challenging commission was awarded to a local artist. He placed his signature in silver-inlaid capitals on the underside of the barrel, visible only to fellow gunmakers: “DEONDERE WIDIE WARDDENE ACHARI”. The Sinhalese surname Widiewarddene (in various spellings) is still common today. *Deondere* is possibly a variation of the Dutch *de oudere* (the elder). The name suffix Achari indicates that the maker belonged to the blacksmith caste. The ebony stock and the flintlock were probably also made in

Sri Lanka. On the inside of the lock is a maker's mark MiW accompanied by a bird – possibly a reference to the coat of arms of Colombo, which depicted a dove (Latin: *columba*) on a mango tree. The silver-inlaid decorations on the lock and side plate are probably not attributable to Widiewarddene: apparently, a European-trained manufacturer attempted to replicate the motifs on the barrel.

August III received the gun on 7 October 1749 as a birthday present from his distant relative Johanna Magdalena of Saxe-Weissenfels, the widowed Duchess of Courland. She was resident in Leipzig and may have purchased the object at the trade fair there. SR

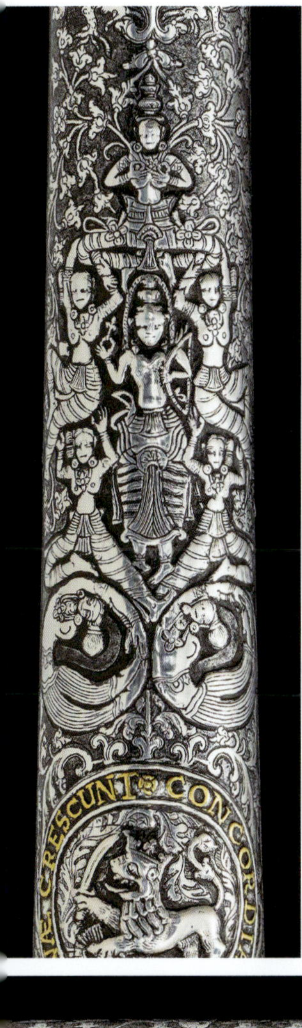

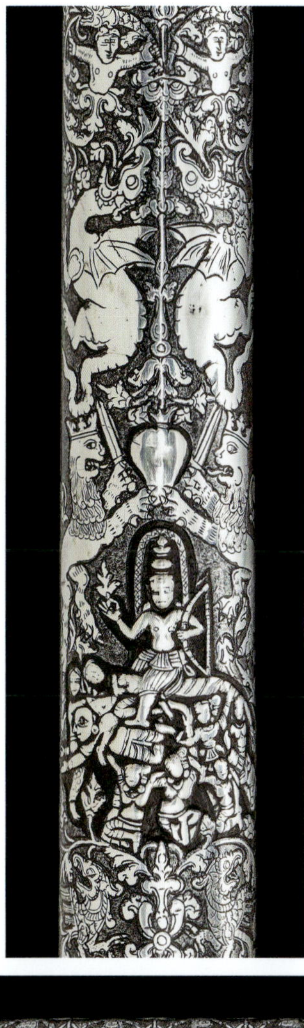

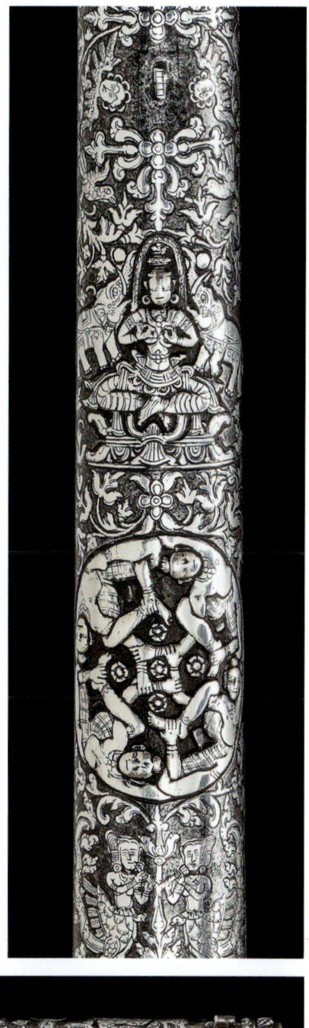

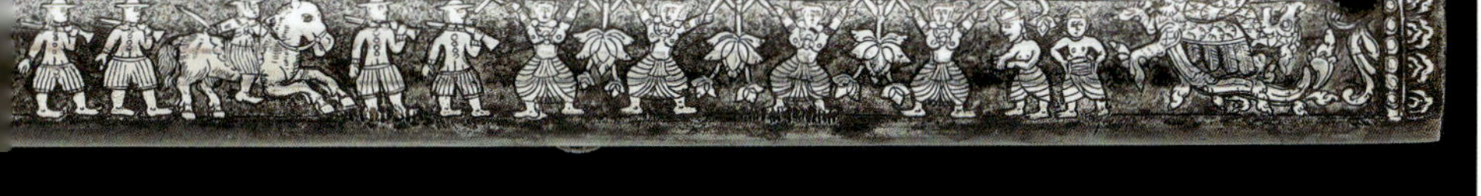

Showcases 12 and 14

Poland, Baltic region, Russia

The coronation of August the Strong as King of Poland in 1697 prompted Saxony to shift its political and cultural focus eastwards – a development that was also reflected in the objects acquired for the Firearms Gallery. Electoral Saxony now became part of the complex balance of power around the Baltic region, where Poland-Lithuania, Sweden, Denmark, and Russia vied for supremacy.

These regional tensions had already resulted in a high volume of firearms production. In the initial phase of the Thirty Years' War (1618–1648), the Swedish King Gustav II Adolf had founded several state-owned arms manufactories – including the one in Norrköping, which was established in 1620 on the initiative of an industrialist from Liège. Early in the eighteenth century, for strategic military reasons, Tsar Peter I commissioned the building of the Tula Arms Factory, to which western gunmakers also made important contributions. In peacetime, these armaments manufactories increasingly produced luxury and hunting weapons.

A striking observation from a technical point of view is the sustained prevalence of snaplock and snaphaunce lock variants in the territories under Swedish control. By contrast, Eastern European gunmaking tended to be dominated by influences from the West, which can probably be explained in part by the strong presence of German-speaking minorities. In ornamental design, however, individual touches inspired by local decorative styles are often visible. SR

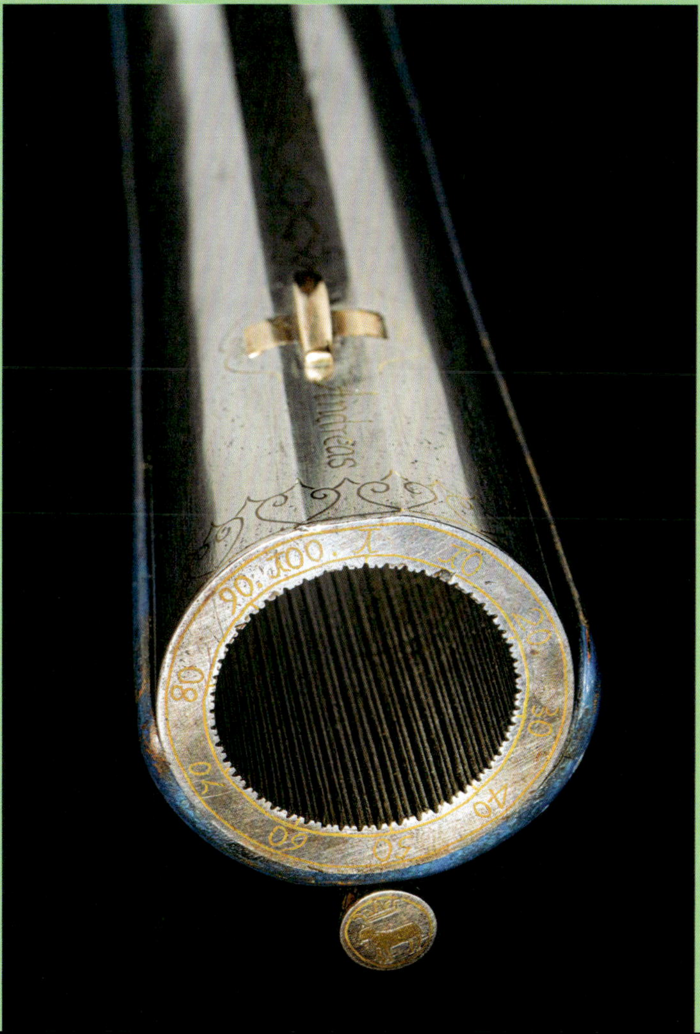

Three-shot flintlock gun

Johann Hildebrandt, Toruń/Thorn, before 1716
124.3 cm, Ø 14 mm, 4714 g
Inv. no. G 71

The trading town of Toruń (German: Thorn) was home to a Polish and a German-speaking population. The gunmaker Johann Hildebrandt, who is documented as a citizen in 1691, belonged to the latter community.

The gun on display features a rare mechanism that made it possible to fire three shots in succession from a single barrel using two flintlocks. To do this, three bullets, each with their own powder charge, were inserted one after the other. Each charge was ignited via a separate touch hole positioned at the appropriate point on the barrel. The first shot was fired using the left lock, the pan of which was connected to the front touch hole by means of an external powder channel. For the second shot, the right lock was operated, which ignited the middle charge via a similar powder channel. Now the right lock had to be re-cocked, and the pan pushed to the side: underneath was a third pan and the rear touch hole, which were used for the last shot. The heavy barrel has a smooth bore. August the Strong received this complex weapon before 1716 from a "Count Bielinskij" – probably the influential magnate Franciszek Bieliński. SR

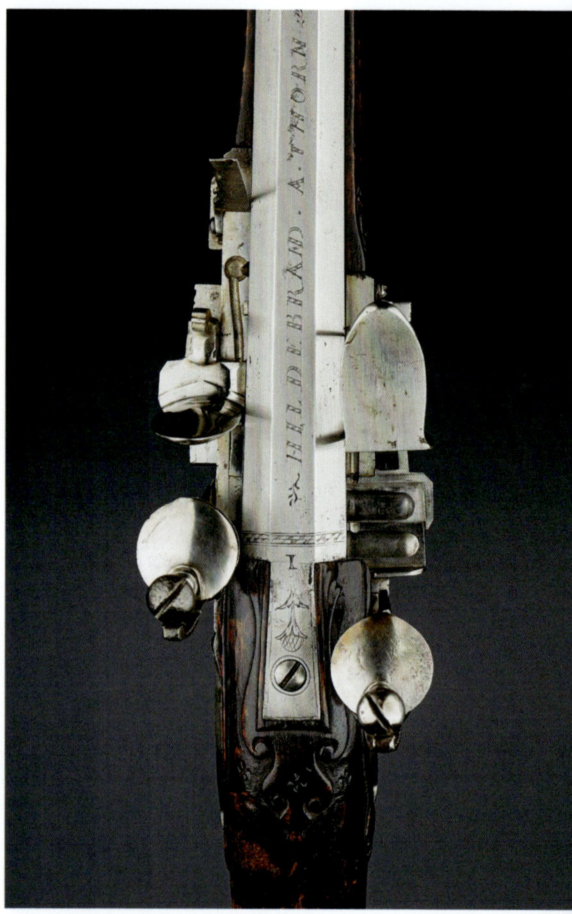

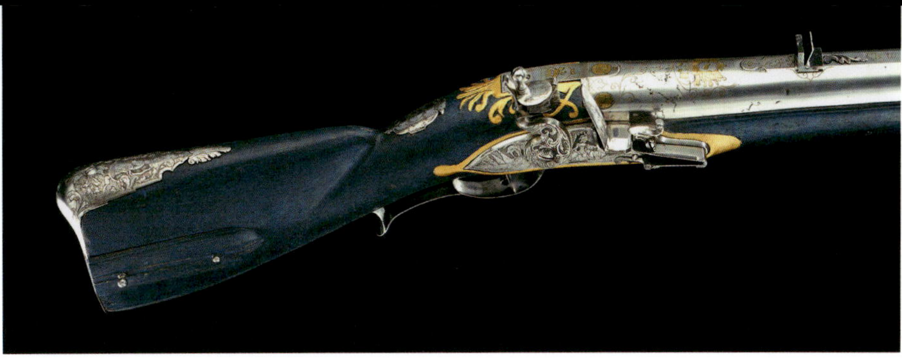

Large-calibre flintlock rifle

Barrel: Daniel Thiermay, Liège or Paris, before 1739
Refurbishing: Master Andreas, Volhynia (?), 1739
136 cm, Ø 38 mm, 9276 g
Inv. no. G 959

This enormous rifle is a typological curiosity. Its weight and oversized dimensions suggest that it would have had to be supported on a rest for firing. The barrel is unique, with an impressive calibre of 38 mm: to stabilise the flight path of the trajectory, it is equipped with exactly 100 alternately deep and shallow hairline grooves – a masterpiece of the barrelsmith's craft (→ cf. fig. p. 141). The barrel chamber bears the mark of the Liège gunmaker Daniel Thiermay.

According to the historical inventory of the Firearms Gallery, August III received this rifle in Warsaw in 1740 as a gift from the Polish magnate Michał Bieliński, Voivode of Chełmno (German: Kulm) and brother of the aforementioned Franciszek. According to this source, the gun was made by a farmer in Volhynia. This region, now part of Ukraine, belonged to the Polish aristocratic republic until 1795. However, whether a farmer there could have produced the technically sophisticated weapon seems questionable – and is demonstrably untrue in the case of the barrel. Rather, this statement must refer to the comprehensive refashioning of its ornamentation, which gave the object its somewhat eccentric appearance. The stock was painted blue and gold, the lock and mounts were decorated with rather rustic engravings, and an elaborate combination of gold-inlaid pictorial images and text appeared on the barrel. This decorative artist signed the lockplate and the barrel with his name 'Andreas'.

A prominent element of the décor is the *Junosza* coat of arms borne by the Bieliński family (a lamb in a crowned escutcheon). This motif appears on the barrel, on the thumb plate, and on the ramrod tip. The barrel also bears the date 21 November 1739 and another coat of arms (possibly that of the Swiatopełk-Czetwertyński magnate family). Two inscriptions in Polish and Latin proclaim how strange and marvellous the object, and hence God's creation, is. This probably refers to the design of the barrel, which was of special interest to Andreas: at its muzzle, he meticulously numbered the 100 hairline grooves with gold-inlaid numerals. SR

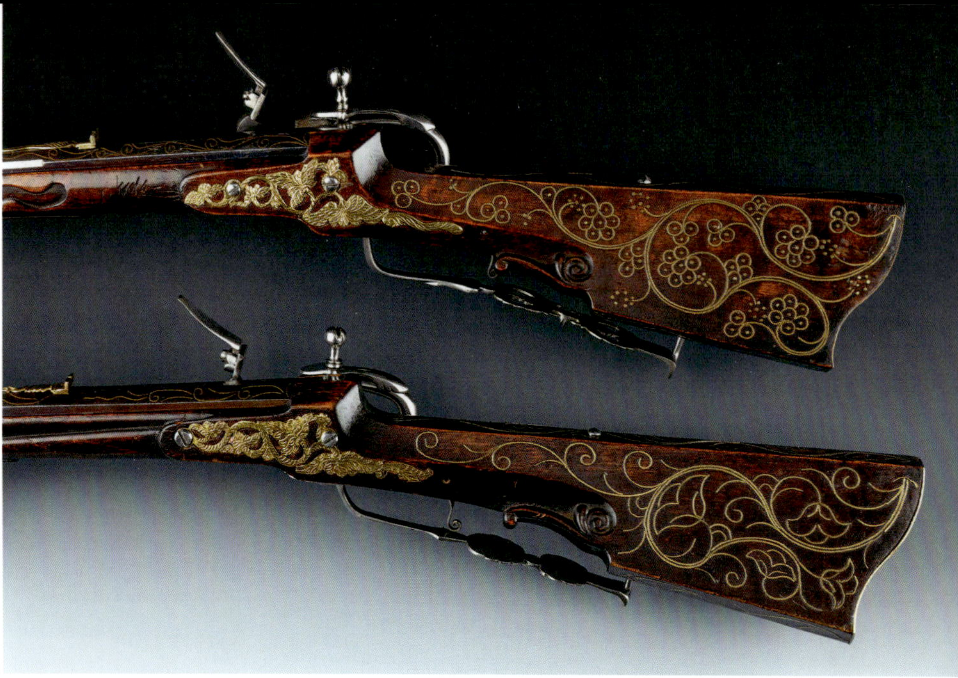

Two snaplock rifles

Courland, probably late 17th century
101.7 cm, Ø 6 mm, 2528 g
95 cm, Ø 8.5 mm, 2332 g
Inv. nos. G 151, G 154

In Sweden and throughout the Baltic region in the late seventeenth century (and beyond), snaplock firearms were frequently produced – while elsewhere the more modern flintlock had long been standard. These two very similar small-calibre fowling rifles (each being one of a pair) came into the Firearms Gallery in 1735 and 1736 via different routes. According to the inventory, both originate from Courland. The firing mechanism corresponds to a snaplock variant (known as the Baltic lock) with an internal spring and characteristic cock design that was widespread in the Baltic region. The battery also serves as a safety device: the vertical steel can be turned sideways so that, in the event of unintentional activation of the trigger, no sparks are produced and the priming pan remains closed. SR

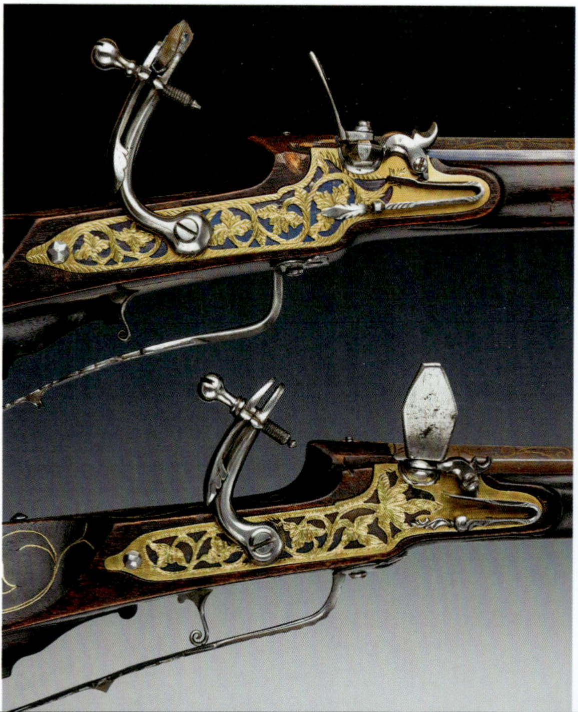

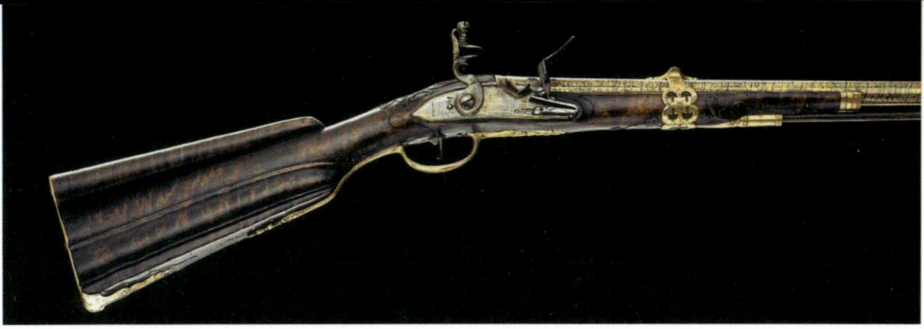

Two flintlock shotguns

Tula, before 1751
Tula, 1749
126 cm, Ø 14 mm, 3316 g
136.5 cm, Ø 17 mm, 2808 g
Inv. nos. G 1581, G 1582

Tsar Peter I founded a state small arms factory in the city of Tula, south of Moscow, in 1705. Gunmakers from Germany, Sweden, and the Baltic worked there alongside local manufacturers. In addition to equipping the Russian army, the factory also produced luxury firearms for the St Petersburg court. Tula is still a centre of the Russian armaments industry today.

The two shotguns shown here demonstrate different European influences, the one having a Madrid-style stock and the other having a stock in the French fashion. A feature that is characteristic of Tula is the gilding on the barrel, which was produced using different etching techniques (→ cf. fig. p. 140). In the case of the 'French' gun, an etching ground was applied to the barrel surface and a motif etched into the metal, which was subsequently copper-plated and fire-gilded; the remaining areas of the steel were blued. The result is an opulent array of scrolling vines on a golden background. On the 'Spanish' shotgun, on the other hand, the Damascus barrel was etched over its entire surface, bringing out the 'watered' pattern produced during forging as a result of the varying carbon content of the metal. The subsequent fire gilding was applied to the deeper etched areas only, creating a rippling surface pattern in blue and gold.

King August III received these two shotguns in October 1751 from the Saxon general Karl Sigmund von Arnim, who had recently returned from a diplomatic mission to St Petersburg. The thumb plate on the 'French' specimen shows the Polish-Lithuanian coat of arms combined with a Saxon-Austrian alliance coat of arms: hence, the intended user was probably Queen Maria Josepha of Austria. SR

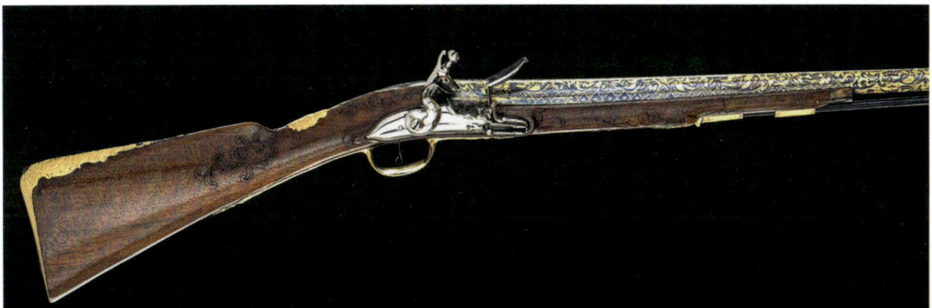

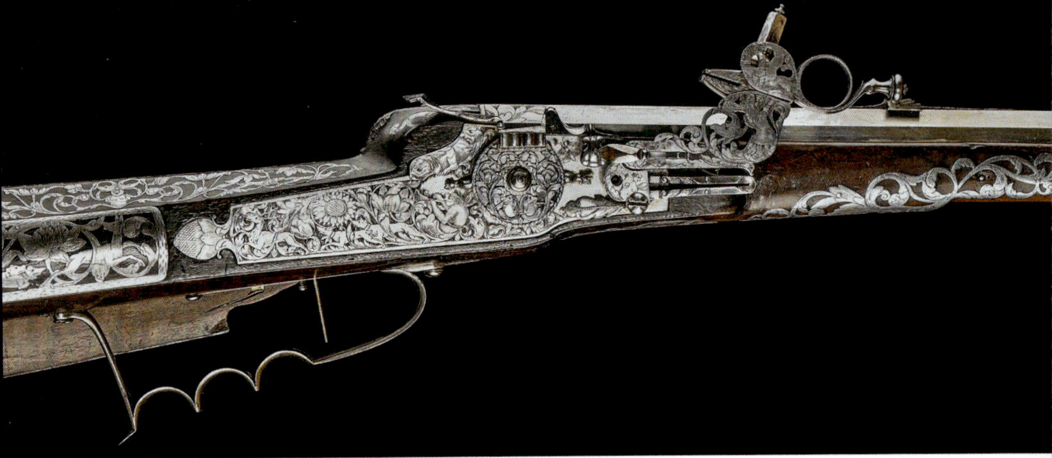

Self-spanning wheellock rifle

Wenzel Fischer, Riga, late 17th century
111.8 cm, Ø 15 mm, 6008 g
Inv. no. G 371

The former Hanseatic city of Riga was caught in the middle of a complex geopolitical power struggle. Having been under Polish-Lithuanian rule since 1581, the city was conquered by Sweden in 1621 and developed into its most important Baltic stronghold. In 1710, Riga was finally conquered by the Russian Tsar Peter I during the Great Northern War.

It is obvious that this rifle closely adheres to German gunmaking practices, for example in the type of stock and in its mechanical features (a self-spanning wheellock). However, the animated engravings on the lock and the decorative metal inlays on the butt are distinctive. August the Strong received the rifle from "a Polish gentleman" around 1700. SR

Snaphaunce rifle

Samuel Ridderspore, Norrköping, late 17th century
127.7 cm, Ø 13 mm, 4367 g
Inv. no. G 647

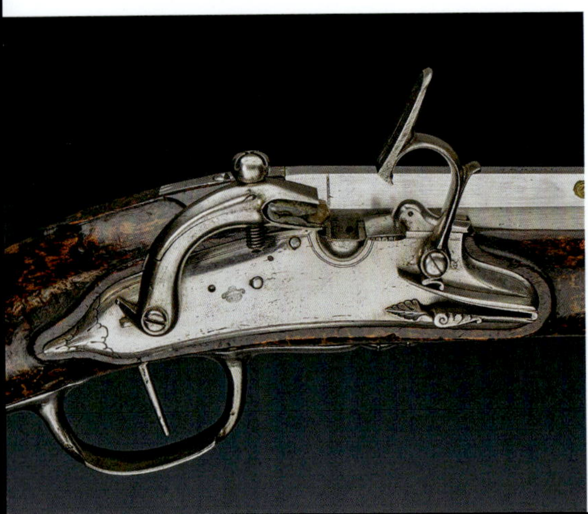

This rifle, which has a stock of stained birch burl wood, has a typical Swedish snaphaunce lock. The pan cover is similar in design to that of wheellock guns and had to be slid open by hand before firing. A simple internal safety mechanism ensured that when the steel was in the rest position, the pan cover was locked shut. SR

Flintlock shotgun

Musket barrel: probably German, before 1700, restocked in 1752
Lock: Heinrich Kappel, Copenhagen, before 1718
139.1 cm, Ø 19 mm, 3746 g
Inv. no. G 1619

August the Strong's failed siege of the then Swedish city of Riga in 1700 heralded the start of the Great Northern War. After this inauspicious beginning, the conflict was to have even more dramatic consequences for the Elector of Saxony, culminating in his (temporary) loss of the Polish throne.

The verse inscribed in inlaid gold on the barrel is a reference to the siege of Riga: "Bey Riga brauchte mich August / Anstat des Ernsts · zu seiner Lust" (At Riga August used me / not in earnest but for pleasure). The meaning of this inscription is explained in an inventory of the *Büchsenkammer* (Rifle Chamber) in the Jägerhof in Dresden. The barrel originally belonged to an old musket "which was given to His Majesty by a musketeer near Riga, and with which he shot ducks": thus, he enjoyed a moment of relaxation in the midst of the rigorous warfare. The fact that August attached sufficient relevance to this episode to include the simple musket in his collection is consistent with his well-known penchant for theatrical self-aggrandizement. The marks on the barrel indicate that it was indeed intended for a military weapon.

In 1752, the barrel was restocked – probably due to the unimpressive nature of the original musket – and combined with an elegantly carved capercaillie shotgun made by the Copenhagen gunmaker Heinrich Kappel. The decision to use a gun from Denmark (Saxony's ally in the Great Northern War) can hardly have been coincidental. The resulting prestigious weapon, distinguished by its illustrious history, was then displayed in the Firearms Gallery. It is unclear whether the inscription on the barrel was also created in 1752 or whether it was already in existence before then. SR

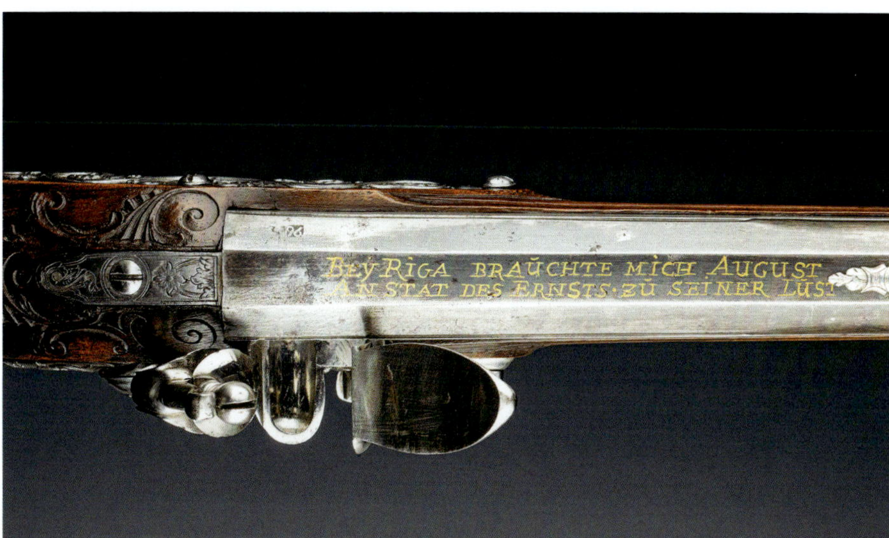

Glossary

Airgun: Pneumatic weapon fired by means of compressed air (usually with a smooth-bore barrel).

Battery: In snaplock and flintlock firearms, the component combining steel and pan cover. Also called **frizzen.**

Blunderbuss: Firearm with flared muzzle (**blunderbuss barrel**) for firing a number of lead balls at short range.

Breechloader: Type of firearm in which the projectile and powder are loaded not through the muzzle (as in a **muzzle-loader**) but directly into the barrel chamber from the rear.

Breech screw: Screw at the rear end of the barrel, attached to the stock by the **barrel tang.**

Butt: Rear portion of the stock, to be braced against the shooter's shoulder or cheek; in the type known as a French stock, it is connected to the rest of the stock by the **small.** The butt is often reinforced at the back with a **butt plate** or **butt cap** made of iron or bone (sometimes fitted with a metal ball). Butt caps are also used on pistols.

Butt trap: Deep recess in the butt for storing wadding or tools, for example. Closed by a **butt trap cover**, usually made of bone, horn, or wood.

Calibre: Internal diameter (bore) of the barrel, determining the size of projectile that could be used.

Carbine: A short shotgun (starting in the 19th century also a rifle), especially for horsemen.

Chamber: Rear section of the barrel, where the ignition of the propellant takes place.

Cheek piece: In firearms with so-called German stocks, the left side of the butt, which is braced against the user's cheek when taking aim.

Cock: In snaphaunce, snaplock and flintlock firearms, the part of the lock that holds the sparking material (flint) and brings it to the pan (cf. **dog** in wheellock firearms).

Dog: In wheellock firearms, the part of the lock that clasps the sparking material (pyrite) and holds it on the pan (cf. **cock** in snaplock and flintlock firearms).

Double-barreled rifle or shotgun: A firearm with two barrels.

Dreimalumschläger: Special type of wheellock in which the wheel rotates three times around its axle (→ cf. pp. 38, 60, 70–71, 86).

Fork rest: Fork-shaped pole for resting the firearm on when shooting.

Lock: External mechanical device of a firearm for igniting the propellant charge. For this purpose, a small amount of powder (primer) is ignited in the pan, which is connected to the barrel chamber via the touch hole. The sparks for ignition are generated differently in different lock types. In a **wheellock**, they result from the friction of a piece of pyrite on a rotating steel wheel. In a **snaphaunce lock**, a flint strikes a steel plate (called a steel); in a **snaplock** the flint strikes a battery, in which the steel also acts as a pan cover. The **Miquelet lock** is a snaplock variant with an external mainspring – this form was widespread in the Mediterranean region (especially Spain). The **flintlock** was a French development in which the cock can be rotated into the half-cock position (with a safety catch) and then pulled into full-cock. Whereas the cock of the snaplock is blocked externally, by a lever protruding outwards through an opening in the lockplate, the trigger mechanism of the flintlock is located inside the lock. In the early nineteenth century the **percussion lock** was developed; this uses caps containing shock-sensitive explosive materials as primers for igniting the main charge.

Mainspring: Activates the wheel of the wheellock or the cock of the snaphaunce lock, snaplock or flintlock.

Mounts: Metal components installed on the stock (side and thumb plate, butt cap, trigger guard, sights, ramrod pipes, etc).

Musket: In the 16th-17th century, a heavy military rifle that was placed on a fork rest when firing; later, a long infantry rifle.

Over-and-under shotgun: A double-barreled shotgun in which the two barrels are positioned one above the other, rather than side-by-side.

Pan or **flash pan:** Small tray-like component of the wheellock, snaphaunce lock, snaplock, and flintlock, for igniting the priming charge; is provided with a sliding **pan cover** (or tilting **frizzen**) to contain and protect the priming powder.

Pommel: Usually spherical end section of a pistol butt; makes it easier to remove the firearm from the saddle holster.

Primer or **priming charge**: Small amount of fine gunpowder (primer) placed in the pan of the lock and used for igniting the main charge (propellant).

Propellant: Main charge of gunpowder, inserted into the barrel chamber behind the projectile.

Ramrod: In muzzle-loading weapons, a wooden rod for inserting the bullet, usually kept in a groove beneath the barrel (often with a metal **ramrod pipe** as a holder and guide). The front end is reinforced with a **tip** made of bone or metal; the rear end is sometimes fitted with a ball puller or hook for use as a **cleaning rod**.

Repeating weapon: Multi-shot firearm with a magazine for storing balls and powder.

Rifle: A firearm with a spirally grooved (rifled) barrel.

Rifling: Spiral grooves in the interior of a gun barrel. The **rifled barrel** gives the projectile a twist, which stabilizes its trajectory. The number of grooves and the cross-section of the rifling vary; so-called **hairline rifling** is narrow and shallow, with numerous grooves.

Self-spanning wheellock: Special type of wheellock in which the wheel is automatically spanned when the dog is pulled down and positioned on the pan (→ pp. 70, 83, 146).

Set trigger: Trigger device for rifles that minimizes trajectory deviation when the shot is fired. The mechanism is activated by pulling a second trigger blade. The shot is then released by pulling only very lightly on the needle-shaped main trigger.

Shotgun: A firearm with a smooth-bore barrel, suitable for firing balls or a charge of shot.

Side plate: Metal plate on the opposite side to the lock, serves as a base for the lock screws (→ cf. fig. p. 97)

Sights: Aiming device consisting of rear sight and front sight. The former can be designed as a fixed V-shaped sight or as a **folding sight** (for aiming at different distances).

Spanner or **wrench**: Tool for tensioning the lock in a wheellock firearm, usually square-section.

Stock: Component connecting the barrel and lock of a firearm, which also serves as a grip or support, usually made of wood. Common types were the German (→ cf. fig. p. 37) and French stocks (→ cf. fig. p. 98), as well as the Madrid and Catalan stocks in Spain (→ cf. figs. pp. 111, 110). In a **half-stock** weapon, the front part of the barrel extends beyond the stock.

Stutzen: A short hunting rifle.

Target rifle: A heavy rifle for shooting at targets.

Thumb plate: Small metal plate on the upper side of the small, for resting the thumb on.

Tilting barrel: Type of breechloader in which the barrel is hinged, giving access to the chamber for loading the charge.

Touch hole: A hole drilled into the side of the barrel that connects the pan of the lock with the barrel chamber. The sparking of the primer charge produced by the lock mechanism is transferred through it to the main charge of propellant in the barrel.

Trigger guard: Protective loop surrounding the trigger of a firearm.

Selected bibliography

Die Ahnengalerie der Wettiner, exhibition catalogue Festung Königstein, edited by Heinz-Werner Lewerken, Dresden 2006

Jutta Bäumel, Rüstkammer / The Dresden Armoury. Guide to the permanent collection in the Semper building, Munich / Berlin 2004

Angelica Dülberg, Der Stallhof. Bemerkungen zur malerischen Ausgestaltung des Langen Ganges, in: Das Residenzschloss zu Dresden, vol. 2. Die Schlossanlage der Renaissance und ihre frühbarocken Um- und Ausgestaltungen, edited by Landesamt für Denkmalpflege Sachsen, Petersberg 2019, pp. 440–442

Max von Ehrenthal, Führer durch die königliche Gewehr-Galerie zu Dresden, Dresden 1900

Gewehrgalerie, edited by Dirk Syndram / Stefano Rinaldi / Gernot Klatte, Dresden 2020 (Dresdener Kunstblätter 64, no. 4 / (2020)

John F. Hayward, The Art of the Gunmaker, 2 vols., London 1962, 1963

Arne Hoff, Feuerwaffen. Ein waffenhistorisches Handbuch, 2 vols., Brunswick 1969

Esther Hoppe-Münzberg, Das kurfürstliche Stall- und Harnischkammergebäude mit Langem Gang und Stallhof – eine neue Bauaufgabe im Komplex des Dresdner Residenzschlosses, in: Das Residenzschloss zu Dresden, vol. 2. Die Schlossanlage der Renaissance und ihre frühbarocken Um- und Ausgestaltungen, edited by Landesamt für Denkmalpflege Sachsen, Petersberg 2019, pp. 417–439

Gernot Klatte, Frühe schottische Pistolen in der Dresdener Rüstkammer, in: Dresdener Kunstblätter 54, no. 1 (2010), pp. 16–29

Gernot Klatte, 21 Gewehre und 2 Porträts. Heinrich Graf von Brühl und die Dresdener Rüstkammer, in: Dresdener Kunstblätter 58, no. 2 (2014), pp. 36–45

Gernot Klatte, Zwei Meisterwerke des Dresdener Hofbüchsenmachers Christian Herold für Kurfürst Johann Georg II., in: Dresdener Kunstblätter 59, no. 2 (2015), pp. 50–57

Gernot Klatte, Die Büchsenkammer des Kurprinzen Friedrich August auf Schloss Hubertusburg, in: Schloss Hubertusburg, edited by Martin Schuster, Tim Tepper, Sabine Webersinke, Beucha 2022 (Arbeitshefte des Landesamtes für Denkmalpflege Sachsen, no. 30), vol. 1, pp. 566–576

Torsten Lenk, The Flintlock: its origin and development, New York 1965 (original Swedish edition 1939)

Heinz-Werner Lewerken, Zur Geschichte der Dresdner Gewehrgalerie, in: Jahrbuch der Staatlichen Kunstsammlungen Dresden 27 (1998/1999), pp. 93–98

Heinz-Werner Lewerken, Dresden's Royal Firearms Gallery, in: The Glory of Baroque Dresden. The State Art Collections Dresden, exhibition catalogue Mississippi Arts Pavilion, Jackson / Miss. 2004, pp. 233–235, 254–265

Friedrich Nollain, Die Königliche Gewehr-Gallerie in Dresden, Dresden 1835

Ulrike Ortrere / Christine Voigtmann, Kurfürstlicher Stall und Stallhof Dresden: das erste Museum der Neuzeit, Berlin 2025

Stefano Rinaldi, Six horses for the king of Poland. Making and staging a diplomatic gift at the court of Louis XIV, in: The Burlington Magazine, vol. 166, no. 1457 / 2024, pp. 810–825

Bernhard Roosens, Feuerwaffen als Familiengeschenke an Kurfürst Friedrich August II. von Sachsen/König August III. von Polen, in: Dresdener Kunstblätter 59, no. 2 (2015), pp. 72–79

Bernhard Roosens/Gernot Klatte, Die Feuerwaffen des Kurprinzen Friedrich August auf Schloss Hubertusburg 1733, in: Die königliche Jagdresidenz Hubertusburg und der Frieden von 1763, edited by Dirk Syndram/Claudia Brink, Dresden 2013, pp. 143–146

Dieter Schaal, Katalog Dresdener Büchsenmacher 16.–18. Jh., Staatliche Kunstsammlungen Dresden, Historisches Museum, Dresden 1975

Dieter Schaal, Katalog Suhler Feuerwaffen 17.–18. Jh., Staatliche Kunstsammlungen Dresden, Historisches Museum, Dresden 1979

Dieter Schaal, Die Gewehrgalerie, in: Barock in Dresden, exhibition catalogue Villa Hügel Essen, edited by Ulli Arnold/Werner Schmidt, Leipzig 1986, pp. 260–276

Dieter Schaal, Aus der “Württembergischen Verlaßenschaft” zur Gewehrgalerie. Ein Stück Sammlungsgeschichte des Barock, in: Jahrbuch der Staatlichen Kunstsammlungen Dresden 22 (1991), pp. 37–47

Dieter Schaal, Fürst Günther I. und die Schwarzburg-Sondershausener Verlassenschaft von 1741. Ein Beitrag zur Sammlungsgeschichte der Gewehrgalerie, in: Jahrbuch der Staatlichen Kunstsammlungen Dresden 23 (1992), pp. 37–49

Dieter Schaal, Die “Merseburgische Verlaßenschaft” von 1738. Eine fürstliche Büchsenkammer in der königlichen Gewehrgalerie, in: Jahrbuch der Staatlichen Kunstsammlungen Dresden 24 (1993), pp. 47–57

Johannes Schöbel, Princely Arms and Armour. A Selection from the Dresden Collection, Leipzig 1975

Ulrike Weinhold, Steinschlossfeuerwaffen des französischen Hofbüchsenmachers Bertrand Piraube in der Dresdner Rüstkammer, in: Jahrbuch der Staatlichen Kunstsammlungen Dresden 28 (2000), pp. 17–32

The authors would like to thank the following for sharing their advice and expertise: Heiko Berger, Marta Golik-Gryglas, Magda Kozar, Rafał Ochęduszko, Yevgeny Rodionov, Holger Schuckelt, Maria Söhnel, Hans-Christoph Walther.

Imprint/Image credits

Imprint

Published by: Staatliche Kunstsammlungen Dresden, Rüstkammer, Marius Winzeler

Authors: Stefano Rinaldi (SR), Gernot Klatte (GK), Marius Winzeler
Consultant: Robert Pelzl
Restoration: Manfred Biedermann, Kirsten Frank, Andreas Frauendorf, Robert Pelzl
Proofreading, photo editing: Susanne Sonntag
Translation: Geraldine Schuckelt

Project management publishing house: Imke Wartenberg
Production publishing house: Heike Strempel
Series layout, cover design, typesetting: Kathleen Bernsdorf, Berlin
Image editing: bildpunkt Druckvorstufen GmbH, Berlin
Printing and binding: Beltz Grafische Betriebe GmbH, Bad Langensalza

The Deutsche Nationalbibliothek lists this publication in the Deutsche Nationalbibliografie; detailed bibliographic data are available on the Internet at http://dnb.dnb.de.

www.deutscherkunstverlag.de
www.degruyterbrill.com

Questions about General Product Safety Regulation:
productsafety@degruyterbrill.com

ISBN 978-3-422-80313-8

Image credits

Bibliothèque de l'Institut national d'histoire de l'art, Paris: p. 101

Foto Marburg & Zentralinstitut für Kunstgeschichte, Photothek: Inge Schön: p. 13

Frank Hoff, Schweinfurt: p. 4

Sächsisches Staatsarchiv, Hauptstaatsarchiv Dresden: p. 11

SLUB Dresden/Deutsche Fotothek: Walter Möbius, df_hauptkatalog_0061524: p. 14; Photo: DDZ, 2010.11, df_dat_0007111: p. 18; Unknown photographer, df_hauptkatalog_0086683: p. 25

Staatliche Kunstsammlungen Dresden, Gemäldegalerie Alte Meister: Elke Estel/Hans-Peter Klut: p. 10

Staatliche Kunstsammlungen Dresden, Münzkabinett: Mirko Schöder: p. 56

Staatliche Kunstsammlungen Dresden, Rüstkammer: Elke Estel/Hans-Peter Klut: pp. 20 bottom, 21, 62, 111, 116, 143; Photo archive: p. 30; Jürgen Karpinski: pp. 12, 35, 37 bottom, 41 top, 42, 43 top, 46, 47, 54 right, 58, 60, 70 top, 73, 77 top, 79 bottom, 82, 83 top, 84, 85, 86, 87 top, 90, 93 bottom, 94, 95, 96 bottom, 97 top, 98, 99, 100, 102, 103 bottom, 104, 108, 110 bottom, 127, 134, 145; Hans-Peter Klut: pp. 27 right, 44, 78, 103 top, Jürgen Lösel: front cover, pp. 7, 15, 16, 19, 20 top, 23, 27 left, 32, 33, 34, 36, 37 top, 38, 39, 40, 41 bottom, 43 bottom, 45, 48, 49, 50, 51, 52, 53, 54 left, 55, 57, 59, 61, 63 top, 70 bottom, 72, 74, 75, 76, 77 bottom, 79 top, 80, 81, 83 bottom, 87 bottom, 91, 92, 93 top, 96 top, 97 bottom, 106, 107, 109, 110 top, 112, 114, 115, 117, 118, 119, 120, 121, 122, 123, 124, 125, 126, 128, 129, 131, 132, 133, 135, 136, 137, 138, 139, 140, 141, 142, 144, 146, 147; Jörg Schöner: p. 89; Thomas Seidel: pp. 26, 28, 29, 88, Lukas André Suthe: p. 113; Jana Vallot/Lukas André Suthe: p. 71

Stiftung Preußischer Kulturbesitz/Staatsbibliothek zu Berlin: p. 63

Front cover: Georg Geßler, Wheellock rifle, Dresden, 1611 (→ cf. pp. 38–39)
Fig. p. 4: The Long Corridor. View of the south façade facing the Stallhof (Stableyard)
Fig. pp. 32–33: View of the Firearms Gallery facing east, from the entrance